THE MANAGEMENT
OF PUBLIC RELATIONS

WILEY SERIES ON MARKETING MANAGEMENT

Series Editor: FREDERICK E. WEBSTER, Jr., *The Amos Tuck School of Business Administration, Dartmouth College*

GEORGE S. DOMINGUEZ, *Marketing in a Regulated Environment*

ROBERT D. ROSS, *The Management of Public Relations: Analysis and Planning External Relations*

VICTOR WADEMAN, *Risk-Free Advertising: How to Come Close to It*

The Management
of Public Relations

ANALYSIS AND PLANNING EXTERNAL RELATIONS

ROBERT D. ROSS

A WILEY-INTERSCIENCE PUBLICATION

JOHN WILEY & SONS, New York • Chichester • Brisbane • Toronto

Library of Congress Cataloging in Publication Data:

Ross, Robert Davis, 1908–
    The management of public relations.

    (Wiley series on marketing management)
    "A Wiley-Interscience publication."
    Includes bibliographical references and indexes.
    1. Public relations.   I. Title.

HM263.R597   659.2   77-9288
ISBN 0-471-03109-7

Printed in the United States of America

10 9 8 7 6 5 4 3 2 1

Series Editor's Foreword

Marketing management is among the most dynamic of the business functions. On the one hand it reflects the everchanging marketplace and the constant evolution of customer preferences and buying habits, and of competition. On the other hand, it grows continually in sophistication and complexity as developments in management science are applied to the work of the marketing manager. If he or she is to be a true management professional, the marketing person must stay informed about these developments.

The Wiley Series on Marketing Management has been developed to serve this need. The books in the series have been written for managers. They combine a concern for management application with an appreciation for the relevance of developments in such areas of management science as behavioral science, financial analysis, and mathematical modeling, as well as the insights gained from analyzing successful experience in the marketplace. The Wiley Series on Marketing Management is thus intended to communicate the state-of-the-art in marketing to managers.

Virtually all areas of marketing management will be explored in the series. Books now available or being planned cover advertising management, industrial marketing research, brand loyalty, sales management, product policy and planning, public relations, overall marketing strategy, and financial aspects of marketing management. It is hoped that the series will have some effect in raising the standards of applied marketing management.

Hanover, New Hampshire
June 1977

FREDERICK E. WEBSTER, JR.

Preface

The purpose of this book is to suggest the elements and factors necessary for effectively managing external relations (public relations). We cannot afford the alternative, which would result in further eroding the already low public confidence in and credibility of most of our institutions.

The almost universal tendency has been to focus on "cosmetic" communicative efforts (largely journalistic) rather than situation analysis and good management. It has not been effective. As a result, continuing public demand for regulation of both business and nonbusiness institutions has been answered by legislation that is sometimes as punitive and contrary to the public interest as it is corrective.

Insufficient attention has been given to the importance of good performance throughout all departments and competences of the organization (as viewed by customers and the publics). Not enough attention has been given to the social climate (public environment) and to the public interest.

The principles outlined in this book are important, therefore, to all levels of management concerned with business and public administration, to those concerned with specific public relations responsibilities, to engineers, lawyers, financial people, and journalists. They should be of particular importance to faculties and students of those same competences and disciplines.

The book is concerned with the management processes as applied to public (or external) relations and also with the source and nature of attitudes, communication, communicative tools, and the management of change.

Los Altos Hills, California   Robert D. Ross
April 1977

Acknowledgments

I gratefully acknowledge the assistance of my wife Gladys F. Ross in preparing the manuscript for this book and of my son Robert H. Ross for his editorial comments and suggestions.

R. D. R.

Contents

Important factors in the environment. The information explosion.

The relations of three basic principles to the functions of public relations management. Perceiving the social climate or environment. Influencing management decisions. Defining opportunities and problems. Counselling all parts of the organization. Determining attitudes and opinions. The communicative function. Management of public relations workers and their efforts. Public relations managers as analysts. Validity of information. Public relations budgets. Cost control. Accountability.

Defining specific objectives. Determining underlying problem causes. Advantages of management by objectives. Objectives not a list of activities. Plans for measuring results. Interim, problem corrective and adaptive objectives. Steps in setting objectives. Upper management approvals. Three kinds of public relations objectives. Who should set objectives. Role of the public relations staff.

Research helps perceive the environment. Research objectives. Importance of quality. Research one of many decision factors. Reporting and using research figures. Media research. Newspaper and magazine circulation. Television audience measurement. Fishing expeditions and focus group interviews. Tests of readability and interest. Making better use of research data.

The communicative process. Communication in terms of audience interests. Basic forms of communication. Communication and attitudes. Factors important to effective communication. Ways of communicating. The effect of the company a message keeps. Facts versus inference. Other meanings of words. Illustrations. Group dynamics. Symbols and symbolic events. Listening. Communication with employees.

Importance of specific objectives. Sources to which advertising and publicity may be credited. Publicity. Double check the facts—Keep records of information sources. Illustrations. Magazine articles. Press interviews. Advertising. Newspaper and magazine advertising. Advertising illustrations. Readership. The air media. Basics for purchasing advertising space. Other communicative tools. Motion pictures. Placards, displays, exhibits. Open houses and tours. Booklets, leaflets, direct mail. Communicative tools for informing employees.

Public affairs. Effect of "under the table" activity. Public affairs problems and functions. Special kinds of knowledge needed. Community relations. Community relations and employees. Knowing the community and vice versa. Contributions. Financial public relations.

Benefits of specific plans. Tieing public relations plans to the organizations plans. Barriers to implementing plans. Developing the plan. Setting objectives—plans for measuring results. Undesirable side effects. Plan formats. Pricing out plans. Getting clearance and support. Keeping records. Carrying out the plans. Keeping people informed. Coordination and integration. Direction, supervision and leadership. Reviewing results—innovation.

Social aspects of the industrial revolution. Change in social beliefs and customs—the culture. Growth and centralization of government. Social responsibility. Growth of population-urbanization. Knowledge workers.

Consumerism. Attitudes toward profit and business. The capital crisis. The energy crisis. The physical environment. The shift in emphasis from the technical to humanism. The information explosion. Recognizing change and the need for change.

Introduction

Most discussions of management focus primarily on internal operations. Yet an organization's external relations in today's world are as important or perhaps more important to its success than its internal operations. For despite the greatest internal effectiveness and efficiency, if an organization's plans, policies, or actions affecting relations with its publics are unacceptable, it may be severely regulated, it may loose important parts of its markets, it may have difficulty surviving. Its management may be forced to waste a large percentage of its time, energy, and resources defending itself before regulatory bodies and the courts.

At a meeting of The Conference Board early in 1976, Daniel Yankelovich, able opinion research leader, pointed out that in 1968 about seven out of 10 people felt that business did a very good job in balancing the pursuit of profit with service to the public. That standing has fallen precipitously and in 1976 was only 19 percent.[1] But it was pointed out (as this book does again in many references) that distrust of business is only one piece of a much more widespread problem of distrust of most of our society's institutions.

The cause goes far beyond mere lack of rapport or good communication. Too many organization leaders (and organizations) have been shown to have "feet of clay." Their protests to the contrary, their denial of problems, or their protests that solutions are contrary to "economic necessity" gain them little or nothing.

Yankelovich also expressed the view that business is being criticized

[1] The Conference Board, Report No. 701, *Business Credibility: The Critical Factors.* New York, 1976.

today for doing things that seemed acceptable only a few years ago. Business has not changed, he says. Society has changed. The recognition of changes in and by society is one of the requirements in managing external relations (public relations).

The failure to manage external relations effectively is rampant. During the last few years, the government and the news media have brought to light one serious failure after another by all kinds of organizations.

Foreign bribes by numerous firms, the Penn Central fiasco, Watergate, the scandals in Congress, and the failure of the U.S. National Bank are but a few of almost countless examples. Each one is an example of the failure to have the proper balance between the desire for profit, power, or votes on the one hand and the public interest on the other. Each one is an example of the failure to give proper consideration to external relations (relations with the publics). Each failure further erodes public confidence in and acceptance of business, government, and other institutions and also the professions (witness the medical malpractice furor).

Important problem areas that concern the management of external relations (public relations) include consumerism, the growth of government and government regulations, discriminatory practices, the negative attitude toward profit and business, the capital requirements crisis, the energy crisis, concern for the physical environment, *and the loss of public credibility and confidence in business, in government, including Congress and the courts, in political organizations, and in most other major institutions.*

Such problems greatly affect and should be of vital concern not only to every business but equally to every nonbusiness organization, including government, political organizations, doctors, lawyers, accountants, the courts, schools, and so on. Thus they should be the subject of effective corrective action not only by business managements at all levels but also by nonbusiness organizations.

These problem areas should be the subject of study by faculties and students of schools of management, business administration, public administration, public relations, journalism, finance, and engineering. All men and women with advanced degrees in such fields should have a knowledge of the effective management of external relations and what is involved.

External relations are subject to constant change. They may be concerned with social matters (the public in general and special publics), government, laws and regulations, economic matters, political matters, external (or internal) changes in technology, and so on. Collectively they are the factors of the environment in which organizations operate currently and will operate in the future. New events occur. The political scene changes. Power struggles between people, groups, and countries take place constantly.

Achievement needs, as a powerful motivating factor, change for whole societies, which increases or decreases economic and cultural growth. The needs for power and affiliation as motivating factors change, affecting a society's culture and its aggressiveness.[2] People's achievement, power, affiliation needs, and other motivating factors affect international relations and psychographic matters that concern the marketplace, education, the professions, government, and so forth.

The development of new and the improvement of old information, knowledge, and technology also bring change in the marketplace, education, the professions, government, and other areas.

All long-range (largely strategic) planning and a considerable part of short-range (largely operational) planning must focus on external relations. The management of external relations (public relations) depends on constant and careful analysis of the various situations, factors, problems, and opportunities that confront every organization.

SCOPE OF EXTERNAL RELATIONS (PUBLIC RELATIONS) CONSIDERATIONS

Effective management of external relations requires knowledge and understanding of the important interrelationships between such complex matters as the nature of attitudes and public opinion, communication, the environment, and the management processes.

External relations consists of the relationships of every part of the organization with the general public, as well as with each of the special or subpublics. It involves the favorability or unfavorability of the relationships that result from all business and other activities, including those of marketing, legal, governmental, financial, engineering, and manufacturing departments. It consists of the relationships between political parties and their members as well as voters and government. It concerns a school's relationships with students, alumni, and outside businesses. It concerns the relationships between government and its constituents.

Effective management of external relations is generally difficult, because of its own complex nature and because of the relationships with the managements of the various other departments, functions, and systems of an organization. There must be a good understanding of the other functions, and care must be taken not to infringe unnecessarily on the responsibilities of their managements.

---

[2] Discussed in David C. McClelland, *The Achieving Society*. New York: Van Nostrand Reinhold 1961.

In various parts of this book we include discussions concerning employee relations. Employees are not an "external public," but they are perhaps the most important "public" of an organization because they are vital to good performance and good external relations.

EXTERNAL RELATIONS—PUBLIC RELATIONS

As mentioned earlier, external relations consists of relationships with the general public and each of the special or subpublics. In essence, it consists of "public relations." However, our definition of public relations will not be the traditional one primarily involving emphasis on communications and publicity. Rather, it will be that of "relations with the public."

Effective management of relations with the public is an important field generally neglected in the study of management. One reason for this neglect is the prevalent and historical viewpoint that good public relations is determined to a large degree by the activity of public relations specialists with emphasis on communications—primarily publicity. However, as a precept of the management of the function, there is an urgent need to enlarge on that narrow concept.

In the past, people have frequently failed to recognize the vital importance of public relations considerations in every decision and every action. This is true not only in business organizations but in every other kind of organization—governmental, philanthropic, social, church, to name a few. With the mounting importance of external relations, however, the need for recognition of public relations as one of the key considerations becomes more and more necessary. Much greater emphasis on the effective management of the public relations function and a much better understanding of what determines the quality of an organization's public relations are needed. A fundamental change is necessary in the concept held by most management people that the function of public relations workers is primarily that of publicists.

The importance of public relations as a pivotal consideration in the long-range success of an enterprise can be illustrated by innovations made by Theodore Vail when he headed the Bell Telephone System early in the twentieth century. Vail made it clear that the primary goal of the Bell System was to anticipate and satisfy the service requirements of the public. He established the Bell Telephone Laboratories, ensuring the ability progressively to improve and expand telephone service technology. He was responsible for setting up an internal system for measuring and ensuring a quality of service that led to providing telephone service unmatched in most other parts of the world. He was instrumental in the development of a concept of public utility regulation, protecting the public and at the same time being fair and equitable to utilities. This farsighted concept undoubtedly helped protect the Bell System from the governmental take-over that happened to the telephone industry in most other parts of the world many years ago.

None of Vail's decisions were labeled as public relations. Yet all pointed to good performance from the public's viewpoint.

MANAGEMENT OF THE PUBLIC RELATIONS FUNCTION

Much has been said about the need for those working in the public relations function to have a knowledge of the behavioral sciences. Such a professional need is evident. Relatively little, however, has been said about the management of the public relations function. To a large extent those working in the field have been considered practitioners but not managers. Yet, since a large percentage of an organization's opportunities and problems arise from good or bad relations with the public, probably the greatest requirement is that those responsible for the function have an excellent understanding of the principles of management. *The public relations function not only can be managed—to be successful it must be* well *managed.*

THE PURPOSE OF THIS BOOK

Good public relations is important to all disciplines. It is important to the effectiveness of all departments of an organization and to all competences, as well as to the organization as a whole. Because of the impact of every management decision and action on public relations, it is important that management personnel have a good understanding of their roles with regard to it.

The purpose of this book is to suggest principles of management of external relations—the public relations function. The book is designed to be a tool of management as well as of faculties and students of management, business administration, public administration, and public relations. Besides discussing the management of the public relations function, the book provides a view of what determines public attitudes (and therefore the favorableness of relations with the publics) and of attitude research and communication. Since a knowledge of the tools of the public relations function is essential to understanding and managing it, the book provides an overview of those tools and of specialized public relations functions including public affairs, community relations, contributions, and financial public relations.

Chapter 11 discusses the management of change, which is of particular importance because all management is primarily concerned with results in the future—the future being from a few hours to many years away. It is to the advantage of all organizations to consider how changes can be made most advantageous or least harmful to the organization and to society. Chapter 11 will be helpful to those concerned with the management of any part of an organization.

ONE

THE Purpose

OF THE PUBLIC RELATIONS
(OR EXTERNAL RELATIONS)
FUNCTION

In the effective management of any function, the very first consideration must be to define the purposes of the function. What is the purpose of the public relations function? Very simply, it embodies the considerations necessary to develop and maintain good relations with the public. We state this purpose in different terms a little further on.

Public relations is one of the most misunderstood terms and perhaps one of the most misunderstood functions. The public relations function in management is only vaguely understood even by many key executives and is no better understood by the majority of lower management. The following story illustrates this point.

Not too long ago telephone calls in most metropolitan areas of the United States were charged for in various numbers of "message units." The number of message units a call cost depended on the distance and length of the call. At the end of the month all the charges for the various calls were lumped together on the customer's telephone bill as one bulk amount. No detail was provided. Most customers did not understand or accept this kind of billing. Even those who did understand it, did not like it. The practice led to very unfavorable public relations.

However, the managements of the telephone companies conceived of the public relations function as using the right magic words. Management felt that if only the public relations department would do a better job, people would accept their telephone bills with message units and the public relations problems would go away. Of course, management was disillusioned. Eventually it was forced by public pressure and the Public Utilities Commissions in some states to change the method of billing. Message unit billing simply did not come up to the level of performance acceptable to the customer. The idea that good performance from a public viewpoint is the key to good public relations had never dawned on management. Its attention was entirely focused on its own accounting and engineering departments' viewpoints.

OBSOLETE VIEWS OF THE PUBLIC RELATIONS FUNCTION

Many people still think of the public relations function as being primarily concerned with press agentry. Some conceive of it as always agreeing with such influential persons as city, state, and national officials or officers of important organizations.

Not long ago some people began to give great emphasis to "corporate identity" as the important factor in public relations, emphasizing such things as logos, emblems, attractively painted vehicles, and the like. However, corporate identity *really lies in the character, the integrity and performance* of the organization, not in the superficial design of its logotypes, emblems, or the color of vehicles.

Many of the people who work in the field of public relations and who do not consider themselves mere publicists, still associate the function almost exclusively with communication. They are still inclined to view public relations activity as work involving dealing with the news media. And communication is regularly suggested as the cure-all for unfavorable views held locally, nationally, and internationally. However, in a half century of explosive expansion in communicative media and ability, there has been no improvement in relationships on either a local or worldwide level. One needs only to look at the Middle East, Vietnam, Ireland, or the continuously turbulent domestic scene to realize that mere communication is not the answer.

It is true that public communication is an important tool of the public relations function. However, as pointed out in the introduction, today there is an urgent need to enlarge on that somewhat narrow concept.

Various groups such as political campaign managers, fund raisers, promoters of special events bill themselves as public relations specialists. Such groups meet the needs of the organizations they serve. Their businesses are usually quite legitimate. However, there should be a distinct difference made between the promoter and the public relations professional. There is little similarity between their objectives and the kind of work they should perform.

The public relations function had (and still has in many quarters) the connotation of ballyhoo and exaggerated claims—an attempt to sell appearance instead of substance. It has sometimes been held in ill repute. On the other hand, others say that public relations is just a matter of following the Golden Rule.

None of these viewpoints adequately describes the public relations function today. What, then, should be the real purpose of the public relations function? What should the function accomplish?

THE PURPOSE OF THE PUBLIC RELATIONS FUNCTION

The single purpose of the public relations function should be to help the organization develop and maintain a social climate or environment in which it can prosper best. Good public relations is based on good performance and behavior as seen from the public's viewpoint. Thus the public relations function is concerned with helping to ensure that the organization's performance and behavior are good, both as to what it does and what it says. And it is concerned with helping ensure that what the organization does is in the public interest.

We refer to the public interest throughout this book. In considering the public interest, one of the important concerns (but certainly not the only one) is with ethics. We define and briefly discuss ethics so that the reader will have a better understanding of the meaning we imply from the outset.

Ethics is the discipline dealing with what is good or bad and with moral duty and obligation. As applied to the organization and to its managers, a fundamental rule of ethics is that they must take great care that their

THE SINGLE PURPOSE OF

PUBLIC RELATIONS ACTIVITY IS

TO HELP THE ORGANIZATION

OBTAIN AND MAINTAIN A SOCIAL

CLIMATE IN WHICH IT CAN

PROSPER BEST.

Figure 1

behavior is such that they do not knowingly do harm. This is one of the basic responsibilities as concerns the public interest.

The ethical responsibility and duty of the organization (business, political, government, professional, and any other) and its managers are even greater than for society in general because organizations are in a position of leadership in society. They have authority. They stand out and occupy a position of visibility.

In addition to the consideration of ethics and behavior, the organization has the responsibility to ensure that both what it does and what it fails to do will not be harmful to the public. This is one of the basic areas of performance and is in addition to the area concerning the quality of an organization's products, services, its treatment of its employees, and so on.

An organization's performance is fundamentally more important than what it says. The communicative function is important, but actions speak louder than words.

Because public relations functions are concerned with the environment or social climate, those working in public relations should be vitally interested in the practical theories and findings of the leading sociologists, management scientists, and persons in allied fields. For example, Peter Drucker's books, such as *The Age of Discontinuity,* give some valuable insights.[1] A knowledge of the viewpoints of leaders of contemporary thought on such subjects as motivation, group dynamics, organizational development, and management is essential. The thinking of these people can give much-needed perspective to those responsible for the public relations function.

With a purpose of helping the organization to obtain and maintain an environment or social climate in which it can prosper best, it is apparent that the public relations function has a definite, specific purpose. And it requires the best in management methods and thought to accomplish that purpose. Those working in the function should be students and advocates of the best principles of management. The mere ability to communicate well is of secondary importance for necessary effectiveness.

PUBLIC RELATIONS: AN INVESTMENT IN THE PRIVILEGE TO OPERATE

The public relations function in reality is an investment in the privilege to operate. Thus it is perhaps more an investment in the future than an operating expenditure for the present. It is necessary to help ensure successful operation five, 10, or 20 years from now. Without this investment, without this function or activity an organization can lose its freedom to operate at

---

[1] Peter F. Drucker, *The Age of Discontinuity.* New York: Harper and Row, 1969.

all, or it can have its freedom to operate curtailed by a multitude of laws and government regulations.

Each year brings new congressional, Federal Trade Commission, Federal Food and Drug Administration, Securities Exchange Commission, and other hearings that result in curtailment of the freedom to operate as well as unfavorable publicity to many organizations. An unremitting stream of legislation and new government regulations translates unfavorable public attitudes into law.

The public relations function of the past was ineffective in preventing the insensitivity to the public interest that brought about the deterioration of confidence. It was preoccupied with communication and did not recognize its true purpose. The importance of such matters as the public interest, performance, and so on were not brought out in top management councils. Thus the decision mix of major institutions has not in many instances included those things that the public relations function should have supplied.

The public relations function can no longer be a subsidiary consideration. It must be recognized as one of today's most important considerations, but this can happen only as a result of effective performance by public relations management. It requires gearing up to perceive what is in the public interest. It places responsibility on the public relations manager for effectively informing his colleagues in top management of potential public relations problems and their probable consequences as well as their potential opportunities.

THE SOCIAL CLIMATE AND THE PUBLIC INTEREST

Let us enlarge on what is meant by "social climate" or environment. It is made up of the attitudes and reactions of the general public—the interrelationships between the organization and all the special publics, such as government groups, consumers, minority groups, educators, and others.

The environment is to a large degree the result of management decisions and actions or indecisions and inactions. It is the result of the innumerable contacts of many kinds by institutions with people and organizations of all manner of backgrounds, viewpoints, educations, intelligence, traditions, experiences, religions, races, abilities, weaknesses, strengths, aspirations, and economic well being, as well as ages and sexes. It includes the results of everything the organization says and has said or fails to say.

Because the public relations function is concerned with the social climate or environment, it is much concerned with the public interest. An organiza-

THE ORGANIZATION EXISTS

ONLY BY PUBLIC CONSENT AND ITS

EXISTENCE IS JUSTIFIED ONLY IN

TERMS OF ITS CONTRIBUTION TO

SOCIETY AS VIEWED BY SOCIETY.

Figure 2

tion exists only by public consent, and its existence is justified only in terms of its contribution to society as viewed by society.

How does one determine what is in the public interest? Good perception of what is most desirable from the long-range standpoint of the community and the nation, together with a strong sense of ethics and integrity are the key factors.

Sometimes what is in the public interest may not be popular from a short-term viewpoint. There can be a great difference between the long-term public interest and what the public desires at any given time. The business and political systems have been more intent on providing the short-term desires of the publics than what is in the public interest.

As Philip Kotler points out, the food industry has been oriented to producing products with high taste appeal.[2] Nutrition has tended to be a secondary consideration. The packaging industry has produced nonreusable containers, but consumers pay for this convenience in the form of solid waste pollution. Food companies and the packaging industry both have come under attack by consumer organizations and government for failure to heed the public interest.

Government provides countless services to meet the various public desires, but in doing so it has gone further and further into debt through deficit spending. This has been a major cause of inflation, which is not in the public interest. Inflation has caused the loss of public confidence and tremendous economic problems. One might be tempted to blame the result on the democratic process through which the political system heeds the desires of the public. *However, the real problem is the failure of leadership,* which includes the failure to effectively communicate in terms the people can understand. Little has been said to bring out that people in a democracy have responsibilities as well as rights and privileges. These failures have been to a large extent those of the public relations function, which did not consider the importance of the public interest.

[2] "What Consumerism Means for Marketers." *Harvard Business Review*, May/June 1972.

A great deal has been said about consumerism during the last few years. Opinion research findings show that the consumer issues are not primarily the product of consumer activists. In reality the consumer issues arise primarily from the marketplace. In essence the research shows that the public feels that business does not have the proper balance between important and necessary profit (money, lust for power, peer group approbation, ego,) on the one hand and the public interest on the other. This is a public relations problem. Therefore, one of the primary purposes of the public relations function is to help management and the entire organization understand and achieve this balance. In doing this the public relations function must be successfully coordinated and integrated with the functions of other parts of the organization.

As brought out earlier, the best principles of management will be needed. In a matter as complex as public relations, with its ever changing problems and situations, nothing is more important to success than the application of the best management principles. Later chapters in this book will deal with management principles as they relate to the public relations function.

Effective public relations activity will not result in "giving away the store," as some people may occasionally infer, but rather still having a store and continuing to do business in spite of tremendous public and governmental pressures. The public relations function is concerned with the best ways of guiding the organization so that it has the kind of environment in which it can prosper best.

Nicholas Murray Butler, former president of Columbia University, once said that there are three kinds of people—those who make things happen, those who watch what goes on, and those who don't know what has happened. The public relations management must be of the first group—those who make things happen.

WHAT REALLY DETERMINES CUSTOMER ATTITUDES?

At the beginning of the chapter, we said that the public relations function is concerned with performance and behavior. That an organization's performance and behavior must be the first consideration of the public relations function cannot be overemphasized. The effect of behavior or performance on customer attitudes is shown by an important research study completed in 1967. This milestone research project was conducted by the Pacific Telephone Company to find out what really determined their customer's attitudes. The study was designed by prominent specialists in the field, including Paul Lazarsfeld, former chairman of the sociology department at

Columbia University. It was conducted by examining the differences between the experiences and other characteristics of customers having the most favorable attitudes and those having the least favorable attitudes. (Chapter 2 discusses attitudes in detail.) Characteristics examined included:

- Customers' personal experience with the service.
- Their attitudes toward the company.
- Exposure and attitudes toward the company's advertising.
- Demographic characteristics (age, education, etc.).
- Attitudes toward other businesses' services, costs, images, and the like.
- Ideology (political orientation measured by attitudes toward big business, government control, and so forth).

The analysis was done in two ways:

- By study of the differences in the experiences of those with the most favorable and the least favorable attitudes.
- By simple and complex correlation analysis. (Factor analysis and multiple regression analysis were conducted by John Myers, professor of marketing, University of California at Berkeley.)

Let us look at some of the key findings. The difference between those with most favorable attitudes and those with least favorable attitudes in terms of their personal experiences is shown in the following table.

Number of Unfavorable Experiences	Least Favorable Attitudes	Most Favorable Attitudes	Difference
None	5%	32%	27%
One or two	20%	44%	24%
Three or more	75%	24%	51%

Of all the factors studied, those with the most favorable attitudes and those with the least favorable attitudes differed most in respect to their unfavorable experiences. Those with the least favorable attitudes had a much larger number of unfavorable experiences.

As shown in the table above,[3] 5 percent of those with the least favorable attitudes had no unfavorable experiences. This compares with 32 percent of those with the most favorable attitudes. On the other hand, 75 percent of

[3] Printed by permission of The Pacific Telephone and Telegraph Company, San Francisco.

the low attitude group had three or more unfavorable experiences compared to only 24 percent of the high attitude group—a difference of 51 percentage points.

Results of computer analysis of the relationship between unfavorable experiences and unfavorable attitudes showed that nine times out of ten unfavorable attitudes were the results of unfavorable experiences. In other words, performance as seen by the public is the primary determinant of peoples' attitudes. Since favorable attitudes are a key to good public relations, it is apparent that good public relations starts with good performance.

However, it does not necessarily follow that good public relations will result from good performance alone. Good performance must be publicly recognized and acknowledged, and it must be appreciated for it to result in good public relations.

COMMUNICATION

Communication is an important tool of the public relations function. Public recognition and acknowledgment of performance require communication to effectively bring the good performance to the attention of the public, which is another very important purpose of the public relations function. Effectively implementing this purpose can be much more difficult than it may first appear. Whatever is said must compete for attention and acceptance with a great volume of other information with which the public and its individual members are bombarded.

In addition past abuses such as false and misleading advertising, misrepresentation, poor labeling, and failure to stand behind warranties and guarantees have reduced the credibility of all organizations. Opinion research shows that although the public distinguishes between an individual organization that is doing a good job and those that do not, all organizations are faced with problems of communicating in a climate of distrust. The innocent and the guilty are tarred with the same brush. Legitimate claims boomerang. Motives are questioned. Yet it can be tremendously important to the organization that the public be well informed. Both performance and communication must be good in the broadest sense.

Good communication should effectively provide information that is in the public interest. One important example in which the public has not been sufficiently informed concerns the energy shortage. The public interest required an effective job of informing not only the general public but particularly the government, automobile manufacturers, architects, and so on. The need to conserve gasoline and other kinds of energy was not effectively communicated until a crisis developed. The government and the general public were caught unaware. Automobile companies continued to make bigger and heavier cars using more and more fuel per mile. Many architects gave scant or no attention to such matters as conserving heat and other forms of energy in designing houses and buildings.

Another important example concerns the food business and the future effect of the rapidly growing world population on food supplies. Information has not been effectively provided to the public or the government concerning possible world food shortages owing to increasing population. Yet shortages can greatly affect both availability and price. And as supply and price problems occur more and more frequently, they can effect the credibility and public relations of the food business. Effective communication could promote measures resulting in increased supplies.

THREE KINDS OF PERFORMANCES DETERMINE PUBLIC RELATIONS

Recognizing the importance of both performance and communication to good public relations, we can derive one of the fundamental definitions of the public relations function. *Good public relations results from good performance publicly acknowledged and appreciated.*[4]

In reality the public relations of any organization is determined by three kinds of performance. The first kind concerns the degree of satisfaction with the products or services of the organization and involves such things as sales, delivery, billing, and maintenance as well as the quality of the product or service itself and the effectiveness with which it meets the real needs of the potential consumer. "Product and service" apply whether they are provided by a business, government, a church, or some other organization.

The second kind of performance concerns policies set by management as regard to such things as:

• The organization as a place to work.

• Relations with the communities where the organization operates.

• The organization's attitudes toward the quality of its goods and services.

• The organization's policies toward using its skills in doing what is in the best interest of the customer rather than being skillful in making the customer do what suits the interest of the business.

• The policies toward keeping a proper balance between profit on the one hand and the public interest on the other.

[4] Cutlip and Center, *Effective Public Relations.* Englewood Cliffs, N.J.: Prentice-Hall, 1964.

GOOD PUBLIC RELATIONS

RESULTS FROM GOOD PERFORMANCE

PUBLICLY ACKNOWLEDGED AND

APPRECIATED.

Figure 3

The third kind of performance relates to the traditional communicative functions of the public relations staff. These functions include keeping the public informed concerning products, services, and policies.

The objectives of the public relations function should encompass all three areas of performance. The communicative objectives, however, must always reflect those of the other two. At every level of the organization, including the policy-making councils of top management, it is important that the public relations function effectively influence decisions so that they will be acceptable to customers and in the public interest. The public relations function should take the lead and initiate change when change is desirable.

KNOWLEDGE OF THE ORGANIZATION VITAL

To be successful, the public relations function should be cognizant of the functions, viewpoints, and problems of all the other parts of the organization. This knowledge is necessary for proper rapport and is vital to the formulation of practical and workable recommendations. It is essential to the management and conduct of the public relations function.

Earlier we pointed out that the purpose of the public relations function is to develop and maintain a social climate or environment in which the organization can prosper best. In the business world this relates directly to profitability. The public relations function includes recognizing its responsibility with respect to profit.

There is little real public quarrel with profit objectives. The quarrel is with viewpoints that enterprises are in business strictly to make a profit, with no thought for the public. Without sufficient profit, nothing can be accomplished by business organizations nor can they exist. There should be proper balance between sufficient profit on the one hand and the public interest on the other.

At the start of this chapter we said that in the effective management of any function the first consideration must be to define the purposes of the function. We have discussed the purposes of the public relations function. But what about the functions of management? There are many views of management, and even some managers can only vaguely define the management process. We briefly describe that process as it is viewed in this book. Other chapters, particularly Chapter 4 on the functions and responsibilities of public relations management, Chapter 5 on objectives, and Chapter 10 on developing and carrying out plans, broaden the discussion.

Sometimes management is construed as being primarily concerned with the supervision of people. The management process really consists of four orderly steps:

1. Analysis and definition of opportunities and problems.
2. Making decisions as to what will be done.
3. Getting the decisions carried out.
4. Analysis of the other three steps and their results after the decisions are partly or fully carried out.

These steps include planning, organizing, supervising, coordinating, controlling, and leading.

Many people are concerned with defining opportunities, problems, or situations, but their work does not include making decisions as to what will be done about their findings. These people can be extremely important to the success of an organization, but their work may not involve managing. Included, for example, are many accountants, economists, and research people.

People may make decisions, yet have no supervisory authority over those who will carry out the decisions. Nonetheless they get the decisions carried out. Decision makers may operate through others to get their decisions implemented. For example, one may have responsibility to make decisions for the president of an organization and to recommend specific actions. The president, who has the supervisory authority, makes it clear that the decisions and actions are to be carried out. In reality both the president and the person who made the decision are managers. Of course, if one merely offers two or more alternatives as possible decisions but makes no choice or decision, he or she is involved only in the first step of management—the analysis and definition of opportunities and problems.

For effective management, feedback of results and their analysis are important. Such feedback and analysis may include reviewing original problem analysis, the decisions as to what should be done, and the implementation of the decision. We should know what happened as a result of our actions, and why, in order to make possible future improvement. If the overall results do not come up to expectation, we should find out why so that corrective action may be taken.

The four steps needed for effective management that have been described work well in management by objectives, which is discussed in Chapter 5.

TWO

THE NATURE OF
Attitudes AND
Public Opinion

What is the nature of attitudes and public opinion? What are some of their effects? These are the primary concerns of public relations management. Therefore, anyone working in the field must have a special interest in these subjects.

We should be sure that we have a common understanding of what we mean by "public." By general public we mean the entire population—the rich and the poor and the middle class, men and women, young and old, educated and uneducated, all the racial, ethnic, and religious groups. A public, for the purpose of our discussion of public relations, is a group of people with some kind of common interest with which we are concerned.

Most people have some idea of what constitutes the general public. However, frequently we have a tendency to classify the people we know as the general public. In reality the attitudes of those we know personally may be biased one way or the other and not at all representative of the majority of people. Sometimes that is one of the problems of management. You may have heard stories about the heads of corporations who get the opinions of their dinner guests or their wives and then go down to the office and change the company's public relations or advertising program accordingly. A good example of this concerned a vice president of a large corporation and the head of a large department store. The company the vice president worked for was using radio programs to recruit employees. The program consisted of five-minute interviews with company employees who had had unusual experiences. It was a successful supplemental effort to classified newspaper ads.

The vice president and his wife had dinner with the president of the large department store, who did not like the program. Next day instructions were given to substitute a semiclassical music program. Unfortunately, the company could never identify a single applicant who came in as a result of the music program in the half year it ran.

Such an approach to arriving at decisions can be very hazardous. There are tools for finding out what the public thinks. For example, opinion research, if well done and properly used, can usually give us much better information than can our dinner guests.

SPECIAL PUBLICS

In public relations, we frequently have to consider particular groups of people for one reason or another. For example, there may be a reason to approach a particular group about a government regulation that you wish changed or put into effect. Therefore, government people are a "public." The suppliers your organization buys from are a special public. Each of the various minorities may be another special public. Employees are still another public. And so forth.

Large organizations may have many thousands of employees who are a very important public, not only because of their own views but also because they influence their families and may influence their relatives, friends, neighbors, people in other institutions and government offices, and so on. Among employees of a given organization there will be several different publics with diverse attitudes and viewpoints. Each department may be a public. Women, men, minority groups, nonminority groups, lower management, middle management, young people, and those ready to retire may each be a separate and important public.

Employees are an especially important public because an employee is regarded by his friends as an expert on his organization. If he is not properly informed about important matters concerning the organization, his job, and his department, he may be embarrassed when asked about them. Thus his attitude toward the organization he works for may be lowered. It follows that he may speak less favorably about his organization, or the quality of his work may suffer.

The stockholders of a business are a "public." If you want to borrow money or sell stock, the banks, security dealers, and security analysts are a very important public. They are such an important public that there is a

A "PUBLIC" IS A GROUP
OF PEOPLE WITH SOME KIND OF
A COMMON INTEREST WITH WHICH
WE ARE CONCERNED.

Figure 4

specialized branch of the public relations function known as financial public relations.

Youth is an important public that may consist of several subpublics by level of education attained or by age group. Certain of the youth, college students in particular, will become the leaders of tomorrow, and this gives them special importance.

Educators are a public important to us, not only in their own right but also because they influence the attitudes and beliefs of both youth and the general public. And more and more educators are taking part in government today. They write books, are members of commissions, and run for office. In relations with educators it is important to give faculty members as much first hand knowledge as possible of the organization to which they may or may not send their graduates for employment. Well-conceived organization-sponsored aids to education in the form of films, guides, and demonstration material along the lines of the organization's special competences may also be helpful.

Church leaders constitute a public. Through their influence, contacts, and sermons, they may sometimes help to create a favorable or unfavorable opinion of an organization.

Government is an important public. Regulatory groups such as the Federal Trade Commission, the Food and Drug Administration, the Federal Communications Commission, the Interstate Commerce Commission are examples of several different government publics. The tax people are another. The people who make government purchases of goods and services may constitute several more. The federal government is the largest customer of many businesses, and it can make its weight felt in the marketplace. According to Philip Kotler in his book *Marketing Management,* by 1974 government purchases came to $277 billion a year of products and services, or 21 percent of the gross national product.[1] Federal government purchases account for 65 percent of the total spent at all levels.

People from a particular kind of business may be a public. For example, automobile dealers may have strong feelings about an organization's pur-

[1] Englewood Cliffs, N.J.: Prentice-Hall, 1976.

chasing a large number of foreign-made vehicles. People from other businesses in general may be another public. For instance, to a newspaper, businesses in general could all be potential advertisers. Racial groups are special publics—the Black, the Mexican-American, the Chinese, and so on. Particular economic groups can be publics. The importance of these special publics to businesses and other organizations should be apparent.

A person may be a member of a number of different publics. He may be a member of a particular ethnic group, of a particular age group, of a particular industry group, of a particular union. He may be a Republican or a Democrat or an independent.

It may be necessary or advantageous to search for and take special cognizance of any of the special publics or several of them, not only as to what and how we communicate with them but also as to how we deal with them in other ways. For example, special training may be given to underprivileged people so that they may obtain jobs and become self-sufficient.

New special publics constantly emerge. For example, in the last 10 to 15 years, groups interested in protecting the environment have become important, as have those interested in consumer protection. Special publics frequently influence political action and the social environment a great deal more than the so-called general public. Special publics spearhead the changes. They arouse interest on the part of the public as a whole. Recognizing the various special publics that can affect an organization's public relations favorably or unfavorably is one of the keys to good public relations.

ATTITUDES AND PUBLIC OPINION

Now that we have defined what publics are, we will discuss public opinion. What is public opinion? An opinion is an expression of an attitude. To have an opinion implies that there can be differences in belief or opinion.

An attitude is an emotional feeling toward something—for example, toward an issue, a situation, or an organization. Note the word "emotional." Differing political attitudes are a fine example of attitudes as emotional feelings.

One often sees people attempting to change attitudes by presenting so-called "facts" from the viewpoint of the presenter, but opinions of what the facts really are may vary greatly depending on one's self-interest. Facts have little or no emotional impact in terms of the listener's self-interest. For example, a large public utility, in applying for higher rates, made a practice of providing vast quantities of data and testimony in the best legal fashion. However, the state regulatory agency seldom gave the utility the higher

AN OPINION IS AN EXPRESSION
OF AN ATTITUDE.
AN ATTITUDE IS THE EMOTIONAL
FEELING TOWARD SOMETHING, FOR
EXAMPLE TOWARD AN ISSUE, A SITUATION
OR AN ORGANIZATION.
PUBLIC OPINION IS THE COMPOSITE
OF THE OPINIONS OF ALL OF THE PEOPLE
WHO MAKE UP THE PUBLIC.

Figure 5

rates it desired. The utility stuck to the "facts" as it saw them and did not express its needs in terms of customers' self-interest.

Public opinion is the composite of the opinions of all the people who make up the public. To influence public opinion, therefore, one must influence the attitudes and beliefs of individual people and ultimately individual groups or publics.

Attitudes are basically determined by what one conceives to be his or her own self-interest. Once self-interest is aroused, attitudes are not easily changed. People tend to avoid exposure to communication inconsistent with their existing beliefs and attitudes.

What are people's self-interests? Sometimes it is not as easy to know as one might presume. Economic interests (wages or salaries, for example) may frequently take a back seat to other interests. In his book, *The Evolution of Management Thought,* Daniel A. Wren discusses the much-publicized investigations that were carried out during the lates 1920's at the Hawthorne plant of Western Electric Company.[2] Western Electric Company is the equipment-producing and supply arm of the American Telephone and Telegraph Company. The Hawthorne plant is located in the Chicago west-side industrial area. The investigations were first conducted by the National Research Council of the National Academy of Science and later by the Harvard University industrial research people.

Before the investigations were conducted, it was generally thought that people reacted primarily to economic and physical incentives, but the investigations showed that it was not special wage incentive plans but rather *interpersonal relationships* that led to improved output. Physical needs were not as important as social needs. The investigations showed that people

[2] New York: Ronald Press, 1972, pp. 276–290.

reacted more favorably to communicative efforts in a supervisory climate of openness, concern, and willingness to listen.

People act in their self-interest to protect their group status. People are social beings and therefore frequently may seem illogical as to what they conceive of as in their interests. They want social recognition, social satisfaction, and the security of social relationships. They may owe their allegiance to more than one group. For example, a person may be a member of an informal work group, his family, a professional society, and a political party all at once.

Attitudes are influenced by many things. A person's own experiences, of course, are a tremendously important source of his attitudes. His religion may be the source of or may influence his attitudes. He may have chosen his religious beliefs, he may have taken the religious beliefs of his parents. His economic status can be an important source of his attitudes. In addition one of the greatest influences on attitudes is the family. The family contributes greatly to personality, which in turn contributes greatly to attitudes.

One of the things that makes educators such an important public to all organizations is that they can have a considerable effect on children's attitudes that may remain with them throughout life. Family and educators influence attitudes during a person's formative years.

Some attitudes can be the result of the social group to which a person belongs. Attitudes may have been acquired or inherited from the social group of which a person is a member. People's attitudes are greatly affected by the groups to which they belong or to which they would like to belong, or groups they dislike. An important reason for this is that people are rewarded for conforming to the attitudinal dictates of the group.

The country in which a person lives or from which his parents came can have a lot to do with his attitudes. The common law of the land reflects attitudes developed by centuries of experience. Thus persons living in countries with a background of English common law may have a different viewpoint from those with a Spanish background. Such differences may influence attitudes considerably.

ATTITUDES ARE DETERMINED

BY SELF-INTEREST. ONCE SELF-

INTEREST IS AROUSED, ATTITUDES

ARE NOT EASILY CHANGED.

Figure 6

A person's motives and goals may have an important bearing on his attitudes. Sex, job, age, and health are also keys to attitude. How a person was treated by his parents and the training he received from his parents are not only important to attitudes but may be the primary key to how responsible he is and how he acts as a member of society. Maybe a person's mother was Victorian or his father a banker or a union organizer or perhaps his family lost everything in the great depression of the early 1930s. Such things can greatly influence attitudes.

THE COMPLEXITY OF ATTITUDES

A person's basic overall attitudes and how he perceives himself and the world can have complex foundations. Every person is apt to be quite different from every other person, because each one is influenced and molded by his own multitude of experiences throughout life. It is as if one were looking through a church window with each of his experiences being one of the countless pieces of differently colored stained glass.

The fact that each person is different can sometimes make the public relations function especially difficult, because those concerned with public relations judgment must perceive public attitudes through their own stained glass windows. This calls for great care and good perception. Fortunately, we can frequently examine attitudes concerning one thing at a time. However, this procedure can sometimes lead to pitfalls and erroneous conclusions. Computer analysis of the correlation between attitudes toward different things can be helpful in avoiding wrong conclusions.

INFLUENCING ATTITUDES

One may ask: Why can we not give the people the facts and then they may come up with the right attitudes? What are the facts? How often can we really get the facts? As we said earlier, most frequently we get only opinions as to what the facts are. Such "facts" are facts only in light of the experiences, viewpoints, and wishes of the people expressing them. Even when they have the facts, people are influenced more by their emotions than by facts. This leads us to three basic precepts of importance to the public relations function. Consideration of these three basic precepts is important to success in attempting to influence attitudes.

1. People will ignore ideas, opinions, and viewpoints unless they are affected by them personally in some way.

PEOPLE WILL IGNORE IDEAS,

OPINIONS AND VIEWPOINTS UNLESS

THEY AFFECT THEM PERSONALLY IN

SOME WAY.

YOUR MESSAGE MUST BE STATED

IN TERMS OF THE INTEREST OF YOUR

AUDIENCE.

Figure 7

2. Your message must be stated in terms of the interest of your audience.
3. People are apt to change their attitudes only when there is "something in it for them."

The implications of these three precepts for communication and for motivation are tremendous. Think of the implications for communications with employees, for example. Upper management often attempts to communicate with employees in terms of *its* interests, failing to recognize the interests of the employees.

People may not accept facts as facts. The extent to which this goes can be illustrated by a viewpoint held by a person who professed that whether it was going to rain could be determined by looking at the moon. If the edge of the crescent of the moon was tilted downward, according to this person, it meant that water would spill and it was going to rain. Sound silly? Well, how many other viewpoints seem equally as foolish? But such ideas are difficult to change.

That is why public relations decisions can be so difficult sometimes and why one cannot write a public relations rulebook giving all the answers. The answers depend to a large extent on the public's perception of the particular situation at the particular time. Success in public relations efforts depends a great deal on developing the best possible perceptive abilities.

We have said that good public relations results from good performance publicly acknowledged and appreciated. We have also suggested that good public relations depends on favorable attitudes. Favorable attitudes in turn depend on good performance. We also said that people will ignore ideas, opinions, and viewpoints unless they are personally affected in some way. To affect people personally requires making performance more visible, that is, changing performance or engaging in new performance from the public's viewpoint. Communicative effort is important to get performance noticed and appreciated.

Public attitudes are based on what people know or think they know about performance. In regard to many social issues, performance and events are felt to be synonymous. For example, inflation, recession, and Watergate are events, but to most of the public they are synonymous with performance. Thus events, not communicative action, are the key elements in bringing about changes of attitudes on social issues. Again, however, communicative effort may call attention to the events, giving visibility and gaining acknowledgment and appreciation. The communicative effort can get either favorable or unfavorable "appreciation," which will be illustrated by an example discussed in the next paragraph.

That events, not communicative activity, have the greatest affect on attitudes has great importance in the political world. Thus Watergate and inflation played the greatest role in defeating large numbers of Republican Party candidates in the 1974 elections. Communicative activity by the Republicans had little effect in overcoming what the public perceived as performance problems. Communicative activity by Democratic Party candidates called attention to the perceived performance failures of the Republicans, thus helping to get acknowledgment and unfavorable "appreciation" of them. The lesson to politicians and those interested in political science may be that political parties should give more attention to performance in the public interest. Thus they may help to shape and control events in the direction necessary for favorable attitudes.

Inflation is another example of how events, not communicative activity, are the key elements in changing and shaping attitudes. The perils of inflation have received publicity for years, but relatively few people paid any attention until the inflation started to affect them noticeably. The event of rampant inflation changed public attitudes. Suddenly everyone was talking about it and demanding that government do something immediately. Business and labor were accused of being the cause, thus further impairing the favorableness of their public relations.

Likewise, warnings of impending shortages of energy supplies have been given at intervals for years, but it took an embargo on oil by the Arab nations to drive home the seriousness of the energy situation. Even then, as gasoline and other energy supplies became more abundant again, people were not personally affected sufficiently to cause them to worry greatly. Interestingly, proposals have been made in the United States to place a heavy tax on gasoline to drastically curtail its use. The futility of this measure is shown by the experience in other parts of the world where prices of "petrol" at $1.25 to $1.80 a gallon has done little to curtail its use appreciably.

Much publicity has recently, been given to impending serious food shortages, but in a great part of the world no real food shortages yet exist. People do not see the event, so to a considerable degree the warnings go unheeded. Thus the problem of public relations managements of the food industry is difficult and is made more so by the loss of credibility by all business. Yet an effective public information program directed especially at government is essential. Without it, as we will discuss later, the food industry and business in general will take the blame when more drastic shortages develop.

One hears it said that the press molds and sways public attitudes for or against one side or another as concerns political and other events. In reality events themselves have the major effect in molding public opinion. Of course, biased reporting of the event, in which one side or another of an issue is given predominant treatment, can incorrectly portray the event and wrongly influence attitudes. And there is a good bit of biased reporting. Frequently, however, what is desired by one side or the other of a controversy, however, is that events be played down or that information be withheld altogether so that it does not become public knowledge. Such was the desire in the case of Watergate and Nixon. In the case of Watergate it was primarily the event, not the press, that influenced public opinion. The press merely provided the information about the event to the public.

People interpret events in terms of what they conceive as their own self-interest. Whenever possible, people avoid being exposed to information that is contrary to their experiences and beliefs. If a situation forces them to be exposed to such information, they may become angered and will usually give as little attention to the information as possible. Information programs wind up talking to people who already agree with what is said and who have the same beliefs and attitudes expressed in the programs. Since these people do not need persuasion, the effort is largely wasted.

People are constantly bombarded by an endless stream of information and attempts to mold and change their beliefs and attitudes. However, unless the communicative effort is coupled with some aspect of performance or some emotional consideration of interest to them, it will be ignored. It will have little more effect than water on a duck's back. This principle should be of major interest to public relations management and should be of particular concern to those responsible for the communicative aspects of the public relations function. Millions of dollars have been spent on ineffective public information programs by business, government, and other organizations because those responsible for the public relations function failed to understand this fundamental principle.

THE EFFECTS OF ATTITUDES

What are the effects of attitudes and opinions? They are what determine the course of events, the direction an organization can go, the direction the country or the whole world moves. Let us consider an example.

A few years ago the University of California campus at Berkeley was the scene of many disorders. In addition to disturbing the public, the disorders disturbed the alumni-who most people would agree are a key public as far as any university is concerned. With each succeeding disorder on the campus, more alumni became disturbed. As a part of the university's centennial celebration, it set out to collect a large endowment fund, but the alumni questioned whether the university was an institution to which they wanted to contribute. A large number decided not to give. The university found it could not get the original sum, so it reduced the figure successively through a number of steps and finally received only a small fraction of the amount it had set out to collect. That is the sad story of what adverse opinion by a key public can do.

The record is filled with other examples of how adverse public opinion has affected organizations. The bankruptcy of the Penn Central Railroad is an example. The attitudes of passengers and shippers toward the railroad's performance had a major effect on its public relations and thus its business. Passengers and shippers' attitudes were the result of the attitudes of railroad management and workers. Poor performance caused shippers to avoid the railroad whenever possible. Railroad cars and sometimes whole trainloads of shipments became hopelessly lost. Joseph R. Daughen and Peter Binzen, authors of *The Wreck of the Penn Central,* relate that the son of the president of the railroad complained to his father that the passenger trains were always late, dirty, and too hot or too cold. His father replied, "If you don't like it, walk."[3]

The public relations problems of Consolidated Edison Company of New York, beginning in the late 1960s, is another example. As reported by *The Wall Street Journal,*[4] power failures, high rates, and customers outraged by treatment such as service shut off because of clerical errors drastically affected public attitudes toward the company. Generally poor performance, low employee morale, and inefficiency contributed further to public relations problems. Poor repute with investors added financial public relations difficulties and to money problems. Inability to deal effectively with the New York State regulatory agency—a public of prime importance to Consolidated Edison—further complicated matters. The company's management hired a consulting firm to help "achieve a better identity." It

[3] Boston:Little, Brown, 1971.
[4] August 26, 1968.

repainted its trucks a different color and adopted a new slogan, but the problem, as the consulting firm soon found out, went deeper than so-called "identity."

The examples of the Penn Central Railroad and Consolidated Edison emphasize the importance of performance to attitudes and public relations. It is obvious that good public relations has a high value and that poor public relations can lead to failure and bankruptcy. An organization's good performance stands out as the key factor in good public relations.

THREE

Public Environment
AND ITS IMPORTANCE TO
PUBLIC RELATIONS
MANAGEMENT

In the introduction to this book and in our consideration of the purposes of the public relations function in Chapter 1, we stated some of the reasons why attention to public relations (or external relations) is so necessary. We pointed out that the public relations function is an investment in the privilege to operate. Without this investment, without the public relations function or activity, an organization can lose its freedom to operate at all, or it can have its freedom to operate curtailed by a multitude of laws and government regulations. The public relations function is responsible for sensitivity to the public interest. The public relations manager is responsible for informing his colleagues in top management and throughout the organization of the potential consequences and opportunities of public relations problems. The purpose of the public relations function is *to help develop and maintain an environment in which the organization can prosper best.*

The quality of a management may be judged by its ability to correctly perceive its environment and to effectively do something about it. Correctly perceiving the environment is essential to making good decisions that will enable the organization to prosper. With this in mind, having discussed attitudes, we now examine more fully the environment and its influence on public relations.

In our discussion of the public relations environment, only some of the more important factors can be included. There are many other factors, some of great importance, that are relevant to particular organizations. The ability of public relations management to discern these factors will depend on its perception and its use of problem and opportunity analysis (situation analysis).

SOME IMPORTANT FACTORS IN THE ENVIRONMENT

Some of the more important factors in the environment include the following:

1. *More and more people are better educated.*   This causes them, among other things, to observe more, to be more discriminating, and to be more demanding. A larger percentage of the population is younger, and public opinion research shows that this leads to the same results. At the same time, the amount of knowledge available on almost every subject has multiplied. Improved communication and transportation have expanded the scope of activities and interests and areas of concern tremendously—sometimes to include the entire world. Interrelationships between various major fields of study have become more important.

Thus although many people may seem better educated, frequently their knowledge is relatively superficial and insufficient for proper understanding of a problem. Their knowledge may be narrowly focused on a given area without knowledge of important interrelationships with other areas. Situations and solutions that seem simple to them may be in fact tremendously complex.

Many examples of these facts plague organizations of all kinds. For instance, in the political area senators, presidents of important national organizations, as well as people in general, have speculated as to why government leaders did not take the simple steps that were advocated to quickly curb inflation. The public's knowledge of the causes of inflation is superficial and insufficient. As concerns the physical environment, many are impatient at the delay and seemingly needless obstacles to cleaning up air and water pollution. They do not understand the interrelationships with other key matters. Some people wonder why governments do not quickly come to agreements on stopping conflicts. Many are annoyed at how long it has taken for man to recognize people's needs for growth, for development and utilization of potential, or for the aesthetic things of life.

Solutions frequently seem simple because people are not sufficiently informed. Lack of information on the part of the public can often present special challenges to public relations management.

2. *Greater affluence is an important factor in the public relations environment.*   Even during recessions, more people have more money than in past decades. Money whets the appetite for "more and better" and helps to

remove the reluctance people once had for demanding better performance from the suppliers of goods and services. Affluence also enables people to be more discriminating.

3. *Communications reach more people more quickly.* Today radio, television, newspapers, magazines, and books, as well as the telephone and the worldwide mail system spread information, biased or unbiased, quickly and thoroughly. This increases the visibility of both good and bad behavior on the part of organizations and makes it easier for people to discover malfeasance.

The ever more crowded world and urbanization of large areas lend increasing importance and visibility to the failure to recognize the public interest and to act with social responsibility. Such failures are more apt to be publicized. An example is the pollution of air and water.

4. *The growth of population.* Little has been said about the tremendous effect of the exponential growth of world population as it affects public relations. The world now has over four billion people—and only eight billion acres of arable land. With a world growth rate of about 2 percent per year, the population will double by the year 2010.[1] Although the rate of growth in the United States and some other places is much less, worldwide consumption is the problem. The resulting increasing world shortages can have a large effect on the social environment and therefore public relations. The scarcity of raw materials will increasingly raise world and domestic prices, curtail availability of products in the marketplace, and require substitute products. In such a situation, without the best attention to public relations, suppliers and government will be blamed and will take the brunt of the problems.

What measures can public relations people take to be aware of impending shortages? In many organizations potential shortages are already recognized, at least to some degree. In others public relations management may use such things as discussion with knowledgeable people in other departments, careful watch of magazines, newspaper articles, new books, upward changes in prices that signal a change in demand or supply, new uses without new sources, and good perception to become aware.

An example of a business that failed to take appropriate action during a shortage is the canning jar industry in 1974. Given the inflated prices for food, it was not hard to predict that housewives would can large amounts of fruits and vegetables. Yet the industry failed to perceive this. When canning season arrived, it was not long before not a jar or jar lid was to be found on

---

[1] Paul R. Erlich and Anne H. Erlich, *Population, Resources and Environment.* San Francisco: Freeman, 1970.

grocers' shelves. The industry lost the business. It also failed to heed the public interest. It contributed to the general lack of confidence in business and all other institutions. And specifically, its own public relations were damaged.

Public relations managements of organizations that may be affected should see that potential shortages are effectively made known internally. They should see that the legislative and executive branches of government and institutions that have a voice concerning the use of materials in potentially short supply are effectively informed. Prudent use and conservation of materials within the organization should be required. Other businesses, government, and the public should be effectively encouraged to be prudent. Substitutes for potentially scarce items should be developed whenever possible.

The scarcities may bring conflicts of interest between world markets and a demand that sale of scarce commodities abroad be embargoed. The political reactions to scarcities and rising prices may make favorable public relations even more difficult to achieve for business, government, political parties, and others. Shortages may force abandonment of viewpoints currently held by some concerning such things as natural foods, chemical fertilizers, and pesticide residues.

During a period of shortages, crime and violence may increase as more people seek to forcibly take what they cannot get otherwise. This also is a part of the social environment that public relations people must recognize. One possible action in such an event is to ensure that the organization has good relations with the police authorities. Plans may be made for use in event of various contingencies.

The growth of population also increases the interdependence of people in almost every phase of life. Individual action becomes more difficult. People are dependent on public transportation to get them to work. Large distribution systems are needed. Communications facilities become more complex and more important.

Particularly in urban areas, government becomes more costly and complex as such services as education, the provision of water, the removal of waste, the handling of traffic, and law enforcement burgeon. Such events as strikes, the weather, and natural catastrophes have a greater effect.

The growth of population is an important factor in the public relations environment that is apt to be overlooked.

5. *Resistance to change and customs carried over from an earlier day* is also a factor in the public relations environment and may invite a failure to progress with the times because management, through habit or failure to perceive changed conditions, continues outmoded ideas and practices.

Management, employees, or other groups within organizations may defend the status quo because they believe change constitutes a threat to their status.

Of course, change merely for change sake offers no advantages. Resistance to truly unnecessary or undesirable change is not only justifiable but desirable. However, resistance to change per se can reduce innovation and prevent progress.

6. *The increasing rapidity of change* is of growing importance and is a factor in the environment that imposes two problems. The first concerns management's keeping abreast of the new—of keeping up with the times. Lack of innovativeness on the part of many organizations prevents change. Obvious needs do not occur to them until a competitor takes the opportunity the organization was unable to recognize.

The second problem stems from a failure to manage change in order to help the organization develop and maintain an environment in which it can prosper best. Chapter 11 is devoted to a discussion of the management of change.

7. *Impersonality.* Impersonality is a factor that has become a part of the environment without many people specifically noting it. The relationship between most organizations and the people they serve has become extremely impersonal. For example, in the marketplace at one time in history the customer dealt personally with the one who made the article or furnished the service. The supplier is now almost always remote and impersonal.

This impersonality has led to many abuses by businesses and other organizations, including lack of service, insufficient supply, and indifference of employees, many of whom have a "couldn't care less" attitude. It has resulted in salespeople who know little or nothing about their wares, thus frustrating inquiring customers. Such employees and their negative motivation cause high product failure and poor service with catastrophic results to public attitudes. In large businesses, large government, and other large organizations, impersonality is also a problem in employee relations, adding to negative motivation.

8. *Bigness.* Bigness, too, has become a major factor in the environment. It is looked at favorably and defended by some and decried by others, but as illustrated by big corporations, big government, big labor unions, big churches, and so on, bigness is a major factor in the environment and cannot be ignored.

One of the causes of impersonality is bigness. There are many advantages of bigness, but bigness also brings many disadvantages that the wise public relations manager will seek to overcome. It may hinder initiative, delay decisions, bring lack of coordination, foster internal politics, cause disregard of people as individuals, reduce desirable motivation, and nourish arrogance.

Bigness frequently brings lack of coordination between departments. For example, in a major company's special promotion introducing a new toothpaste, a $1.00 refund offer was displayed in California. However, the refund certificate on display stated that the offer was good only in Michigan. In another case a department head of one of the country's largest businesses was in a large supermarket. It was the last day of a major special promotion using extensive advertising that was a part of the executive's responsibilities. However, the sales department had failed to get the essential point-of-sale material to a single store other than the one the department head was in. The whole effort and a lot of money went down the drain. The benefits of the promotion were lost. A negative attitude was left with the public whose interest had been whetted by national advertising.

A major food company widely promoted a special offer on cooking oil, but none of the oil was to be found on the shelves of the supermarkets in the area. A service company's business offices with great politeness regularly accepted orders from customers, only to have the service department just as regularly fail to keep the commitments made.

The top managements of a great many large companies have the highest ethical intentions, but they are so remote and frequently uninformed that they are unable to prevent serious violations in parts of their organizations. For example, a part of one district of a national grocery chain began to ignore the company's advertised special promotion prices. Customers at checkout stands were charged regular prices instead of those advertised. Only a letter to the president of the company corrected the situation. In another case, a national oil company mixed up its billing between customers and ignored requests to correct the billing errors. For several months it sent the bills of a California customer to a Florida customer of the same name. Then it charged the California customer a late payment penalty. Only communication with its head office in Houston, Texas, remedied the situation.

Examples like these contribute to a lack of public confidence and to unfavorable attitudes.

9. Another factor in the environment is *the increasing recognition of old injustices and a demand that they be corrected.* An example is racial, religious, age, or sex discrimination. There is a literal explosion of views, demands, and actions in this controversial area. Government laws and regulations concerning equal employment opportunity, education, and housing have made this area an important part of the public environment.

The need to eliminate discrimination based on color, religion, age, sex, or favoritism is apparent. Equal employment opportunity also concerns the need for rewards to be based on performance. This need is based partly on integrity and ethics, but it has other important bases. From an organizational viewpoint, only with the best performance can one deliver goods and services in the public interest. Only with the best performance can one cope with competition. From a national viewpoint, only with the best performance can one successfully cope internationally in the areas of commerce and defense. These are important reasons for basing rewards on performance. Both factors–the need to eliminate discrimination based on race, religion, age, sex, and favoritism and the need for reward based on performance—involve controversy and are important parts of the environment.

10. *Large and inquisitive government with a malignant and insatiable appetite to expand, spend, and control more* is much discussed. As a part of the environment, government has a major influence on public relations. Coupled with this influence is the growing population and urbanization. In turn has come willingness and sometimes need to turn over to government the responsibility for more and more functions. In addition failure by individuals or organizations to recognize and meet obvious needs leaves a vacuum to be filled by government.

In the area of regulation, particularly, government will probably take an ever-expanding share of the private organizations' attention and take away an ever-expanding share of their perquisites. Federal agencies and commissions have grown in power as various practices, which the public believed were not in its interests, caused Congress to enact laws providing more and more authority.

Some of the principal United States agencies are the Federal Trade Commission, the Food and Drug Administration, the Securities Exchange Commission, the Federal Communications Commission, the Interstate Commerce Commission, and the Consumer Products Safety Commission. Regulatory agencies and commissions have also been established by the states. To give an example of the growth of regulatory agencies, by 1974, 57 government agencies looked after consumer interests in milk at a cost of $3 billion annually.

Another important effect of the growth of government concerns the ability to finance business and industry. During the past decade particularly, growth of government expenditures has been enormous. According to A. Gerlof Homan, *by 1974 41 percent of the annual gross national income in the United States was being spent by government.*[2] (The amount spent, which includes expenditures for education, defense, foreign aid, welfare payments, and so on, should not be confused with the amount of government

[2] Speech delivered to the Society for Advancement of Management, San Francisco Chapter, November 21, 1974.

purchases mentioned in Chapter 2.) Government is taking more and more of the total pie of finance available.

One result of this huge amount of government expenditure is the financial starving of business. Business is unable to raise the needed capital, which prevents modernization and the building of new capacity. However, if the economy is to be strong, there must be a continuous strong push for new capacity and modernization. (The growth and centralization of government and the capital requirements crisis are discussed further in Chapter 11 on the management of change.)

No organization can prosper for long in a sick economy. Healthy businesses cannot exist in a sick society. This is a very important aspect of the public environment, and public relations management, even in the field of financial public relations, has largely neglected it.

With the growth of government expenditures has come constantly increasing taxation and deficit spending, which is the major cause of inflation. All three have a tremendous effect on the public environment and therefore should be of concern to public relations management.

11. *Vociferous special groups and activists have learned to gain attention,* frequently unwarranted, from politicians and from the press, radio, and television. These groups must be contended with as a part of the environment.

12. *The growing voice of the consumer.* Consumerism is one of the most important factors in the public relations environment. Many people relate consumerism to commerce and the marketing of goods, but it is also important to the professions. Lawyers, medical doctors, real estate brokers, insurance businesses, accountants, contractors, and others are greatly affected by consumerism.

Some people feel that consumerism is the result of the activities of such workers as Ralph Nader, but opinion research shows that although activists and government agencies have a great deal to say about the shortcomings of businesses and the professions, in reality the consumer issues arise primarily directly from the marketplace. The public feels that business does not have the proper balance between profit on the one hand and the public interest on the other. People feel that a breach of contract has occurred between the buyer and the seller. They complain about such things as false and misleading advertising, misrepresentation, overcharging, poor product quality, unsafe and harmful products, service problems, poor labeling, and failure to stand behind warranties and guarantees. People favor government regulation when they see the public interest ignored. More people believe that large companies should not be allowed to grow as much as they wish. Regulation, litigation, and unfavorable publicity add greatly to the complexity of business and to the cost of doing business. Thus consumerism, which causes them, is a major factor in the public relations environment.

Some business people contend that consumerism is a passing problem, but there is no indication that it will cease to be an important consideration to business and the professions. The causes of consumerism and of subsequent government intervention generally result from failure on someone's part to heed the public interest. More is said about consumerism in subsequent chapters.

13. Anyone who has read the newspapers of the past decade is aware of the *importance of ecology* to the public relations environment. Clean air and clean water are among the leading public demands.

14. *The atmosphere of unconcern, avoidance of responsibility, lower morality, and disregard of principle and ethics. Lawlessness.*

All of these factors are interrelated. One cause, of course, is greed for profit, power, votes, peer approval and so forth, without regard for the public interest. But greed is as old as mankind.

Population growth, impersonality, and bigness contribute to the opportunity for lower morality, disregard of principle and ethics, and lawlessness. They provide the chance of not being caught or punished. But this, too, may be only a small part of the problem.

Collectivism, discussed in Chapter 11, makes it possible for groups to obtain unwarranted advantages at the expense of other groups and individuals. This may result in retaliation.

The information explosion spreads information about malfeasance in high places with little or no punishment. Others emulate what they hear or see.

The tendency by courts and the legal profession to emphasize procedure and technicalities rather than real justice contributes to the problem.

In this ever more crowded world, the public interest becomes increasingly important. Failure to consider it becomes more harmful.

The adversary relationships between government and other organizations may contribute to the problem, as does ineffective management of government agencies and departments.

Unconcern and avoidance of responsibility come partly from bigness and impersonality. They may also come from penalties, either legal or by social groups, which may result from becoming concerned and taking responsibility. Responsibility and authority go hand in hand. Without authority, the tendency may be to avoid responsibility.

The primary cause of these related undesirable aspects of the environment may be the lack of leadership. As brought out in Chapter 1, the ethical responsibilities and duties of all organizations and their managers are greater than for society as a whole because they are in a position of leadership. They have authority. They stand out and occupy a position of visibility. It is their duty to set the example, to provide desirable objectives, and to motivate people to try to reach them.

It may be primarily in the realm of leadership and insistence on leadership by all parts of management that the public relations function can best help meet these environmental factors.

15. A part of the public relations environment is *the shift in emphasis to what is termed "the quality of life."* With the necessities (such as having enough to eat and reasonable shelter) better provided for large parts of the population, many people have the time and money to be more concerned with "the quality of life." They do what they prefer to do even if, for example, it means less affluence. They may stop working for a business, take time out to get a Ph. D., and then join the academic world. Or they may take time out to travel or play golf, for example.

16. Many of the lower motivational requirements are being met, so that what motivates people to work has changed. As brought out in Abraham Maslow's hierarchy of needs,[3] after the basic needs of survival (food, shelter, sleep, sex, safety, and security) are met, other higher needs emerge. Some of these are the need for love and belonging, self esteem, esteem by others, meaningfulness, justice, and beauty.

As Maslow pointed out, "What a man can be, he must be." Therefore, the need for growth, development, and utilization of potential have increased in importance as has the need to know and understand and the aesthetic need for beauty. Today, the growth needs, the need to know and understand, and the aesthetic needs have greater importance in motivating people.

17. *Inflation.* We referred to the inflationary effect of large and inquisitive government as our tenth factor. Inflation has a profound influence on public relations. With high prices, many customers cannot afford some products or services at all, and prudent customers may curtail their use. Businesses take the brunt of the blame for the higher prices, which creates public relations problems with political overtones. Nonbusiness organizations must curtail their operations because of high costs. Inflation also fosters carelessness about the quality of products and service. The results of inflation on markets, costs, and finance, can have catastrophic effects on an organizations' environment and its ability to prosper.

18. The *negative view held of profit and business.* There is a widely held negative view of and hostility toward profit. This view and hostility are a great danger to society and to both business and nonbusiness institutions. Those holding negative viewpoints include many among the superficially

---

[3] *Motivation and Personality.* New York: Harper and Row, 1954.

well educated, the leaders and members of some consumer organizations, the leaders and members of some labor organizations, and a considerable percentage of the youth. Many politicians, members of legislatures, regulatory agency staff members, people working in government departments, school teachers, and church leaders have unfavorable attitudes toward profit.

However, business profit and savings from past profits not only finance every business and all economic growth and jobs, they also make possible and finance all nonbusiness institutions and activities. This includes government, which is supported by taxes, the money for which is initially derived from business profits and wages. It also includes the schools and universities, churches, and other social institutions. Business must produce enough goods and services not only to supply itself and its people but also a surplus to supply all the rest of society. The surplus is the difference between the value produced by business activity and the cost. It is profit.

Peter Drucker states in his book, *Management: Tasks, Responsibilities, Practices,* that even the Soviet Union recognizes the need for profit.[4] The commissars who run Soviet enterprises do so on a higher margin of profit than do managers in the West. Probably one of the primary causes of the negative attitudes toward profit is the concept held and expressed by many business people that the purpose of business is only the maximization of profit. Drucker suggests that this is the major cause of the misunderstanding of the nature of profit and the deep-seated hostility toward it.

There has been an extreme focus on profit by business leaders, and this has had a decided effect on the public relations environment. Business success has come to be judged by many people almost entirely in terms of short-term profit. Too often the race for profit supersedes integrity and ethics. Drucker points out that many managers define the goals of their businesses only as profit maximization, yet they constantly complain of hostility to profit.

Profit for both the present and the long term must always be the first consideration and the first requirement of every business because without profit the business will cease to exist and can assume no social responsibility whatever. However, the function of business is not only profit. The key to the situation is the requirement for balance between the need for profit on the one hand and the public interest on the other. The business must have integrity, good ethics, and responsibility from a public point of view.

In any pluralist society, Drucker observes, responsibility for the public good has been the central problem and issue. He quotes Joseph Schumpeter, economist, who pointed out that capitalism has become less acceptable the more it has succeeded. Some businesses have been and are noteworthy in their ethics and their concern for the public interest. But they may not be in the majority, and unfortunately they are tarred with the same brush as those who have too little regard for the public interest. Profit and capitalism are key and controversial parts of the public environment.

Earlier we referred to the public's negative view of business. The attitude of business toward profit undoubtedly contributes a good deal to this negative view. A second contributor is the failure of marketing to be in the public interest. The principal task of the marketing function, as defined by J. B. McKitterick, is not so much to be skillful in making customers do what suits the interest of the business as to be skillful in conceiving of and then making business do what suits the interests of the customer.[5] E. Jerome McCarthy, noted marketing authority, said that a firm should seek to meet the needs of the customer at a profit.[6]

As pointed out by Philip Kotler in his book, *Marketing Management,* selling and marketing are based on different concepts.[7] Selling focuses on the needs of the seller, whereas marketing focuses on the needs of the buyer. Good public relations demands focusing on the needs of the buyer.

Much emphasis has been given to attempting to create customer needs that are not really in the customers' best interests. Too often business attempts to be skillful in making customers do what suits the interests of business. Too many businesses conceive of marketing merely as selling whatever the business produces, which is designed for the greatest profit. However, business should have as its objective satisfying customer needs.

Much of the failure to concentrate on customer needs comes from the failure of top managements to recognize that every department of a business must be truly customer oriented. Both marketing strategy and marketing operations must be based on good analysis of the characteristics and of the true needs and desires of customers and potential customers.

The failure to concentrate on customer needs can also be caused by products and services that are poorly designed or made of poor materials and by poor workmanship. It can be caused by unsatisfactory delivery or installation, poor instructions in use, insufficient provision for repair, or unsatisfactory repair work. It can be brought about by undesirable credit policies. It can be the result of the way the product was advertised—by the kind of sales promotion used and how it was carried out. It can be caused

[5] "What is the Marketing Management Concept," in *The Frontiers of Marketing Thought and Science.* Chicago: American Marketing Association, 1958.
[6] *Basic Marketing,* 4th ed. Homewood, Ill.: Richard D. Irwin, 1971.
[7] Englewood Cliffs, N.J.: Prentice-Hall, 1976.

by pricing problems. For example, a business may fail to recognize the pricing needs of important segments of the market for an essential product or service.

These problems can be the result of an organizational structure that gives responsibility to engineers, accounting people, and plant managers for such things as pricing and planning products and services, rather than to Marketing Management. They can also be the result of failure to consider the public interest.

Marketing is where the business meets the customer. It is, therefore, a key factor in public relations.

The hostile attitude toward profit and toward business should be of key concern both to those with responsibility for business public relations and to those concerned with the public relations of nonbusiness institutions. The hostility is a vital danger to both. As indicated in our discussion, much work needs to be done within business organizations with regard to viewpoints on profit maximization and concern for the public interest. Equally necessary is work aimed at informing the public and special publics concerning the importance of profit to society.

However, so-called "economic education" of the type so often discussed in recent years can have little effectiveness when it merely preaches the viewpoints prevalent in too many businesses. A change in public attitudes will be based on a change of business attitudes and performance.

19. *The shortage of energy.* The diminishing supply and increasing cost of energy is a key factor in the environment. As brought out by James T. Doudiet, manager of the Financial Planning and Analysis Department of Pacific Gas and Electric Company, more than two-thirds of the known United States petroleum resources have already been used up. The cost of fossil fuels (oil, gas, and coal) will undoubtedly increase considerably as reserves are used.[8]

A reduction in the amount of energy to be used for motor vehicles will be permanent. The cost of manufacturing, which requires large amounts of fuel, will increase materially. The cost of gas and electricity used in homes and elsewhere will of necessity be much higher. This particularly will cause constant contention among utility companies, public utility commissions, and consumers. A good deal of the problem arises from a failure of utility managements and the managements of oil companies and other fuel producers to effectively inform opinion leaders and the public in general of the impending problem long ago. This failure will bring further loss of confidence in business, along with many consumer relations difficulties as

---

[8] Speech delivered to the Society for Advancement of Management, San Francisco Chapter, March, 1975.

prices rise. At the same time, stringent economy in the use of fuel (energy) and a redoubling of efforts to obtain more efficient and effective production, distribution, and use of fuel will be required.

Architects, designers, and manufacturers of heating and lighting equipment must give special attention to the conservation of energy. Failure to do so can lead not only to public controversy but also to wasting much-needed energy. An example concerns the American Gas Association, which was described on a network television documentary in December 1976 as procrastinating concerning action necessary to increase the efficiency of household furnaces.

In the autumn of 1977 the government still had no energy conservation policy or plan. In the public interest producers and distributors of energy have the duty to help bring about the best possible public energy policy and plan. Public relations management will have important public information tasks in connection with the energy supply problem.

20. *Business organizations are asked and sometimes heavily pressured to take what are termed social responsibilities that do not belong in the realm of business.* For example, businesses have been pressured to provide day nurseries for the children of women employees. Yet opinion research shows that the public in general does not feel day nurseries are a business responsibility.

Of course, businesses and those who work for businesses (those who work for other organizations, as well) should participate in desirable community activities, but there is a need to decide what kinds of activities are within an organization's social responsibility. More will be said later about this important factor in the public environment.

These are some of the factors that influence public relations. They, together with many more, make up the environment in which organizations must operate. They are the kind of factor concerning which public relations management must take action for they have a profound influence on how well the organization prospers.

THE INFORMATION EXPLOSION

In a discussion of the environment we should also consider the effect of the "information explosion." Today events in the world are literally moving at a faster pace than ever before. This has brought about "the information explosion," and in turn, the information explosion helps cause everything else to move faster and faster.

Every new discovery opens previously unknown avenues to several more and different discoveries, and when those new discoveries are made, each one opens up several more avenues to further breakthroughs. And so the discoveries come faster and faster.

Think of color television, the outgrowth of black-and-white television. You can trace its antecedents back through the idea of sophisticated radio and then back to the days of World War I when communication was by dot-and-dash code.

Or think of satellite travel into outer space, and then recall that the automobile has come into its own only since 1910. The steamboat was invented during the nineteenth century. It has been a short span of years since the Wright brothers flew the first airplane at Kitty Hawk, North Carolina. Now jet airplanes go around the world in hours. Before the nineteenth century, people sailed boats, traveled in horse-drawn vehicles, rode on horses, camels, or other kinds of animals, or they walked. Those were the only ways to go—even long distances.

Think of the printing press, invented in the fifteenth century. Today we print daily newspapers, countless magazines, and an abundance of books at low cost. All manner of office copying machines make copies of almost anything. We have motion picture cameras with zoom lenses, Polaroid cameras that develop prints immediately, and other kinds of cameras for all kinds of sophisticated picture taking. And it has been only about a century since the telephone was invented. One can talk to hundreds of millions of people in almost any part of the globe with your voice conveyed by satellite or going by cable laid under the broadest oceans.

Computers store great quantities of information. They can automatically send to and receive from other computers. In a short period of time they can correlate information that would take years or centuries for man to do manually. They can deliver overnight printouts of enough correlated information for a large book.

All these things are not only examples of the much faster pace at which the world is moving; they are also all concerned in one way or another with the tremendous information explosion that gets the word out so fast that minutes after something of importance happens, people all over the globe know about it. The information explosion makes books, and therefore knowledge, available at low cost to people everywhere. Compare that with the day when the monks in monasteries painstakingly handlettered scrolls of every page of a document—and every copy had to be on original.

Think of other information speeders. Fast air mail can carry books, letters, and all manner of other documents to anywhere on earth in almost no time. Exact copies of letters and other documents can be sent across the continent over telephone lines in a matter of minutes. Data of all kinds speed between computers and people with undreamed-of speed. Schools of all kinds are coming into being so that the common man can have an excellent education and can better understand the world around him. Man can hear over the transistor radio and can see on television and in the pictures what other people have and can aspire to having the same or better. He can communicate his wishes with less fear of reprisal and punishment than was expected in years gone by. With the information explosion and the almost immediate knowledge by people about almost everything that happens, it is no longer possible to hide situations that in prior times would never have come to light. This forces organizations to pay greater attention to public relations and to be constantly aware of how their publics are going to perceive their actions, reactions, and inactions. We must forever look outward to find out what people think instead of inward at the machinations and problems and viewpoints of our own organization.

Today's world calls for action and performance if we are to have public approval.

OTHER IMPORTANT FACTORS IN THE ENVIRONMENT

Some of the important general factors in the environment have been discussed. As brought out at the beginning of this chapter, many other environmental factors of concern to individual organizations and at particular times should be watched for and considered by public relations management in determining the overall environment of the organization, the recommendations to be made, and the courses of action to be taken. The environment includes such things as the attitudes people have and the opinions they express toward the organization. It includes people's attitudes and viewpoints of its services or products, its employees or volunteer workers (for example, of political parties), its management, its ethics and integrity, its responsibility as a part of the community, and its consideration of the public interest.

With the information explosion and with the number and complexity of other factors that make up the public environment or social climate, one can deduce that one of the primary jobs of the public relations manager should be that of an analyst. Good perception of the environment requires careful and constant analysis.

The public relations manager should make sure that he has every opportunity to be aware of the changing environment in which his organization operates. Careful and constant analysis of the factors discussed in this chapter and other environmental factors are important to successful public relations.

FOUR

THE Functions AND
RESPONSIBILITIES OF
PUBLIC RELATIONS
MANAGEMENT

Public relations (or external relations) management has the responsibility for the favorableness of the organization's relations with all its publics. This is true even though public relations management may not be directly involved with the publics in many matters—for example, marketing, billing, or service.

With responsibility goes accountability. Merely because a desired result requires decisions beyond the authority of the public relations management to implement does not mean that it should not be held accountable, for the authority to analyze a problem or opportunity and to recommend a decision is an important kind of authority.

RELATIONSHIP OF THREE BASIC PRINCIPLES TO THE FUNCTIONS OF PUBLIC RELATIONS MANAGEMENT

Greatly influencing the functions of the public relations management are the three basic principles referred to in Chapter 1 (see pages 9, 12, and 17):

1. The purpose of public relations activity is to develop and maintain a social climate or environment in which the organization can prosper best. It is the public relations management's responsibility to guide the decisions of the organization so that they will help to develop and maintain a favorable environment.

48

2. Good public relations results from good performance publicly acknowledged and appreciated. The public relations manager should study the organization's performance in every area and work with all the other departments to ensure that performance is favorable from a public viewpoint. He should do a good and complete communication job with each of the important publics to ensure that the good performance is acknowledged and appreciated.

3. The organization exists only by public consent, and its existence is justified only in terms of its contribution to society as viewed by society. The public relations management should study the proposed decisions and actions of the organization to ensure that there is the proper balance between profit on the one hand and the public interest on the other. This is a particularly important responsibility because, as brought out in Chapter 1, failure leads to political action that results in restrictive government regulations. However, even if restrictive government regulation were not the result, failure to heed the public interest would, in the long run, harm the organization as much as it harms the nation and the communities in which the organization operates. Therefore, enlightened self-interest requires proper consideration of the public interest.

Some of the areas involved are the physical environment (for example, air and water pollution), the interests of the consumer, and the interests of employees. As discussed in Chapter 3, the consumer area includes such things as avoiding false or misleading advertising, exaggerated claims, misrepresentation, and so forth. It includes focusing on the buyers' needs rather than the sellers' needs.

The interests of employees include such things as equal employment opportunity, the handling of pensions, job safety, and the motivational climate as it concerns the organization's performance as viewed by the public. Maintaining employee morale is vital. Good morale depends to a considerable degree on the extent to which the motives of the majority of the members of the organization are satisfied.

PERCEIVING THE SOCIAL CLIMATE OR ENVIRONMENT

As suggested in Chapter 3, the quality of a management can be judged by its ability to correctly perceive its environment and to effectively do something about it. Since so much of the external environment of an organization consists of its interface with the publics, one primary function of the public relations manager should be to perceive correctly the social climate or environment and effectively and continually to inform his colleagues in top management of it. More will be said about this in later chapters. The public relations manager should also recommend policies and courses of action that will be in both the public's and the organization's interests.

We have referred to the need for perception in public relations management, and it would be well to define what we mean. Perception concerns the way a person senses a situation or experience and depends on his frame of reference. Thus the public relations manager's frame of reference is necessarily quite different from that of an engineer, for example. Good public relations perception involves sensing a situation or experience correctly from a public relations viewpoint. Sensing a situation or experience from a public relations viewpoint might be quite different from what it would be from a plant manager's viewpoint, for instance.

Public relations management should continually study social trends. Social trends should be as thoroughly considered by the top management as the organization's products and sales. For example, there has been an increased public interest in ecology, but businesses, municipalities, and other organizations seem to have been totally unaware of the fact that what they were doing in the area of air and water pollution, for example, would cause a tremendous negative public reaction. However, it really should not have taken too much thought on the part of top managements and public relations managements to have seen that the problems concerning air and water pollution were coming. Public relations management should be totally involved with the environment in which the organization functions and in which it is apt to function in the future. In this era of rapid change and economic stress, this function is particularly important. Changes in social trends can come rapidly. As pointed out, many organizations were caught unaware and were surprised by the surge of public interest in air and water pollution. Businesses were required to spend large sums of money to clean

PERCEPTION IS HOW A PERSON

SENSES A SITUATION OR EXPERIENCE.

THIS DEPENDS ON HIS FRAME OF

REFERENCE.

GOOD PUBLIC RELATIONS

PERCEPTION IS SENSING A SITUATION

OR EXPERIENCE CORRECTLY FROM A

PUBLIC RELATIONS VIEWPOINT.

Figure 8

up waste being discharged into waterways and into the air. Attendant publicity hurt the reputation of the businesses and contributed to reducing public confidence in the whole business world.

New laws were forced through legislatures. Government agencies had to be formed to enforce the laws. Cities found themselves forced to build new sewage disposal systems to comply with the new laws, adding new burdens to already strained budgets.

INFLUENCING MANAGEMENT DECISIONS

The key function of public relations management is to evaluate and anticipate the effect of every proposed objective, policy, plan, and important action of the organization on each of its publics. The public relations management should also evaluate and anticipate the effect of each of its publics on the organization. It should then influence the organization's actions accordingly. It should consider whether proposals should be carried out and the best methods of doing so from a public relations viewpoint.

DEFINING OPPORTUNITIES AND PROBLEMS

A primary function of public relations management is to define the public relations opportunities, problems, and potential problems. It should develop and obtain agreement among the top management on the public relations objectives, policies, and plans of the organization. In examining public relations problems, in defining objectives, and in formulating plans to meet those objectives, the public relations workers' analysis and perception should include all the "publics" that may be concerned.

It should be recognized that attitudes and viewpoints as to what is good performance may vary. One cannot assume that what is good performance to one person or group will necessarily be good performance to another person or group. Also, what the management of an organization considers to be good performance may not be good from the standpoint of the public. For example, situations as seen by college students might be different from the way they are seen by retired people or businessmen. A failure of a key telephone cable would probably be viewed quite differently by the general public than it would be by people in charge of police communications or by those charged with military communications. Employees could easily have a different view of a company or government pension plan or an employee's stock purchase plan from that of the stockholders or the general public.

People in large cities may have viewpoints entirely different from those of people who live in smaller cities or in rural areas. Construction of a new office building might be viewed differently by Chamber of Commerce members than by police authorities. The building's addition to the tax rolls, the need for off-street parking, the zoning laws, or the type of architecture to be used might be viewed differently by the two groups. The people who live near the location of the new building might have still other views—for example, as to the amount of traffic that might be generated or the intrusion of strangers into the neighborhood. All the various viewpoints must be considered in defining opportunities and problems, in setting objectives, and in developing plans to meet those objectives.

It is obvious that one sometimes will be unable to forecast reactions to performance, events, or communication on the basis of any given manager's viewpoints. Thus the only fairly sure way of determining what is good performance in important matters is through the use of market and opinion research, which should be decision oriented. The results of research may show that some group or public does not consider a specific performance to be good. Other groups or publics may find it highly desirable. This may happen, for example, in connection with political considerations.

When there is disagreement concerning good performance, alternatives should be considered. If no satisfactory alternatives are available, then decisions must be made on the basis of what is perceived to promote the best overall environment or to do the least overall harm.

COUNSELING ALL PARTS OF THE ORGANIZATION

Referring back to the public relations considerations in constructing a new office building as an example, new buildings are not constructed by public relations managements. They are constructed by other departments of an organization. Public relations management should accomplish its objectives largely through counseling other departments.

Counseling all the other parts of the organization on all aspects of public relations is one of the key functions and responsibilities of the public relations management. It includes providing the leadership in coordinating and integrating the public relations activity. This requires that public relations people will take the initiative even when public relations counsel is not requested. For instance, should a plant or office of the organization take part in a certain community undertaking? What social responsibility does the organization have, if any, in connection with a particular situation? What would be the probable public reaction to proposed changes in service arrangements? What off-street parking should be provided for employees and customers? What plans have been formulated for use in event of a disaster? What about the appearance of an office or plant? Is the organization considered to be a good employer? If not, why not? Does the organization do business with local companies? What about open houses and family nights? In event of a strike, what should be done from the standpoint of the public interest?

DETERMINING PUBLIC ATTITUDES AND OPINIONS

To do the things mentioned in the preceding paragraph, it becomes extremely important to determine, analyze, and interpret the public attitudes and opinions as well as the attitudes and opinions of the various special publics such as those of educators, college students, professional people, minority groups, and business people. This is an important responsibility of public relations management.

As mentioned earlier, opinion research is the most successful way of determining attitudes. Such research should be designed to uncover both the underlying or potential problems and the reason they exist so that one may set specific objectives and take effective action as a result of survey findings. More will be said about opinion research and its use in problem analysis in later chapters.

OTHER WAYS OF UNCOVERING OPPORTUNITIES AND PROBLEMS

Public relations management should also use methods other than opinion research for uncovering public relations problems. For example, letters, phone calls, and verbal comments from customers can be a source of valuable information. Personal observation is important. Comments from other parts of the organization can be helpful. Editorial and column comments in the press, newspaper and magazine articles, and books, as well as experience of other organizations, can provide much needed information. We frequently do not need surveys to tell us the things that good perception will show, although the surveys help to document our recommendations to other departments or top management.

THE COMMUNICATIVE FUNCTION

Still another function of public relations management is to effectively interpret the organization's objectives, philosophy, actions, results, operations, ethics, and programs both to employees and to the other publics. When necessary, either from an organization viewpoint or a public viewpoint, public relations management should inform the public concerning the potential effect of political actions that may be proposed by government or others and that are in the areas of competence of the organization.

Public relations management should also be responsible for effectively informing the public concerning potential problems affecting the ability of the organization to provide the service and products the public expects from it. For example, as suggested in Chapter 1, the public should be kept effectively informed of such things as impending paper, sugar, grain, and fuel shortages. It should also be effectively informed of proposed government or other actions that would be apt to affect the supply or price of service or products produced by the organization. Because credibility of both business and government concerning shortages has been impaired by past performance, much greater care and a more extensive effort may be necessary to be effective. Great care should be taken not to cause panic buying of products potentially in short supply. This may be most effectively done by starting your efforts before shortages will be felt in the marketplace.

Sometimes it is necessary that the public understand why an organization elected to take a particular action instead of an alternative. People should understand the organization's performance. Sometimes getting understanding on important matters is half the battle, but one should be cautious that attempts to get this understanding are in terms of the publics' real interest, not simply in terms of the interest of the organization. Otherwise those attempts may only destroy credibility.

Those persons with communicative responsibilities regarding either the media or employees will undoubtedly run into many situations in which people from other functions or departments will desire to withhold some or all the information on a subject that they feel is delicate to the organization or to them. However, one should remember the old adage that if correct information is not provided, misinformation will take its place. Public relations management should weigh such matters carefully.

MANAGEMENT OF PUBLIC RELATIONS WORKERS AND THEIR EFFORTS

Management is responsible for performance. It is responsible for producing results. One of the key functions and responsibilities of public relations management is to manage those working in the public relations field and their efforts. Without this function and responsibility, the other public rela-

IF CORRECT INFORMATION

IS NOT PROVIDED, MISINFORMATION

WILL TAKE ITS PLACE.

Figure 9

tions functions are likely to be inefficiently and ineffectively carried out. Thus performance and results will probably be unsatisfactory.

Management is not necessarily concerned with the management of people. Managers in the public relations function may have no authority over or responsibility for people. This is true whether the level of management is high or low. *The key factor in defining a manager is that he or she must have the responsibility for contributing to the performance and results of the organization.*[1]

Thus a person in the public relations function who has no one reporting to him but a secretary may be a key person in upper management. Although he may not be responsible for the work of other people, he may be responsible for contributing immensely to the results and the performance of the organization—sometimes a great deal more than another person who has many others reporting to him. Compensation should be on the basis of the contribution and not related to the number of people reporting to a manager. The public relations manager's responsibility both upward and laterally is of great importance. Much of the public relations function consists of planning and of advising those in other functions and in top management.

It is important that every manager regularly consider what specific contribution he is making and should make to the performance and results of the organization. A large business had the practice of filling half its public relations management positions with people rotated from other departments for a two-year period. However, evaluation showed these people made very little contribution to the organization's performance or results. A good deal of the two years was spent trying to learn the rudiments of the job from subordinates and colleagues. It was rarely possible to delegate important responsibility to these people, and they were generally simply given a series of assignments to carry out.

Specific objectives should be set for contribution to performance and results of the organization by every person working in the management of

---

[1] Peter F. Drucker, *Management: Tasks, Responsibilities, Practices.* New York: Harper and Row, 1974.

the public relations function. These objectives should be based on the objectives of the function and of the organization as a whole. They should be integrated with those of other managers working in the function and the organization as a whole. Of course, they should be subject to the approval of the person's supervisor. With specific objectives it is possible to measure one's performance against the objectives.

Management by objectives is discussed in Chapter 5. Although the discussion focuses on and is concerned with the objectives of the function and organization as a whole, rather than those of the individual, the overall principles of both kinds of objectives are the same. Management by objectives is important because it focuses on opportunity for performance and results. It enables management to reward performance, good or bad. It helps to eliminate "management by crony," which can have a devastating effect on the results of the organization. It fosters the integrity and fairness that are vitally necessary.

When we talk of management, performance, and results, we are not referring only to business organizations. Organizations other than business have grown so that today the amount of the gross national product in the United States that goes to or through nonbusiness organizations may be over 50 percent. That means that over half the total income of the country goes to or passes through the hands of organizations that are not connected with business. Thus good management that produces good performance and results is of great importance from the standpoint of both the nonbusiness organizations and also the public interest.

As Peter Drucker points out in his book, *Management: Tasks, Responsibilities, Practices, nonbusiness institutions do not need management less than business.*[2] *They need it more.* He suggests that management of nonbusiness organizations is apt to be the frontier of management for the remainder of this century.

The public relations function is considered to be a staff function, but it includes line work. *The line is concerned with the authority of persons. The staff, on the other hand, is concerned with the authority of ideas.*[3] Thus the correctness of an idea does not depend on the authority of a person. In essence, the line commands, the staff advises. Public relations management has line responsibility over its staff. It also has line responsibility of other kinds—for example, in arranging for advertising.

The management of staff work is different from the management of line work precisely because it is concerned with the authority of ideas. It requires a knowledge of the ideas being managed.

[2] New York: Harper & Row, 1974.
[3] J. D. Mooney, *Principles of Organization.* New York: Harper and Row, 1947.

In addition to a knowledge of the ideas and concepts being managed, the management of staff work requires the same kinds of attention to planning, organizing, coordinating, integrating, directing, leading, and controlling as does line work. But the task of managing people in the function is different from that of line work. The motivations of the two are likely to be quite different.

In dealing with ideas, what is right or wrong in conclusions, decisions, and so on does not depend on a person's authority. When the authority of a person is imposed as the determinant, it may lead to poor morale and to ineffective and incorrect decisions and actions.

A knowledge of the work (the ideas and concepts) is needed not only because decisions cannot be made on the basis of authority of persons, but also to be able to properly plan and properly evaluate results. Proper supervision, leadership, direction, coordination, integration, and control must be on the basis of the ideas. Thus those responsible must be knowledgeable about the ideas. This is a fundamental difference between the management of line and the management of staff. It is one of the reasons that this book, which deals with managing the public relations function, contains chapters providing at least an overview of the key areas of knowledge required in managing the work and the workers.

We should define what we mean by management. In Chapter 1 (page 18), we said that the management process includes four steps:

1. Analysis and definition of opportunities and problems.
2. Making decisions as to what should be done.
3. Getting the decisions carried out.
4. Analysis of the other three steps and their results after decisions are partly and/or fully carried out.

As indicated by the process, management is the organizing of efforts to accomplish objectives. The process and its organization include many subparts. For example, it includes staffing to develop and accomplish objectives and to analyze the results of what was done. It requires developing plans of all kinds, including budgetary plans. It embraces organizing to carry out the plans and directing the work of doing so. It involves supervising to see that the work is carried out properly. It includes coordinating to be sure that all parts of the plan are carried out with proper timing. It requires the closely related process of integrating the efforts of all parts of the organization to see that they fit together and pull together toward common objectives. It embraces control so that the results conform as much as possible to the plan. Good management requires providing leadership that is a key motivating force and authority that stimulates and directs the members of the organization toward the achievement of objectives.

Let us discuss the elements in more detail including staffing, planning, organizing to carry out the plans, directing, supervising, coordinating integrating, controlling, and leading.

1. Good staffing is the first essential of public relations management. It includes setting up and carrying out plans for the selection, training, development, evaluation, and progress of public relations people so that the public relations functions will be carried out most effectively. This is a function that has received far too little attention in years gone by.

Much of the success of the people in the public relations function will depend not only on their original selection, either from within the organization or from outside, but also on the management climate and on the training and development made available to the individuals. Unfortunately, far too little attention has been given to the training and development of people who work in the public relations function. Perhaps because of the great emphasis on communication in the past practically no attention has been given to training and development in public relations management.

Among the subjects included in the training program might be such things as management and supervisory methods, problem analysis and objective setting, organizational development, group dynamics, counseling, the effective use of reference material, the functions, operation, and problems of the other departments of the organization, the financial aspects of the organization, handling and use of opinion research, organizational intelligence, and the elements of communication.

Public relations management's own public relations and status, depend on its performance in carrying out its responsibilities and on acknowledgement and appreciation of that performance by the rest of the organization. Public relations workers have long expressed the feeling that their views should be represented in top management decisions. That is not only a desirable wish—it is a necessity if their organizations are to operate successfully in today's world. One sometimes hears comments that people in other parts of the organization do not seek the views of public relations people frequently enough or that those views are not given sufficient weight. However, to achieve recognition, public relations people must warrant it.

As long as public relations people act primarily as staff writers of other people's views, they will have no place in top management. Top management's objectives and functions concern primarily the decision-making processes, not the work of writers. One should not downgrade written and spoken words. They are important tools of the public relations function, but they must never overshadow the overall public relations function, which must emphasize performance of the organization as a whole.

2. The developing of plans, including specific objectives, is discussed in detail in Chapters 5 and 10. Without specific objectives and good plans for carrying them out, the staff would accomplish relatively little. Planning, including both what is to be accomplished and budgeting for the necessary expense, is a vital part of management.

Besides the development of plans as to what is to be accomplished, planning includes other elements. One should plan for staffing, for the planning activity itself, for organizing and carrying out plans, and for each of the other parts of management. Of particular importance is planning for effective leadership. Leadership is a motivating force and authority that stimulates and directs members of the organization toward the achievement of its objectives. How one should best motivate and stimulate people in a particular organization and under a particular circumstance requires careful planning.

3. How best organize to carry out a particular objective? Carrying out the objective may require the help and cooperation of other departments as well as particular public relations workers. How can the ablest people be most effectively employed in carrying out the public relations function and its specific objectives?

4. Directing is important. It causes things to be done. It gets work under way and decides when it is completed. It ensures effectiveness of the work and effectiveness of the supervision of the work underway.

5. One of the least understood areas of management concerns the role of supervision, yet effective supervision is the key to effective management. Its importance can be seen when it is fully realized that every level of management supervises the next level below, as well as carrying out its other responsibilities.

The most important role of the supervisor is to help his people. Unfortunately, in some organizations many supervisors may not have the experience or knowledge necessary to do so. In such cases it may be necessary for the subordinates to train and "help" their supervisors. This can be a cause of resentment.

Good supervision includes continually training one's people and also seeing that opportunities for other training and development are provided to them. It includes helping to make earned progress possible. It also includes providing information and knowledge not possessed by the subordinates and providing them feedback concerning their performance and results. This is essential if they are to properly evaluate and improve their work.

A good supervisor helps his people to organize their work better and also helps the work group to organize itself better so that it can most effectively and efficiently carry out its functions. A good supervisor also provides his people with as much responsibility for their work and results as possible.

The good supervisor's role includes keeping his people continuously informed about the group as a whole and the organization as a whole, including their problems, opportunities, plans, decisions, operations, and results. A good supervisor promptly lets his people know about the important happenings in other parts of the group and in the organization as a whole.

The supervisor should be the chief source of information of his people. Sometimes too much dependence is placed on printed bulletins and various other printed and auditory material to inform people about important matters. Opinion research among various levels of management and nonmanagement in one large organization showed that one of the most important complaints about the management concerned its failure to keep people informed about important happenings. The research showed that people were much concerned about what was happening in the organization because they knew it was important to their welfare.

An essential role of good supervision is to be the liaison with higher management concerning the group's needs and also to provide higher management with information about the group's work, problems, opportunities, innovations, and results. One constantly hears complaints about the lack of upward communication in organizations. Part of the cause is a failure to consider this function of supervision. At the same time, the supervisor has final decision responsibility for the work of his group.

Supervision oversees the details of the work and ensures that it is efficiently and properly done. For example, it includes such things as seeing that the workers are on hand and performing their tasks, that information is checked for accuracy, and that the work is done on time.

6. Coordinative efforts in management are essential if we are to be sure that all parts of the plan are being carried out and at the proper time. Coordination ensures the orderly arrangement of group efforts necessary to provide unity of action. It is also discussed in Chapters 5 and Chapter 10.

The result of the lack of coordination can be somewhat like a chain with one or more links missing. The links may be late in arriving or missing altogether, but whatever the reason, the chain cannot perform its function with one or more missing links.

7. Integration of the efforts of various parts of the organization is also important and should result in unifying the work so that it achieves common objectives. Without integration, parts of the organization may go merrily off doing their "own thing."

The public relations department of one of the major corporations had problems due to a failure to integrate the efforts of its parts. The advertising group's objectives were completely different from those of the publicity people, and the people concerned with community relations, lectures, displays, and exhibits all went their own ways. There was great jealousy between group heads. Needless to say, from the standpoint of organizational objectives, little was accomplished.

Management should reward work done from a total organization viewpoint rather than from a departmental or functional viewpoint.

8. Control ensures that the results conform to the plan. The purpose of control is also to see that the work is done as effectively and as economically as possible. Control includes the evaluation of the work and also the performance of the workers. It includes making certain that expenditures are in line with estimates of cost for each objective and activity. Costs and cost records should be systematically classified and kept according to both objective and the kind of work done. Control includes such things as the use of opinion and other kinds of research to determine bench marks by which to measure results.

9. Leadership can help to make possible the esprit de corps that can be an important element in the success of an organization. Esprit de corps is the result of unity of purpose and accomplishment, harmony, a desire by the workers for organizational achievement, and leadership toward reaching specific organizational objectives. Good leadership can help bring about harmony, unity, and a desire by the workers for organizational achievement. *Leading is more than administering or superintending in that it emphasizes motivating and stimulating workers toward the achievement of common objectives.*

If leadership includes leading members of organizations toward definite common objectives, then without definite objectives there can be no leadership. This applies to business leadership, government leadership, leadership of the public relations function, leadership in the education field, and throughout society. We discuss objectives in Chapter 5.

The management of the public relations function ought to be a studied effort taking into consideration each of the points discussed in the preceding few pages. These points and what is being done about each of them individually should be periodically reviewed to be sure that none is being overlooked or lost by default and that all are being efficiently and effectively carried out.

Public relations management should keep abreast of new theories and development in management thinking and adopt or try those that seem to promise improvement. It should also continually think through its own management process and organizational structure to be sure that they fit new situations, opportunities, and problems. Besides borrowing from the new ideas of others, it should also innovate to constantly develop and maintain the best management structure and methods for its own use. Neither in the management of the public relations function nor in the carrying out of work should consensus of opinion be allowed to replace logic or creativity.

Collective wisdom cannot be achieved by groups of people who as individuals are uninformed and without knowledge. On the other hand, creativity should not be confused with imagination, for creativity is imagination that has been disciplined to meet specific objectives.

THE PUBLIC RELATIONS FUNCTION AND ORGANIZATIONAL STRUCTURE

Because his functions are vital and his counsel of key importance to all parts of the organization, the top public relations manager should be on a level equal with the heads of other departments reporting to the chief executive of the organization. With the great diversity of kinds and sizes of organizations, however, it would be folly to prescribe an organization structure for the public relations function. However, those in the management, planning, and counseling parts of the function should be separate from those concerned with media and other journalistic endeavors. Lean, well-motivated organizations with the ablest and most experienced people obtainable are apt to be the most effective.

PUBLIC RELATIONS MANAGERS AS ANALYSTS

We concluded Chapter 3 with a reference to the public relations manager as an analyst. With the number and complexity of the factors to be considered, one can deduce that one of the primary functions of public relations management is that of analyst. For example, in Chapter 3 we discussed the importance of the environment and some of its complex factors that require a great deal of analysis. Public relations management must take an objective view of all the facets of the organization as seen by many different groups such as customers, employees, government people, suppliers, the financial world, stockholders, and the public at large.

Two important tools available to public relations management in its role as analyst are opinion research and the computer. Opinion research, which we discuss in more detail in a later chapter, aids the public relations manager in getting the real facts. Once he has these facts in hand, the computer can help to organize, correlate, and store them for quick and convenient marshaling when needed. It can also help to prevent valuable data from becoming lost and unused in file drawers of forgotten study reports.

However, care must be taken not to provide an explosion of data just because the computer can provide it. The object is not to overwhelm the manager with data but rather to provide useful information.

VALIDITY OF INFORMATION

We said that opinion research helps to get the real facts. In the public relations decision-making process particularly, it is important to be careful of the validity of the information used. If one is going to use data from opinion research, for example, he should make sure who issued the data originally. Stay clear of recommendations biased by the recommender, such as predictions of their own coverage issued by newspapers, radio, and television stations. Be careful of opinion research organizations who write reports and bend data to please those in authority. One should also remember that the ultimate source of all data is the originator—not the issuer or some intervening person.

There are many examples in which failure to check facts and opinions have led to problems. One example of failure to check the facts led to the marketing of the Edsel automobile a few years back. In that case, as reported by Harold L. Wilensky, University of California professor of sociology, the Ford Motor Company policy makers were blinded by stereotype and oversimplification.[4] Conventional studies convinced them that low-income owners of Fords, Plymouths, and Chevrolets would turn in these "symbols of poverty" as soon as their earnings increased sufficiently. Based on this preconception, Ford projected a huge market for large, medium-priced cars with heavy ornamentation and gadgetry. Ford's policy makers were shown data on the rising sale of smaller cars, and they dismissed the buyers of the small cars as the "teacher trade." When the Edsel hit the road, it was the "year of the compact."

How uncritical organizations can be in the use of information is illustrated by the case of the salad oil swindler who took 51 companies for $174 million—another example of failure to get the facts at the source. As related by Wilensky, the perpetrator of the swindle obtained warehouse receipts for nonexistent oil from a subsidiary of American Express Company.[5] Using the receipts for nonexistent oil as collateral, he secured loans. With these loans and a modest supply of oil he became the nation's largest dealer in salad oil. Good business practice would have required the lenders to verify that the oil was actually in the warehouses, but they failed to do so.

[4] Harold L. Wilensky, *Organizational Intelligence.* New York: Basic Books, 1967.
[5] *Organizational Intelligence.* New York: Basic Books, 1967.

SOMETIMES IT AIN'T THE

THINGS WE DON'T KNOW THAT

HURT US ..... IT'S THE THINGS

WE DO KNOW THAT AIN'T SO.

Figure 10

Only when the swindler's firm went bankrupt did American Express and 50 other companies discover shortages worth $174 million. Acceptance, trust, and faith in routine pieces of paper were the flies in the ointment.

How does one get good information? Great care must be taken that data are valid. Data should always be checked for accuracy and completeness at the official source. But that will not always ensure that the data are correct or complete. One may receive misinformation because of rivalry between people and groups. Within the organization there may be distortion or the blockage of information. It is good to remember that people tend to hold back problem information from the boss and that many organizations motivate people to keep silent. Therefore, public relations management should also use information outside official channels. The manager should keep his eyes open and should go out to observe and to talk firsthand with people of various levels of the organization to be sure of an effective flow of information. He should also make it a point to observe and talk with people outside of the organization.

In connection with observing and talking with people, either inside or outside of the organization, it is of interest to consider the value of viewpoints arrived at as a result of observation as compared with those arrived at from inference. Viewpoints derived from observation can be made only during or after observation.[6] They are restricted. On the other hand, viewpoints derived from inference may be made at any time. Viewpoints derived from observation must stay with what one observed and must not go beyond that, but viewpoints derived from inference can go well beyond those of observation. One can infer to the limit of one's imagination. Thus viewpoints obtained from inference should not have the weight of those from observation.

Viewpoints arrived at from observation can be made only by the observer, but as we all know from experience, anyone can have a viewpoint arrived at from inference. Thus, statements of inference involve only degrees of probability, but statements of observation approach certainty.

[6] William V. Haney, *Communication and Organizational Behavior.* Homewood, Ill.: Richard D. Irwin, 1967.

VIEWPOINTS FROM OBSERVATION

· CAN BE MADE ONLY AFTER OR DURING OBSERVATION.

·MUST STAY WITH WHAT ONE OBSERVED. MUST NOT GO BEYOND.

· CAN ONLY BE MADE BY THE OBSERVER.

· STATEMENTS OF OBSERVATION APPROACH CERTAINTY

Figure 11 Reprinted with permission from *Communication and Organizational Behavior:* Text and Cases by William V. Haney (Homewood, IL: Richard D. Irwin, Inc., 1973c).

VIEWPOINTS FROM INFERENCE

· CAN BE MADE AT ANY TIME.

· CAN GO WELL BEYOND OBSERVATION. ONE CAN INFER TO THE LIMIT OF ONE'S IMAGINATION.

· CAN BE MADE BY ANYONE.

· STATEMENTS OF INFERENCE INVOLVE ONLY DEGREES OF PROBABILITY.

Figure 12 Reprinted with permission from *Communication and Organizational Behavior:* Text and Cases by William V. Haney (Homewood, IL: Richard D. Irwin, Inc., 1973c).

It is desirable to verify official information frequently through informal and unofficial channels. It is easy to fall into the trap of undue defense of established policy. And it is wise to watch out for stereotyped and wishful thinking, or oversimplification. It is a good idea to remember that even if original data are accurate, they may be distorted or held back completely before one receives them. People generally want to make things look good.

SELF-CONVINCING ARGUMENTS—DOCTRINAIRE

So-called facts, arguments, or propaganda directed at friends and enemies can be self-convincing and lead to costly and poor public relations. The validity of information is a key consideration, and public relations management must be fully accountable for the results of its recommendations based on the information it receives.

Public relations management must guard against being carried away by wishful thinking, by organizational doctrinaire and techniques, mistaking them for facts. If they get carried away, they may find they have failed to recognize some of the most important public relations problems or have failed to grasp important opportunities.

Look out for the organization's self-image. Organizations have self-images, and these self-images may be crucial psychological blocks for them just as they are for individuals. One of the responsibilities of public relations management is to help the organization see itself as others see it. The public seldom sees us as we see ourselves. What is of crystal clear importance to us may get a "so what?" from the public—or perhaps disbelief—if it does not fall on deaf ears.

THE PUBLIC RELATIONS BUDGET—PLANS AND OBJECTIVES

A responsibility of public relations management embodying all the foregoing is the development of a realistic budget for public relations activity. The budget should not be a "guesstimate." Rather it should be a documented list of anticipated expenses for all the personnel and activities under the direct supervision of public relations management for the period of time covered.

Public relations management should have specific objectives and develop specific plans for carrying out those objectives. By pricing out the plans, much of the guesswork can be taken out of preparing the budget for public relations activity. More will be said about the important work of defining objectives and planning in later chapters.

THE MANAGEMENT OF COST—COST CONTROL

The management of cost is an important function. The public relations manager should keep careful records of all costs. All expenditures should be classified according to four categories. The first is according to the location or place where they were made. The second should show the medium, activity, salary, or personal expense for which they were paid. The specific reason for every personal expense should be kept. The third classification should show all expenses by task, project, or objective. The fourth category should provide data as to the amounts expended by each person working in the function. No expense should be paid unless it has been properly classified into all four categories. In doing so salary, office expense, or personal expense may have to be prorated to more than one category. With this information it is possible to make cost analyses on the basis of place, media and activity, task-project or objective, and the persons making expenditures.

Expenses should be reviewed each month and compared with the budget. Necessary adjustments should be made in the amounts and kinds of expenditures. Careful analysis should be made at least every six months to ensure that expenditures are as planned. Costs should be compared with measured results of activity at least annually. The public relations manager should give great attention to managing cost. He should insist that all those in the function do likewise.

ACCOUNTABILITY

After everything has been said and done, the proof of the pudding is in the eating. How well did public relations management accomplish its objectives? How well did it plan its expenditures? The number of press clippings obtained is really of no consequence. The ability of public relations management lies in correctly perceiving the environment, in opportunity and problem analysis, in setting appropriate objectives, and in counseling the organization, including top management.

How good was the organization's performance from a public viewpoint? Is the social climate or environment as good as it could be in enabling the organization to prosper over the long term? How effective was the communicative effort in reaching the objectives set for it? Public relations management should be held accountable for all those things by top management.

Public relations management should set up and carry out plans to evaluate its accomplishments in relationship to its objectives as a means of continuing management and improvement. As a public relations function it should on its own behalf regularly and effectively inform its colleagues in the managements of other competences, as well as the rest of the organization, concerning its accomplishments.

SUMMARY

In discussing the functions and responsibilities of public relations management, we said that it has the responsibility for the favorableness of relations
with all the organization's publics. This is true even though the public relations management may not be directly involved with the public in many
matters—billing, for instance.

Public relations management's functions concern three basic principles:

1. The purpose of the public relations function is to develop and maintain a
   social climate in which the organization can prosper best.
2. Good public relations results from good performance publicly
   acknowledged and appreciated.
3. The organization exists only by public consent, and its existence is justified only in terms of its contribution to society as viewed by society.

A primary function of public relations management should be to correctly perceive the social climate or environment and to continually inform
top management about it. This is an important function because the quality
of a management may be judged by its ability to correctly perceive its environment and to effectively do something about it.

Another key function is to evaluate and. anticipate the effect of every
proposed objective, policy, plan, and important action of the organization
on each of its important publics and to counsel the organization accordingly. Public relations management should also evaluate and anticipate the
effects of the various publics on the organization. It should define public
relations opportunities, problems and potential problems, and obtain
agreement on the public relations objectives, policies, and plans of the organization. It should counsel all parts of the organization on all aspects of
public relations and should provide the leadership in coordinating and
integrating public relations activity. Another important function of public
relations management is to determine public attitudes and opinions.

The communicative function is important in that the organization
depends on public relations management to effectively interpret its objectives, philosophy, actions, results, operations, ethics, and programs to
employees and to the other publics.

A very important responsibility of public relations management concerns
the managing of public relations workers and their efforts, which includes
the selection, training, development, evaluation, and progress of the public
relations staff so that the function will be carried out most effectively.
Public relations management's own public relations depends on its good
performance, appreciated and acknowledged by the rest of the organization.

One of the key requisites of public relations management is analytical ability. Tying in closely with that is ensuring the validity of information used in problem analysis and in communicative material.

The public relations manager should be on a level in the organization equal with the heads of other departments reporting to the chief executive officer of the organization.

Public relations management should be responsible for developing and securing approval for a realistic budget for public relations activity.

Finally, public relations management should set up and carry out plans to evaluate its performance as a means of continuing management and improvement. Effective evaluation may use periodical public relations audits. Such audits should include (a) the environment, (b) public attitudes and their causes, (c) effectiveness of public relations management, (d) the effects each part of the organization is having on public relations. The audits might be made by an independent outside review source or by a board of directors committee.

FIVE

PUBLIC RELATIONS
(EXTERNAL RELATIONS)
Objectives

The application of the principles of good management, including problem analysis and management by objectives, has long been neglected by most of the public relations field. Of even greater importance is the general lack of realization by top managements of the effect this neglect can have on an organization's public relations. The discussion of management by objectives in this chapter is centered on organizational (corporate, for example), department, and group planning as it regards the public relations function. It is discussed as a means of better ensuring managerial effectiveness of the function. Thus our discussion here differs from most, which center on the individual. This is not to detract from also using the latter technique. Excellent works on management by objectives as applied to the motivation and managerial effectiveness of the individual are available by well-known authors such as George S. Odiorne[1] and W. J. Reddin.[2] *Defining Advertising Goals for Measured Advertising Results* is a well-known work on the need for specific objectives in advertising.[3]

The use of specific objectives is the basis for much of the rest of our discussion of public relations activity. By public relations objectives we mean written specific objectives as compared with broad philosophical goals of one kind or another.

[1] *Management by Objectives.* New York: Pitman, 1968.
[2] *Effective Management by Objectives.* New York: McGraw-Hill, 1971.
[3] New York: Association of National Advertisers, 1964.

With the increasing rapidity of change and the number of new situations confronting organizations, the day when the management of the public relations function could be successfully carried out on the basis of philosophical goals and generalization is gone. Philosophical goals such as "to give good value," "to be a good employer," "to promote a favorable image," are too indefinite; one is unable to measure results against them. They permit lip-service attempts at attainment. There is no way to measure whether progress is made toward reaching them. They do not lend themselves to accountability. The use of specific public relations objectives is a great deal more apt to be successful.

People with direct responsibility for the day-to-day job recognize broad goals as unreal. An example of this occurred when a department head of a large utility was asked about objectives for his group. Bringing forth a list of broad generalities from a file drawer where they had been for nearly a year, he commented that nobody paid attention to them. Top management asked for them once or twice a year. In the meantime they remained forgotten in the file drawer.

One morning at coffee with four of the vice presidents of a company, the subject of management by objectives came up. All four vice presidents staunchly made the point that their people used this technique of management. There was no mention of themselves. None of them really had any knowledge of the subject. Yet to be effective, the use of management by objectives must always start at the top of the organization.

Too often management by objectives is the popular thing for management people to latch onto. In some quarters it is a cliché—words to be hailed—but with nothing done about it. As Peter Drucker points out in his book *Management: Tasks, Responsibilities, and Practices,* hundreds of companies have adopted a policy of management by objectives, but only a few have followed through to make it effective.[4]

Having generalities as objectives is something like a person setting out to go somewhere without knowing where he is going—without knowing what direction, which road to take, or how far he will have to travel. He can waste a lot of time and money going around in circles. Without specific objectives, we cannot tell whether we are headed toward the right place or going in the right direction. If we do not know where we want to go, how can we measure?

In the past few years there has been much talk about management by objectives in corporate and departmental planning. Where management by objectives has been used, its use has frequently been limited to one phase or

---

[4] New York: Harper and Row, 1974.

A SPECIFIC OBJECTIVE IS

ONE AGAINST WHICH YOU CAN

MEASURE RESULTS.

Figure 13

another of the management job, and it has not as often been used for the entire job. For example, it has been used with regard to budgets, sales, and the numbers and kinds of people on the payroll.

The concept of management by objectives discussed here, however, is the use of objectives as the primary determinant of public relations plans as a means of improving the effectiveness of the function. Under this concept specific objectives are determined to meet each of the situations requiring public relations action. Then plans are developed to meet the objectives.

In management by objectives all parts of an organization must have the same overall organizational objectives. It follows that all parts of the public relations department must also have the same overall objectives. One cannot have those responsible for advertising going in one direction while those dealing with the news media go another. One of the advantages of management by objectives is that it helps to ensure that all parts of the organization pull together toward the same common objectives.

DEFINITION OF SPECIFIC OBJECTIVES

As compared with broad goals, a specific objective is one against which one can measure results. A test of an objective's specificity is to determine plans for measuring results of the activity required to achieve the objective. If you are unable to measure the results against the activity, the objective is not specific and should be changed.

Objectives must always relate to the underlying problem causes or to the underlying obstacles to achieving opportunities. They must define the specific quantitative results to be achieved, and they must define when the results should be achieved. Thus we would not have as an objective improv-

OBJECTIVES MUST ALWAYS

RELATE TO THE UNDERLYING

PROBLEM CAUSES.

Figure 14

ing employee motivation, for example. Instead, after determining the causes of poor motivation, we would set objectives for eliminating or reducing them and for doing those things that will provide a better climate for good motivation. We would state how much progress we expected to make and by what date.

To use another example, we would not have as an objective the improvement of service. Rather, we would determine the underlying causes of poor service. Then we would set our objectives to meet the criteria for good service and to eliminate the causes of poor service. Again, an objective would state how much progress we expected to make by a specific date. By measuring progress, we could tell whether we were on course and how effective our work had been to date.

DETERMINING THE UNDERLYING PROBLEM CAUSES

Determining the underlying causes of public relations problems can be something like a doctor prescribing for a persistent cough. He must be careful to find out what causes that cough and prescribe for the cause rather than merely giving the patient cough syrup. The underlying cause of the cough may be a common cold or something very important such as pneumonia or lung cancer. Treatment for a cold would be very different from that for lung cancer. In public relations the same thing can be true. We have to be careful not to prescribe just for the figurative "cough" but rather to find out what causes it and try to cure the cause.

It is surprising how many people move off to tackle what appears on the surface to be the problem without thinking through what the problem really is—or what the objectives for overcoming it should be. Even in tasks such as preparing a news story, a newspaper ad, or an employee information piece, it is surprising how much good public relations money is spent in writing, producing, and purchasing space in the papers without setting down clear objectives for the piece and then checking the completed job to see if it meets those objectives.

NINE ADVANTAGES OF MANAGEMENT BY OBJECTIVES

As summarized in Figure 15, nine advantages give importance to managing the public relations function through the use of specific objectives:

1. Management by objectives requires tackling the underlying problem causes instead of symptoms. People are apt to tackle symptoms and surface manifestations of the problems. The use of specific objectives requires well-

thought-out definitions of underlying problems and potential problems or opportunities.

Generalized overall efforts based on broad goals and not aimed at specific objectives are rarely as effective as they need to be. They are not aimed at the target. For example, business would not be likely to improve relations with educators through an overall generalized public relations effort. Objectives set to overcome the specific underlying causes of the unfavorable attitudes of educators are needed. Using these objectives, a program can be developed and aimed specifically at improving relations with the educators.

2. With the rapidity of change, new situations and problems constantly confront organizations. The complexion of situations and problems also constantly changes. Since the use of specific objectives requires problem analysis and a review of results, it helps to bring proper recognition and analysis of new situations and changed situations.

NINE ADVANTAGES OF MANAGEMENT BY OBJECTIVES

1.   It requires well thought out definitions of problems.

2.   With today's rapid change, management by objectives permits effectively meeting new situations.

3.   It permits assigning priorities to the most important matters.

4.   It ensures better coordination and enables everyone to know specifically what is to be accomplished.

5.   It helps ensure top management involvement.

6.   People are better motivated.

7.   It permits better budgeting.

8.   It makes possible easier measurement of results.

9.   It makes it easier to evaluate people based on performance.

Figure 15

3. With the use of specific objectives, it is possible to determine more easily the most important problems and to assign them priority. This is essential when one considers the number of different situations and problems confronting an organization at a given time. Within the resources of the organization, which is the most important to solve? Which must be solved first? Time and resources may not be available to meet all situations demanding attention. Analysis of the underlying problems and development of specific objectives will permit public relations management to allocate effort where it will pay off best.

4. Specific objectives help to ensure better coordination of and give more visible direction to the public relations function. Thus they make it easier to make sure everyone in the organization pulls in the same direction at the proper time. Management by objectives helps to provide a common language. This is an important point in organizations where the different departments and different levels of management use different vernaculars. Everyone can have the same understanding of what is to be accomplished. This helps to prevent scattering efforts in as many directions as there are people and situations. Effective action rarely results from scattered efforts.

5. Properly used, management by objectives will help to ensure complete top management involvement and agreement on priorities. Management by objectives must include all levels of management, starting with the chief executive, because each level of management must base its objectives on those of the next higher level. If the next higher level does not have specific written objectives, then the whole system will break down.

6. With specific objectives, people are apt to be better motivated because they know what is expected of them and what the organization is trying to accomplish. In addition if they are allowed to participate in setting specific objectives, they are more likely to be motivated to work harder to reach them.

Thus people will have higher performance objectives. Less supervision will be necessary because work groups and individuals will be able to manage themselves better. When they participate in setting their objectives, they can compare their own performance against them. It follows that they will usually better manage their own performance. Being in on setting the group's objectives takes on added importance in this era when one of the demands of people is that they be allowed to "make a contribution."

Without specific objectives, effective leadership is made difficult because leadership consists of motivating people to try to reach specific common objectives.

7. Specific objectives lend themselves to making specific plans to meet the objectives. These plans may then be priced out. Budgets based on priced out plans will be closer to actual costs than those developed in other ways.

By having specific task-oriented projects, one may make budgeting a logical process rather than only a manipulation of some figures to appease the financial end of the business on an occasional basis. Specific objectives permit better, more precise budgeting of the public relations function.

A certain public relations director always asked for more money than he thought he needed in order to provide a cushion for use in event of budget cuts and because in reality he did not know how to develop a budget. Then at the end of the year, he would hurry to spend the money that was left over in his budget. There is no need for that kind of budget manipulation. With specific objectives and plans for carrying them out, it is usually possible to price out plans fairly closely and to come reasonably close to a budget figure one can live with. One cannot always foresee new situations that may require expenditures of considerable money, but in this event, a request may be made for the budget to be changed. Of course, allowance must be made in budgets for a certain amount of day-to-day demand work not included in the objectives.

8. Specific objectives permit easier measurement of results. Reviews can be made to determine how well objectives are met in considering changes necessary for the future. Objectives set performance standards against which the job done by both groups and individuals can be evaluated.

9. With specific objectives, it is easier to measure employee performance and reward it on the basis of how well the objectives are met.

DEFINING RESULTS TO BE ACHIEVED

Management by objectives organizes all work in terms of achieving specific measurable results. The definition of results must be specific as to exactly what is to be accomplished in terms of the underlying problems to be overcome, and when. The results must be stated in positive terms, and the results to be accomplished, not the activities leading to them, must be defined.[5]

NOT A LIST OF ACTIVITIES

A natural tendency in setting objectives is to list all the public relations activities to be carried out rather than the results to be achieved. This does not meet the requirement of management by objectives. In most every

---

[5] Ernest C. Miller, *Objectives and Standards: An Approach To Planning.* New York: American Management Association, 1966.

MANAGEMENT BY OBJECTIVES
ORGANIZES ALL WORK
IN TERMS OF ACHIEVING
SPECIFIC MEASURABLE RESULTS

- The definition of results must be specific as to exactly what is to be accomplished and when.

- The results must be stated in positive measurable terms.

- The results to be accomplished - not the activities leading to them, must be defined.

Figure 16

endeavor there can be great variation in the direction, the amount of activity, and the outcome if the end results to be reached are not specifically defined. Again, we need to know the results to be accomplished, not the activities leading to them.

The concept provides a great deal more organization and specific approach to the public relations function. It requires meeting issues. One should realize that the inevitable price of meeting issues may at times be controversy. For example, perhaps some of the viewpoints or even basic tenets of the organization should be questioned. However, it should be recognized that good organizational health—good relations within the organization—does not depend on freedom from opposing views. Properly handled, conflicting views frequently lead to better and more effective decisions and organizational adjustment.

PLANS FOR MEASURING RESULTS

A specific objective is one against which one can measure results. Plans for measuring results should be made at the time objectives are set. The results to be achieved should be specifically defined in terms of the underlying problem to be overcome. When the results will be accomplished should also be specifically stated.

The results to be achieved could be changes in attitudes because of improvements in the organization's performance. They could be changes in the amount of information people have on a given subject. Or they might be a measure of the effectiveness of a single communicative effort such as a comprehension study of a newspaper ad. The next chapter discusses opinion and media research, including comprehension studies.

To measure changes in attitudes or in public awareness and the amount of information people have, one needs bench marks or starting points, which may be established by using opinion research or media research conducted before going forward with plans to meet objectives. When the plans have been carried out, then one uses the same research method to find the amount of change from the bench mark. Thus it is possible to measure progress toward an objective.

An example of the measurement of public awareness, and the amount of information people had was the change of all Portland, Oregon, telephone numbers, which was done to enlarge the telephone system there. It was important to know the effectiveness of the public information program concerning the change because premature dialing of the new numbers would result in customers' reaching wrong numbers. If the old numbers were used after the change, the equipment could not complete the calls. So it was essential that the public information program effectively inform customers of the time and date of the change and how to dial calls before and after the change. If people were not getting the message, the information program would have to be revised and intensified.

Low-key publicity was used for nearly a year prior to the change. Just before the start of the intensive public information program, about three weeks before the change, a telephone survey was made to provide a bench mark of public awareness of the essential information.

The information program used the likeness of a very popular elephant in the Portland zoo, named Rosie, as spokesman in newspapers, radio, and television advertising. As the program proceeded, additional telephone surveys were used to measure progress and to determine whether it was necessary to increase the program's intensity.

The last survey, made the day before the change, showed that 99 percent of the people were aware of the vital information. The change was carried out without a problem.

INTERIM, PROBLEM CORRECTIVE, AND ADAPTIVE OBJECTIVES

There are three types of specific objectives depending on the circumstances. One can start with interim objectives that may be used before the necessary information can be obtained to develop problem corrective objectives. The interim objectives can include the research necessary to obtain the information needed for setting problem corrective objectives.[6] In addition, interim

---

[6] Three kinds of action, Interim, Adaptive, and Corrective, are discussed by Charles H. Kepner and Benjamin B. Tregoe, *The Rational Manager*. New York: McGraw-Hill, 1965.

3 KINDS OF
SPECIFIC PR OBJECTIVES

- Interim
    For use before one has information
    to form corrective objectives
- Problem correction and prevention
- Adaptive
    For use when corrective or prevent-
    ative actions are not possible.

Figure 17

objectives can be used in a holding action until corrective objectives can be set. For example, interim objectives can be set at the time one is handed a "hot potato." Such objectives provide time to get and study the facts before setting problem corrective objectives.

The second type of objective is the problem corrective objective. It is the kind one should strive for because it can lead to the ultimate correction or prevention of problems (or the achievement of opportunities).

The best corrective action may not be possible because of circumstances. Such a situation calls for the third type of objective—the adaptive objective. With adaptive objectives an organization adapts to living with a problem and sets objectives to do the best it can under the circumstances. For example, funds may not be available at a given time to correct a problem. So an adaptive objective is set for use until such a time as the necessary funds can be obtained.

Over a period of time, it is possible to have more than one type of objective for a given problem. For example, the organization may start out with an interim objective for use until it is able to obtain more information needed to set problem corrective objectives. Then it may need adaptive objectives because it lacks the financing necessary to carry out corrective objectives. When financing becomes available, then the organization can adopt corrective objectives.

As an example of the use of the three kinds of objectives, after World War II there were not enough telephone facilities. Customers' orders for service were sometimes held up for as much as a year before telephones could be connected. This created a tremendous public relations problem. The problem corrective objective would have been to provide all users with the kind of service they wanted at the time they wanted it, but demand for service was so great that sufficient material, labor, and finance were not available.

Therefore, the telephone companies set an adaptive objective to provide customers with one basic black telephone on a party line with no extensions, to give as many people service as possible. The problem required an extensive public (and employee) information program with an adaptive objective of explaining why it was not possible to provide the kind of service many people wanted.

Sometime later when sufficient equipment was becoming available, an interim objective was set to provide party line telephones, with a promise that by a certain date customers would receive the kind of service they wished. Interim objectives for the public information program were set to fit the new circumstances. Eventually it was possible to provide people the kind of service they wanted at the time they placed their orders. Problem corrective objectives were then possible.

Another illustration involves a public relations staff group. Let us presume that other departments of the organization do not feel that the public relations staff is doing what it should to improve public attitudes. Two interim objectives would be (1) to determine specifically what the attitudes of the other groups are toward the public relations staff, and (2) to determine what the staff is doing to improve attitudes. We can suppose, for the purpose of illustration, that it is found that their entire effort relates to communication. However, it is known that performance problems in certain areas render their communicative efforts ineffective.

With this information, another interim objective might then be set to carry out training programs for public relations staff people to improve their analytical ability, so that they will be able to determine performance problems better. The training program should also improve their ability to persuade those of other departments concerning the necessity to improve performance as viewed by the public. Lack of funds may temporarily prevent carrying out the training program, making necessary adaptive objectives. One objective might be to modify the communicative action in areas where poor performance is apt to harm credibility. Finally, after funds become available making it possible to go ahead with training the staff, corrective objectives may be set, and plans can be developed for corrective action.

STEPS IN SETTING OBJECTIVES

How does one go about systematically setting objectives? Before going into detail on suggested steps, it may be helpful to list them in brief form. The following nine steps are suggested for developing the organization's primary public relations objectives.

1. Determine the current level of performance.
2. Determine and get agreement on the level of performance that is expected.
3. Analyze problems causing current performance to be lower than the performance expected.
4. Consider the relative importance of underlying problems to attitudes and also of the attitudes themselves. Eliminate less important problems and attitudes from consideration.
5. Set tentative objectives.
6. Examine the tentative objectives for undesirable side effects. Revise them as may be necessary.
7. Develop rough plans for carrying out tentative objectives and price them out.
8. Revise objectives if carrying them out is too costly.
9. Get upper management approval for the objectives.

When setting secondary objectives, such as those for news releases, advertising, and so on, much of the analysis should have been completed. Thus the work should be greatly simplified.

Now let us go into more detail on the steps in setting objectives.

1. The first step in setting objectives is to determine current performance as viewed by the publics. In doing this, as brought out in Chapter 4, one should take care to get the real facts and not merely cater to a group's or individual's thinking or personal bias. The initial facts may provide only symptoms of the real or potential problems.

One may ask, "to whom should we listen?" in determining the real problems. Many special groups claim to speak for the public. But do they? Is what appears to be a problem really the symptom of something else? If the problem is real how important is it? How high does it stand in the list of all problems?

How do government agency people and legislators feel? Are they informed? Within the bounds of available resources which should receive attention? Which problems are apt to grow in importance? Which may cause side effects that will to a great extent adversely affect attitudes toward other matters? How much is credibility affected by a problem? Answers to questions such as these are the key to setting objectives.

CLUES TO PROBLEMS

A starting point in getting the facts concerning current performance may be personal observation, letters, telephone or personal comments, and complaints. These may be especially helpful when they come from publics such as regulatory and other government agencies, financial analysts, educators, and the like. Discussion with employees can be invaluable.

Early recognition of problems concerning current performance is important because what was acceptable yesterday may no longer be acceptable today. The change should be discovered as early as possible. Clues to problems or symptoms of problems still only on the horizon may sometimes be obtained from letters to newspaper editors, newspaper column comments, and magazine articles. Bills introduced in state and national legislatures are also indications of problems. A look at the experiences of other businesses can be helpful.

Initial information obtained from these sources may be amplified through the use of attitude research designed to get answers to questions such as those posed earlier.

2. The second step in setting objectives is realistically to determine and get agreement as to the performance expected. This thinking through of the performance one should expect is a primary step.

In some discussions of management by objectives, it is advocated that expected performance should be determined before examining current performance. This practice eliminates the hazard of setting expected performance too low because of the possible large gap between current performance and what expected performance should be. However, with the involvement in attitudinal research and the analysis of attitudes, it is usually necessary that determination of current attitudes come as a first step.

3. The third step is to analyze problems causing performance to be lower than is desirable. To analyze current performance, the attitude research used should find out *why* people feel as they do, rather than merely learning what their attitudes are. If people have unfavorable attitudes, we need to know why in order to understand what the problems really are. In other words, what specific things in performance (or the lack of performance) are causing the unfavorable attitudes? Then we can set objectives to overcome the problems.

In determining why people feel as they do, trained observation and perception on the part of the public relations staff are important factors both in uncovering symptoms and problems and in their analysis.

The underlying problems will be the basis of specific objectives for improvement. Thus the key to setting specific objectives is good analysis to determine the real underlying problems. This may require additional attitudinal research to probe the reasons people feel as they do. Additional research will always be necessary if the original research measured attitudes but did not find out what caused them.

Experience has shown that problem analysis is the most difficult part of the task for most people, but thorough analysis is usually necessary to uncover what really underlies the problem and to avoid setting objectives based on symptoms. One should be careful not to mistake the rash for the disease.

RELATIVE IMPORTANCE

4. The fourth step is to consider the relative importance of the underlying problems in causing attitudes and to discover what the attitudes themselves are. (For example, people may have an unfavorable attitude because most post offices are not open on Saturdays, but they may also have a more important unfavorable attitude toward the cost of mail service. Since opening post offices on Saturdays would add to the cost, the attitude toward Saturday hours is relatively less important.) Considering relative importance permits using resources where they will pay off best, by tackling problems of the greatest relative importance.

Another example of determining relative importance concerned a service business. Among the complaints received about the job done by customer contact people, some had to do with the quality of the work and some referred to the attitudes of the employees. It was found that undesirable attitudes on the part of employees had a much higher relative importance than the quality of the work itself. Customers realize that workers will sometimes make errors and mistakes. To err is only human. But customers do not excuse poor attitudes as indicated by surliness or not caring what kind of a job is done. Thus the greatest effort went to correcting employee attitudes.

5. We have now reached the point where tentative specific objectives should be set to overcome the problems that have been uncovered. What improvements must be made to correct the problems? Long-range objectives should be broken down into short-term steps to facilitate planning and progress reviews.

Research should be planned for use in evaluating results. For objectives requiring a long-range program, periodic research will be desirable for use in reviewing progress and to check on effectiveness and changes in the problem during the course of the program. Chapter 6 discusses opinion research.

6. Tentative objectives should be examined for undesirable side effects, either to public relations or to other functions of the business. Possible alternatives should be considered. Necessary adjustments should then be made to accommodate alternatives and to eliminate undesirable side effects.

PRICING OUT A ROUGH PLAN—COST-BENEFIT ANALYSES

7. A rough plan should be made for reaching the objectives, and it should be priced out to determine whether the plan is within an acceptable financial range. If it turns out to be too costly, it must be modified or eliminated. One must ask: Is the cost within the range that the organization should afford, regardless of the benefits of carrying out the objectives? (2) Do the benefits of carrying out the objectives justify the cost? (3) How much is it worth to achieve the particular objectives?

8. Objectives should be revised if necessary.

UPPER MANAGEMENT APPROVAL

9. If carrying out the objectives presents no cost problems, they and the rough plans for executing them are ready to be approved by upper management. This can be one of the most important steps in setting objectives. It is desirable to get not only top managements' approval but also its active support of the objectives and the work necessary to carry them out.

One may run into situations in which people in other departments of the organization drag their heels and do not cooperate as fully as desirable with public relations objectives. With top management support, the situation can be remedied. Without top management support, those not cooperating fully may get their way. Top management and upper management support is important in getting budgets approved and ensuring proper coordination of efforts throughout the organization.

THREE KINDS OF PUBLIC RELATIONS OBJECTIVES

In Chapter 1, we said that the public relations of any business is really determined by three kinds of performance. The first concerns the degree of customer satisfaction with products and services, including all the customer contacts necessary, and involves such things as sales, delivery, billing, and maintenance. The second concerns the policies set by management and its concern for the public interest. The third relates to the traditional communicative function of the public relations staff. We also said that the objectives of the public relations functions should encompass all three kinds of performance and that the communicative objectives must always reflect the other two. (Objectives should be set for all three in the manner discussed earlier, beginning on page 78.)

WHO SHOULD SET OBJECTIVES?

Who should set public relations objectives? What levels of the organization should have objectives?

To begin with it is essential that the public relations objectives be consistent with the overall objectives of the organization. This emphatically does not mean that public relations management should sit and wait for upper management to set overall objectives. Public relations management, with the active participation and agreement of all the other departments, should set public relations objectives for the organization.

After the objectives have been set, it is desirable for each department, each plant and office, and each work group in the organization to set its own public relations objectives as a part of its overall objectives. Department, plant, office, and group objectives should be based on those of the organization as a whole and the next level above. Higher levels, of course, may approve or not approve the objectives.

In his book, *Every Employee A Manager,* M. Scott Myer says that the most important continuing challenge in the years ahead will be to establish programs that encourage the achievement of compatible employee and organization goals.[7] Giving employees the opportunity to plan and to learn about and evaluate results is an important part of meeting this challenge and increases the prospects of having committed and motivated people. When work groups set their own objectives, reaching those objectives becomes one of their goals. In addition improvements are best made by those who perform the job. Thus they are best able to set objectives for the improvements. Most people work hard to achieve objectives they had a part in setting, but they may ignore or give only lip service to objectives set by someone else. People will also be better acquainted with objectives that they had a hand in setting. Each department and each work group should know and be accountable for the results in meeting its objectives.

Without good performance by all departments, good public relations is difficult to achieve. Every department and every work group has an important effect on public relations. The motivating climate of each group,

[7] New York: McGraw-Hill, 1970.

including its own public relations objectives as a part of the overall objectives, can be an important help in the public relations job. Without the help of other parts of the organization, public relations management can do little.

The improved motivation resulting from each group's setting its own objectives and knowing the results of its work will frequently help rekindle the individual's pride in his work. By stimulating better performance, public attitudes may be improved, assuming, of course, that public relations workers take steps to call the public's attention to the improvement.

ROLE OF THE PUBLIC RELATIONS STAFF

The role of the public relations staff in the objective-setting activity should be that of catalyst, stimulator, coordinator, researcher, counselor, and advisor. Naturally the public relations staff should have its own specific objectives relating to all three kinds of performance.

Having specific objectives is important in every phase of public relations work. For instance, as mentioned earlier, every news story and every newspaper ad should have a specific objective. The objective should be put into writing before a word of the ad or story is put on paper. It is surprising how often catchy sounding copy is prepared without any specific objective. Such copy, however, may have little effect on people's attitudes. The objective of each news story and ad (as well as all other communicative material) should always work toward the overall communicative objectives of the organization.

TOO MANY OBJECTIVES

Care should be taken not to set so many objectives that none can be reached. Objectives with high relative importance should be carried out. Less important ones may be discarded. Resources should be allocated to the place where they will pay off best.

OBJECTIVES THAT ARE TOO DIFFICULT OR TOO EASY

One should take care not to set objectives that are too difficult to reach. They should be reasonable. Neither people nor organizations react well to objectives set beyond their reach. People are stimulated more by success than by failure.

On the other hand, objectives should keep people on their toes. A group should not be permitted to set objectives on the presumption that the status quo is good enough. The public relations management must insist on the solution to perennial problems and the introduction of new ideas to achieve better results.

COST NOT THE FIRST CONSIDERATION

In setting objectives costs should not be overemphasized. Organizations are set up to accomplish purposes—not to lower expenditures. Therefore, objectives should first be defined in terms of what needs to be accomplished before costs are considered. If necessary, the objectives may then be lowered in consideration of the amount of money available for carrying them out. By first setting objectives in terms of what needs to be accomplished before costs are considered, management is made aware of the real situation rather than a watered-down version.

PROPER EMPHASIS AND BALANCE

As objectives are achieved, each part of the organization should be checked to be sure that some objectives are not given undue emphasis. Every organization has some people who overemphasize easy objectives or the ones they like. They may disregard or play down more difficult ones. An example of this concerned a public relations department head in a large organization. He was so deeply interested and engrossed in relations between business and education that he completely ignored his primary public relations responsibilities. Thus vital areas of the public relations function were neglected, and the organization's public relations went from bad to worse, resulting in a financial crisis.

Overemphasis or underemphasis of particular objectives and the resulting underaccomplishment or overaccomplishment of other objectives leads to imbalance and overall loss of effectiveness. No reward should be given people or parts of an organization that shine in accomplishing one objective while neglecting others. Sometimes work on a minor objective may be pushed to create the illusion of commendable achievement. At the same time work on major objectives may go without accomplishment.

IMPORTANCE OF MANAGEMENT BY OBJECTIVE FOR EFFECTIVENESS

The use of management by objectives for the public relations function should lead to the better integration and coordination of the function throughout the entire organization. As the importance of public relations has grown, it has become one of the pivotal ingredients of success or failure for the organization. Effectiveness of public relations management is vital. Management by objectives can make a great contribution to its effectiveness.

ON ESTABLISHING MANAGEMENT BY OBJECTIVES

The establishment of management by objectives is not something that can be done by the writing or the approval of a memorandum authorizing it. A major effort and perseverance over a considerable length of time is required to establish it fully. People must be persuaded to accept it, and they must learn how to use it. It will require more than one step to initiate. For example, the initial opinion research must be arranged for to determine problems before all the objectives can be set. Upper levels should set objectives on which lower levels base theirs. However, the advantages of management by objectives outweigh the problems in establishing it.

SIX

Opinion, Media, and Other Research

Opinion research is a broad and a technical subject. Our coverage in this chapter is designed to give the reader an overview of it and some appreciation of its problems, scope, and benefits. Opinion research and allied kinds of research are primary tools of public relations management for problem analysis and for setting objectives. They are also essential in measuring results. The purpose of research is to provide information that may be used, along with other information and judgment, in making decisions.

Many people have heard about opinion research through newspaper reports of various polls, particularly political polls. An outstanding example of the misuse of opinion research concerned political polls taken by the *Literary Digest,* a well-known news magazine of its day. According to the magazine, its polls showed that Franklin D. Roosevelt could not possibly win the presidential election of 1936. But he did. The magazine lost credibility and went out of existence.

Because election results, for example, are not exactly as indicated by the interviews made several days before the voting, some people take a jaundiced view of polls and opinion research. However, since many voters change their minds or do not make up their minds until election day, it would be unusual for polls taken earlier to predict the results accurately. In addition, political polls are generally representative of the most elemental kind of opinion research. Opinion research has progressed far beyond the scope of most political polls. Most of the problems encountered from political polls made by competent research organizations are the result of erroneous interpretations reached by readers.

As long ago as the early 1930s, progressive businesses such as Procter and Gamble Company and Lever Brothers were successfully using market

THE PURPOSE OF RESEARCH IS

TO PROVIDE INFORMATION THAT MAY

BE USED WITH OTHER INFORMATION

AND JUDGMENT IN MAKING EFFECTIVE

DECISIONS.

Figure 18

and opinion research to determine the effectiveness of advertising and to measure acceptance of products. The effective use of research by the advertising and sales promotion department of Procter and Gamble Company at that time undoubtedly accounted for the company's great success in growing to be the leader in its fields. Research pointed the way not only in advertising and promotion but also regarding the products to be manufactured and the packaging to be used. Astute use of good research by the advertising and sales promotion people helped them to become the leaders of the company. Those leaders became the chairman of the board, the president, and other officers of the company.

However, one still sometimes hears chief executives of large businesses state that they do not believe in opinion research and that they learn all they need to know about public opinion by talking with their peers at the club. Such a viewpoint is dangerous to the business or other organizations involved, for the viewpoints of an executive's peers would seldom be representative of the public.

RESEARCH HELPS PERCEIVE THE ENVIRONMENT CORRECTLY

In Chapter 3, we said that the quality of a management can be measured by its ability to perceive an organization's environment correctly and to effectively do something about it. Sophisticated opinion research, along with other kinds of research, makes it possible to perceive the environment better. It can uncover information needed for problem analysis and for setting objectives. It provides data that, when combined with other information, can result in better decisions.

FINDING OUT WHY AS WELL AS WHAT

Unfortunately, much opinion and market research uncovers only the symptoms of problems.

An example of this occurred at the time Lever Brothers Company began to market Spry shortening. Procter and Gamble had successfully marketed Crisco, another shortening, for many years. But customer research and falling sales indicated attitudes toward that product were unfavorable compared with Spry.

Subsequent research among customers, however, discovered that the problem was really a dislike of the container in which Crisco was sold. The attitude toward the product itself was very favorable. Easily made changes in the container led to immediate improvement of attitudes and recovery of the market for Crisco.

In the case cited, both the true problem and its cause were exposed. But research often fails to determine causes of problems, even when the problems themselves are discovered.

Yet what we really need to learn is what causes the problems, because our public relations objectives should be set to reduce or eliminate those problem causes. Therefore, public relations management should make certain that the research it purchases *finds out not only what people think—but why.*

It is almost impossible to do a good public relations management job without research, including good opinion research and good media research. Conversely, research improperly conceived or carried out can be misleading and dangerous. That is why research should be supervised and analyzed by people knowledgeable in the subject and why only market and opinion research firms of unquestionable knowledge, ability, and integrity should be employed.

RESEARCH OBJECTIVES

In Chapter 5 we discussed the importance of specific written objectives. Research and arranging for research need written objectives, too. The most important requirement when arranging for research is to have specific objectives for the research including a completely thought-out definition of the subjects to be covered. For example, after a series of questionable top

**REQUIREMENTS IN
ARRANGING FOR RESEARCH**

1. A well thought out definition of the problem to be investigated.

2. A clear definition of the specific objectives of the research desired.

Figure 19

management decisions, a large business was having problems with the attitudes of its lower and middle management people. Top management decided to use opinion research in probing the reasons for the poor attitudes.

Among the subjects they could have studied were (1) the attitudes and their causes, (2) the attitudes without determining the causes, (3) the amount of credibility and the reasons for any loss in credibility, and (4) the viewpoints concerning the employee information program used by the business. It elected to study the attitudes (without determining their causes) and the viewpoints concerning the information program. It was decided to make a later study of the causes of poor attitudes "if one was really needed."

The objectives could have included providing a demographic breakdown of results—for example, by level of management, age group, length of service in the business, department, and so on. Perhaps even more important, the objectives could have included investigating psychographic factors. A firm date could have been set for the completion, analysis, and reporting of all research.

As it turned out, although it was recognized as being needed, the later study to determine reasons for unfavorable attitudes was not done. The demographic breakdkown used in the earlier study included only two elements—level of management and age. The research was not decision oriented. *A fundamental requirement of all opinion and media research used by public relations management is that it be decision oriented.*

One should remember that good opinion and media research is quite costly. It is much better to conduct fewer research studies, making sure the results are actionable and used, than to make many studies and have interesting but unusable or unused results. The benefits of all research should be weighed against its cost.

PSYCHOGRAPHIC FACTORS

Psychographic factors and differences among people may be infinitely more important than demographic factors and differences. It has been said that they concern "life styles," but that description is much too narrow. Psychographic factors are fundamentally important because they relate directly to people's motivational needs. In turn, people's attitudes and behavior depend on their needs.

Psychographic factors are directly related to Maslow's hierarchy of motivational needs.[1] For example, the need for achievement as a motivational

[1] *Motivation and Personality*. New York: Harper and Row, 1954.

force relates to Maslow's need for self-actualization. The need for achievement may vary greatly between individuals, specific organizations, groups, and whole nations. The need for power relates to Maslow's need for self-esteem and the esteem of others. The need for affiliation is related to Maslow's need for love and belongingness. All the various needs are inter-related and interdependent.

As suggested by David C. McClelland, the amounts of need in people for achievement, power, and affiliation and the relationships among these needs are important not only to the attitudes and behavior of individuals but to whole nations.[2]

Opinion research has done very little with psychographics, yet they may yield information of great importance to both external and internal relations.

THE IMPORTANCE OF QUALITY

Make sure the people who do research for you are capable and have the kinds of knowledge needed to do high quality work. The results of opinion and media research conducted by those not knowledgeable in the field should be questioned, however competent they may be in other lines of work. The objectives of the research, the validity of the sample selection, the competence of the interviewers, and the interpretations of the answers to the questions used in tabulations must be questioned. A considerable amount of opinion and media research is done by unqualified people.

Too often one finds unqualified people preparing questionnaires and conducting homemade surveys, then peddling the results to unsuspecting managements. Untrained or dishonest interviewers show their personal biases to respondents or complete questionnaires without talking with the respondents. Tabulators improperly code the answers given by respondents under a category where they do not belong. Computer programmers who prepare the data for the survey report make serious errors.

As a ship's navigator takes sightings to calculate his position, public relations management may use opinion research to learn where the organization is in regard to public opinion. If we have the results of previous research for comparison, we can determine what progress we have made in reaching objectives—to learn whether we are on the right course. Research can provide bench marks from which future progress may be measured, but unless we use good quality research done by capable people we, may figuratively go on the rocks. Research techniques are discussed later.

[2] David C. McClelland, *The Achieving Society*. New York: Van Nostrand Reinhold, 1961.

OTHER KINDS OF RESEARCH

We have indicated that other kinds of research, in addition to opinion research, make it possible to perceive the environment and manage the public relations function better. Such research may involve primary data gathered from inside the organization, such as sales figures, cost of constructing new facilities, numbers and kinds of customers served, or the numbers of complaints.

It may also include obtaining secondary data information from outside sources, such as employment data from the Bureau of Labor Statistics or the myriad of data available from the Department of Commerce (census data, for example). The U.S. Department of Commerce publishes a great amount of statistical material on many subjects. The material may be broken down on a county-by-county basis, for example. Some public libraries include up-to-date reference material. Public relations management should be cognizant of where data may be obtained.

In this discussion, however, we are especially concerned with opinion and media research, most of which is done through the use of interview surveys. Basically these surveys consist of asking people questions to find out what they think about some subject, condition, or situation.

WHAT QUESTIONS AND WHAT PEOPLE?

Since surveys consist of asking people to answer questions, one can see that this opens up two problems—what people and what questions? To make the research useful, it is important that we question people who are representative of whatever public we want to measure. We usually would like to have as precise a sample of those people as we can get from a practical standpoint.

Let us assume that we are talking about the general public in a given territory. The demographic characteristics of the people interviewed must be the same as they are for all the people in the territory involved. There must be the same ratio of each of the ethnic groups, age groups, and economic classes in our sample as is found in the territory. We may wish the interviews to be representative of the territory geographically—with the number of interviews we make in the north, south, east, west, and middle in proportion to the number of people who live in each of those sections.

In any survey there may be other considerations. A study of college students could take into consideration the ratio of those who live in dormitories and fraternity and sorority houses to those who live off campus. Or we might consider the ratio of freshmen to sophomores, juniors, seniors, and graduate students.

How many people must be interviewed? Theoretically, a relatively small number of interviews may provide a sample large enough to give the degree of accuracy desired. However, the size of the sample should be large enough so that dependable data will be available for demographic or other break-downs that may be desired. In addition, since the credibility of small samples may sometimes be attacked, a sufficient number of interviews should be obtained so that recommendations based on survey findings are not questioned by those who make the decisions, particularly if they have had no statistical experience. They may question whether a fairly small sample can provide usable results. Survey research specialists should be consulted as to the number of interviews needed for a particular study.

What kinds of questions should be used in surveys? There is a knack to composing questions that will get the needed information without influencing the answers. Questions should always be open-ended so that respondents will answer in their own words. Care must be taken never to use questions which lead respondents to answer in a particular way. Either direct or indirect questioning techniques may be used in opinion and market research. Direct questioning techniques may introduce problems caused by biases. For example, bias can be caused by the kinds of questions asked. It may be caused by the wording of questions asked. Bias may be introduced by interviewers who consciously or unconsciously project a viewpoint. And bias may be introduced by the respondent.

Respondents frequently wish to appear in a good light to the interviewer, for example. They may consider some social connotation in giving their answers to questions. For instance, when asked how many hours they watch television each night, people may feel there is a negative connotation to watching it as much as they do. They may scale down their response to "look good" in the eyes of the interviewer. In addition, although respondents may have views and attitudes on a subject, they may simply not be able to answer the interviewer's direct questions in a way that correctly conveys their views and attitudes.

Thus indirect questioning may often have to be used to get around respondent bias. Indirect forms of interviewing use projective techniques in which respondents are asked to evaluate two (or sometimes more) situations that are structured in such a way that when the individual evaluates them, he provides the information desired. A good example of the indirect technique is a study reported by Mason Haire, made to measure the attitude of housewives toward instant coffee. Direct questioning had not provided results trustworthy enough to use. So respondents were asked to evaluate two shopping lists and state what kind of person might have made up each one. The lists were nearly identical except for the order of the items on them, but one list included a ground coffee and the other an instant coffee. The list with the instant coffee was frequently felt by respondents to have been made by a penny-wise and pound-foolish person who could not manage well. The maker of the list with ground coffee was looked on favorably.[3]

By using an indirect questioning technique, the organization was better able to measure public attitudes and what was back of them, guiding its marketing accordingly.

As another example of an indirect questioning technique, to get more dependable information about the actual feeling on a given subject, a system of trade-offs may be used. A respondent may be asked to choose between two alternatives. Questions may involve the use of many pairs of alternatives, either to find the degree of feeling or to probe more than one subject. For instance, trade-offs may be made in which a change is proposed. The respondent is asked if he would sacrifice some specific thing to achieve the change. Trade-offs may be made with different intensities of sacrifice to achieve a proposal. For example, a question might be, "Would you pay a higher price of five cents a bottle to make possible requiring all beverages to be sold in returnable bottles?" The same question could be used with ten cents a bottle or one cent a bottle. Another example might be, "would you pay $1.00 a month more on your telephone bill to have all phone lines underground?" (Or $2.00 a month more, etc.)

This form of questioning has been used in getting answers to questions such as how should an organization respond to the wishes or demands of people who claim to speak for the public as a whole or for large groups of one kind or another. One may measure how strongly various groups feel about a wish or demand.

Key groups may be selected for interviews. The results for each of the various groups may then be weighted according to what is perceived to be their relative importance in the environment. Combining the weighted results into a composite figure can determine which wishes and demands have the greatest overall importance. One organization making a study for business firms interviewed a sample of state and national legislators. It included as other groups officials of state and federal regulatory agencies and a cross section of national organizations such as labor unions and professional associations. People in the investment world were interviewed as still another group. In addition, the study included stockholders, college students, and the general public.

Another method that may sometimes be used to measure strength of feeling is to ask respondents to indicate how strongly they feel on a scale of one to ten or by other similar numerical scales.

After research experts have prepared survey questionnaires, they usually

---

[3] "Projective Techniques in Marketing Research." *Journal of Marketing,* April 1950.

test them by interviewing people. Then, if the questionnaires seem to put answers into respondents' mouths, to cause a bias in any way, to be misunderstood, or to fail to get the type of information needed, they may be revised before the actual interviewing for the survey begins.

There are many ways of interviewing people. By far the best but the most expensive is in person. For some purposes interviewing in person is too costly or may take too much time, so other means are used. One sometimes hears it said that people will resent fact-finding invasion of their privacy by the personal interviewer. In interviews concerning most subjects there is really no foundation for this worry. Very few people will refuse an interview. Most people are pleased to be interviewed and to have their opinion sought—as long as the interviewer recognizes their time limitations and establishes rapport with them.

OTHER KINDS OF INTERVIEWS

In addition to personal interviews, one may use telephone interviews, mail questionnaires, and questionnaires left to be filled in and picked up later.

The telephone interview is usually reasonably short. It is best used when the information must be obtained quickly at low cost and when the questioning is not too involved.

Mail questionnaires, in most kinds of survey work, should be used with a good deal of care. Only a percentage of the questionnaires are returned, and not all those received are fully completed. People with a strong bias one way or another, or particular demographic groups, may be more apt to return the questionnaires than other people. Therefore, the sample may not turn out to be representative.

In some kinds of surveys, mail questionnaires are the only logical answer because of cost factors. They are particularly useful in checking customers on such things as the performance of employees. For example, mail questionnaires may be used to find out whether delivery was satisfactory or whether repair work was done properly.

Questionnaires left to be filled in and picked up later should be used with caution. Without sufficient testing and care, they can present communication problems that may not exist in personal interviews. For example, different respondents may interpret questions in different ways. There is no opportunity to probe or to be sure that the respondents relate to the question in the right way. Answers to questions may be composite views of a whole family or even include the views of relatives and friends.

An example occurred a few years ago in a "leave and pick up" questionnaire used by the research department of a major business. The questionnaire included a question as to how many people had heard a particular radio commercial. A larger percentage of respondents reported they had heard the commercial in a state where it or similar commercials could not be heard than in locations where the commercial received extensive use. The result was low credibility for the entire survey, which also covered other important subjects.

It is sometimes asked whether respondents give their true feelings and good answers in response to survey questions. With good interviewers, a small percentage of respondents may exaggerate in one direction, but an equal percentage will exaggerate in the other. In a properly conducted survey, results will not be affected.

RESEARCH ONE OF MANY DECISION FACTORS

It is important to remember that surveys are a tool to assist judgment that should be added to all the other information one has in seeking the best possible decisions. Survey results should not take the place of good judgment nor allow one to avoid decision making. Managers should avoid the temptation to allow survey results alone to make decisions for them, failing to properly weigh and consider all the other factors.

Research firms and departments should report the results of research but resist the temptation to recommend action in areas for which they do not have responsibility, since they are apt not to have sufficient knowledge of nonresearch factors.

REPORTING AND USING RESEARCH FIGURES

Since survey figures are based on a sample and not on the entire population, they usually should not be considered as being precise. They should never be reported with greater than slide rule accuracy (even though computers may be able to carry results out to many decimals). They should always be reported in whole numbers with decimals rounded out to the nearest higher or lower figure. The fact that attitudes and viewpoints may have changed some in the relatively short time between interviewing and completing a report is also reason for avoiding the impression that the figures are precise.

In comparing survey results with earlier results, small differences (sometimes as much as three or four percentage points) may have no statistical significance. Survey research specialists should be consulted as to the amount of change necessary to be considered of significance in any given report.

Usually what we seek in survey results is the relative amount of favorableness or unfavorableness, the relative amount of information that people may have, and so on. In comparing new survey results with those of earlier surveys, we may be interested in trends and indications of trends. We may want to know the degree of change. We rarely have need to know the precise percentage of people who have a particular opinion or who have particular information. To acquire such precise information would usually require a great many more interviews and add greatly to the cost of the survey work.

With survey figures we want an indication of acceptance or rejection and how intensely people feel. However, seldom can we look at a percentage and assume that just exactly that percentage of people feel a given way.

MEDIA RESEARCH

Besides opinion research, we may use several other kinds of survey research in public relations work. For example, we would want to determine how well we are communicating with people—perhaps both with people outside the organization and also those inside it. An example of such a survey is the readership study. Readership studies are the oldest way of measuring print advertising effectiveness. Daniel Starch came up with procedures for measuring readership in the early 1920s. George H. Gallup also devised readership study techniques in the mid-1920s. By the 1930s, large business firms such as Procter and Gamble Company made regular newspaper readership studies referred to by many as "Gallups."

The purpose of a readership study is to find out the attention-getting ability of, for example, an ad. Such a study may tell us what percentage of people saw our message, what percentage read it, and what percentage saw or read who sponsored the ad. People are questioned as to whether they have seen and whether they have read specific advertisements in newspapers or magazines. Personal interviews are used. The interviewer first determines whether the respondent has the issue of the newspaper or magazine being studied and has seen or read any part of it. If the respondent has, the interview continues. The interviewer actually goes through the newspaper or magazine with the respondent, inquiring whether the respondent has seen or read each ad being studied. The respondent is also questioned in the same way about the specific parts of each ad that had been seen or read, including the signature of the organization running the ad. Thus we can also learn how many people saw the various parts of the ads such as the illustration, the signature, and the copy blocks.

We can run the ad in one paper for the test before publishing it in a whole schedule of papers. Then if the research indicates problems with the ad's communicative ability and shows a need for change, we have an opportunity to make changes before spending a large sum of money to place it in all the newspapers. This is one form of pretesting an ad. By its use, we are able to stretch our public relations dollars.

In considering the results of readership studies, one should take care not to be confused by the figures. For example, one may hear an advertising executive say that a readership study score was 35 percent. He is referring to the percentage who saw the ad, not the percentage who read it. Most ads are read by only a small percent of people.

COMPREHENSION STUDIES

Another kind of study that may be of great help in measuring how well one is communicating in newspaper and magazine ads, as well as news releases, is known as the comprehension study. As its name implies, this study measures comprehension. It determines if the readers understand what the organization is trying to say. Do they understand the ad or news story's objective? The ad or story is in real trouble if the copywriter did not have a well-throught-out objective. One cannot very well measure whether the reader understands the objective if there really was none. It is a good idea to require a copywriter to include the specific objective when he submits the copy.

In addition to comprehension other information about ads and news releases may be obtained in connection with comprehension studies. One may find out such things as whether the copy and illustration are interesting and believable, whether the reader feels involved, whether there are confusing elements, whether slogans used in connection with logos are noticed and believed. Parts of the ad that are liked or disliked may be distinguished. Most of the elements of communication may be measured. These elements are attention, interest, comprehension, believability, and the power to motivate. More is said about communication in the next chapter.

In making comprehension studies, copies of proposed news releases and ad proofs are used. Sometimes to save expense only a mock-up of an ad showing type-set copy and a rough illustration in the proposed layout is prepared. Comprehension studies may be made of news releases for which time is available.

Studies of newspaper and magazine ads are made well before the ads are scheduled to run so that there will be time to make changes if the study shows changes to be desirable. The studies are made by personal interview.

Since most people's interest in what we have to say may be cursory, the time they give to reading our message may be brief. Therefore, in a comprehension study, respondents are asked first to scan the ad for seven seconds. Then we determine what message they get from it and whether they can repeat the main idea of the ad that we want to get across.

Comprehension is again measured after respondents read the ad taking as much time as they wish. Generally, a considerably higher percentage of people can repeat the correct message after the unrestricted reading. However, this procedure is unrealistic from the standpoint of what people generally do when they read advertising or publicity.

After comprehension is measured, respondents may be questioned concerning the other communicative elements of the ad.

SPLIT-RUN STUDIES

Many different variations of readership and comprehension studies are used by businesses and research firms. One worthy of note utilizes what is known as a "split-run" study in which two different variations of the same ad or two different ads may be studied in one of the newspapers set up to handle split-run research.

Half the paper's circulation with one of the ads is distributed in one part of the city. The other half, with the other ad, is distributed in another part of the city. Both halves are arranged to have the same demographic characteristics. Comprehension studies or other communication studies using personal interviews may then be made with samples in each of the two segments of the paper's circulation. In this way it is possible to compare the effectiveness of the two ads.

One of the simplest forms of split-run studies is to include different special offers in the two versions of the paper to determine which has the better pull. However, sophisticated forms of complete comprehension studies are more useful.

An interesting split-run technique may be used to improve on both readership and comprehension study accuracy and usefulness. One of the problems of standard readership studies is that people may say that they have seen or read ads when in fact they have not. A problem with standard comprehension studies is that proofs of ads are used, and the study situation is not real life. Some ads communicate successfully in the forced reading situations of the standard studies but poorly in real life situations. In the split-run method, which overcomes these problems, two ads may be tested simultaneously using personal interviews made within 48 hours after the ads are published.

A mock-up sheet is used that shows mock-ups of four different ads, two of them being as published in the two segments of the city. Each mock-up ad on the sheet has the correct headline, illustration, and signature but only mock-up copy. The respondents are shown the mock-up sheet and are questioned as to whether they recall seeing any of the mock-up ads in the paper of the day the test ad was run. We can be more confident, when a respondent picks the mock-up of the test ad as one he says he saw in the paper, that it is based on his actually having seen it.

Respondents who pick the mock-up of the test ad may then be asked to describe all they remember about the ad and its elements. They may be asked to tell what the main idea of the ad was and also asked questions about the ad concerning believability, parts liked and disliked, and so on.

Respondents who do not recall the test ad when shown the mock-up sheet may be given the standard comprehension study questions. In addition to the standard examination of data obtained, a comparison of data from the two methods is helpful in considering any desirable improvements in the ads.

In another and older variation of a split-run study, instead of half the paper's circulation being in one part of the city and half in the other, the two ads are printed in alternate papers as they come off the press. One ad appears in one paper and the other ad in the next. This kind of split-run study does not lend itself as well to communication studies, although it helps to ensure like demographic characteristics for both parts of the split run.

Split-run studies are pretests made before ads are circulated in other papers, as are also readership studies and comprehension studies. Such pretests of advertising by testing it in one paper or in proof form before it appears in the whole schedule of papers permits correcting or eliminating ads shown to be deficient.

OTHER COMMUNICATIVE RESEARCH

There are many variations of print ad research studies. For example, the portfolio study is sometimes used in which respondents are handed a portfolio containing a test ad and several others. The respondents are asked to leaf through the portfolio at their own pace. Then the portfolio is closed, and they are asked about the ads just reviewed. Questions are on such things as advertising recall, the main idea of the ad, and comparative ratings of the ads.

Respondents are then asked to reread the test ad fully, following which they are questioned as to its main idea, believability, overall impression, and parts liked and disliked.

NEWSPAPER AND MAGAZINE CIRCULATION

Newspaper and magazine circulation figures are not arrived at by the research method of canvassing the public. They may be obtained from reference books in which the circulation of newspapers and magazines is compiled. One such book most commonly used is *Standard Rate and Data*.[4] Another is published by the N. W. Ayer Advertising Company of Philadelphia, Pennsylvania.[5]

The use of such reference books entails important research to determine the coverage and size of circulation of publications being considered for employment in advertising or publicity. They are also helpful in determining which publications best cover the places where it is desired to use the advertising or publicity. In addition to circulation these references provide advertising rates and may provide the names of editorial and advertising officials of the publications. Circulation figures, together with rates, permit computation of the cost per thousand readers reached by various publications.

Rates for most newspaper advertising are quoted for agate lines of space. There are fourteen agate lines in a column inch of advertising space. Local advertising rates may be quoted for column inches of space without reference to lines. Newspaper rates may be converted to what is called a milline rate, which is the line rate multiplied by one million and divided by the circulation of the paper. This facilitates comparison of the advertising rates for various newspapers, taking into consideration the sizes of their circulation.

Although the milline rate is the most frequently used in comparing advertising rates, from the standpoint of advertising effectiveness a more revealing figure is the cost per thousand readers reached. The approximate number of readers may be learned through readership studies. The milline rate for newspaper space various greatly among papers. There is frequently no relationship between the cost per thousand readers reached and the milline rate for various newspapers.

In general rates for magazine advertising are quoted on the basis of a page or a fraction of a page of space. Readership figures obtained from the use of media research can also be profitably used to determine the cost per thousand readers reached through magazine advertising.

Proper use of these figures can help one to determine which newspapers and magazines provide the best coverage of the locations desired and at the same time the least cost per thousand people to be reached, thus enabling public relations management to make the best use of its budget dollars and to stretch their effectiveness.

[4] *Standard Rate and Data Services*. Skokie, Ill.: Annual.
[5] *Ayer's Directory of Newspapers*. Annual.

Research is also used to measure the communicating ability of radio and television messages, films, exhibits, and other media. The same general principles apply. We test the ability of our message to get and hold attention and its ability to meet other communicative objectives. Studies of television commercials may use a theater audience in which people have been demographically selected to see a television show with commercials in it. Schwerin Corporation of New York originated the use of theater audiences for studying commercials. Since then other research firms such as Audience Studies, Incorporated, of Los Angeles, have initiated similar kinds of study work. People are invited to a theater to watch a television show in which the commercials to be studied are placed. For attending, members of the audience are promised a chance to win some kind of merchandise, frequently provided by the organizations whose commercials are being tested. A preshow questionnaire may be used before the audience sees the show and the commercials to establish bench marks on attitudes or awareness of information. After the showing, the same questions are asked again. Thus some measure of the power of the commercials to change attitudes or convey information is provided.

Considerable emphasis is placed on measuring interest. Audience Studies, Incorporated has devised a method of using individual dials at the theater seats that can be turned by those attending to indicate the degree of interest they have in commercials as they are being run. The dials are connected with a computer that develops a composite graph showing the amount of overall audience interest from the beginning to the end of the commercial.

The measuring techniques employed in theater audience studies are what is known as laboratory techniques, as compared with real-life techniques encountered in the home. The validity of laboratory technique results are sometimes questioned. In general, though, the studies provide a reasonable measure of advertising effectiveness at acceptable cost. Information on such things as sponsor identification, relative liking for the commercial, audience recall of the subject matter of the commercial, comprehension of the objective, involvement (what does the commercial mean to you?), and believability are measured.

For an additional fee from the client, Audience Studies, Incorporated arranges small audience groups for "focus group interviews" after showings. Various aspects of the tested commercials are discussed. A leader is provided who keeps the discussion on the subject, sees that all of the intended subjects are covered, tries to prevent any one person from dominating the discussion, and acts as chairman. The group discussion is tape recorded and the interviews can be transcribed and evaluated for use by the client. The emphasis, however, is on measuring how well commercials build and hold interest. This is a weakness because other communicative factors of equal importance do not get sufficient attention.

In addition there is sometimes a danger that questioning at the time of or immediately after a good show may produce a "halo effect," causing an appearance of greater effectiveness than was really true. The "halo effect" should be guarded against in connection with any measurement of effectiveness of public relations or other advertising in which audience entertainment is employed as a vehicle. The pleasure of having seen and heard the entertainment and the good social feeling engendered by the members of the audience can temporarily cause people to make more favorable judgements than normal. The next day, one may find that the judgements have diminished in favorableness.

Studies may sometimes employ closed circuit television with a show and test commercials piped to various apartments or homes.

Studies of television (and radio) commercials may also be made using house-to-house canvassing in which householders are questioned about the commercials they have seen.

In cities having several television stations, a large number of interviews may be necessary to find a sufficient sample of respondents tuned to the television program and commercial being studied. Therefore, canvass studies are generally limited to cities that have only one or two dominant television stations and that are far enough from other cities so that reception is limited to the local stations.

Using research we can pretest television commercials before they are put into general use and change them if the tests indicate any weaknesses. As with newspaper and magazine ads, mock-ups of television commercials with rough story board illustrations, but voiced with the intended message, may be prepared. They may then be tested at special theater showings or over closed circuit television as discussed.

TELEVISION AUDIENCE MEASUREMENT

A good knowledge of the best television audience measurement systems currently in use is important to any client who uses television spots or sponsors broadcasts. Public relations management should have regular access to the audience reports of one of the national firms specializing in audience measurement, such as the Nielsen Reports prepared by A. C. Nielsen Company. These reports are derived from special kinds of research and give the percentage of the audience tuned to each station at any given time. The number of sets in each listening area is also available. The cost of spots on the various stations and at the different time periods is known by the advertising agency time buyers. Using the average number of viewers per set, we can calculate the cost per thousand viewers. In general it is desirable to purchase television spots on the basis of the lowest cost per thousand.

We know that certain times of the day are devoted more to children's shows than to those for adults and that relatively few men are found in weekday daytime audiences. All such matters should be taken into consideration in arriving at effective audience and cost figures.

The special research on television audiences can be invaluable to public relations management, who should be certain that advertising agency time buyers make proper use of the reports in the purchase of broadcast times. Public relations management should also regularly check the audience size figures for its schedule of spot commercials and program broadcast times. It should check the new spot and program time availabilities offered to its advertising agency by the stations to ensure purchase of time at the lowest cost per thousand viewers of the kind of audience desired.

Audience measurement reports published by the national firms specializing in such research can be subscribed to by the client or reviewed at the advertising agency. The cost and effort required for being sure of obtaining the best available broadcast times can pay big dividends.

It cannot be stressed too much that the use of research in measuring the communicative ability of publicity and advertising and also in the purchase of time and space can greatly stretch public relations dollars. Even more important, it can make the activity much more effective.

FISHING EXPEDITIONS AND FOCUS GROUP INTERVIEWS

Two other kinds of studies that should be mentioned are the "fishing expedition" and the "focus group interview." They are useful to public relations management in such things as determining whether problems or potential problems exist and the nature and causes of problems. They can sometimes be used to obtain initial information about people's viewpoints so that one may prepare effective questionnaires. Or they can help to determine the idiom people use—how they express themselves about a subject so that one may communicate with them more effectively.

The fishing expedition consists of perhaps 15 or 20 interviews in which an interviewer probes a subject in depth, getting the person interviewed to do most of the talking. For example, in the ecology area one can use a fishing expedition to learn enough about the breadth of people's views to enable him to prepare a questionnaire for a full-fledged survey. What else besides air and water pollution is the public concerned about? If one uses only his own experiences and viewpoints, the survey questionnaire may leave out important areas of concern.

In studying employee attitudes the same is true. What areas are of concern to employees? What areas should be explored further? What idiom and nomenclature are used by the people one may wish to include in a survey to study the issue further—for example, minority groups?

Fishing expeditions can be used in connection with almost any subject on which more information is necessary in order to develop a questionnaire. Sometimes fishing expeditions are used to round out and broaden the knowledge of a subject previously explored. Or they are used to determine whether a problem exists that should be explored further later.

The focus group interview serves the same purposes and is relatively inexpensive. Focus group interviews are particularly valuable in adding dimension to knowledge already obtained through another means. The earlier reference to the use of focus group interviews in connection with theater audience studies of television commercials is an example. A half dozen (or a few more) members of the public sit down in a room and discuss a subject. The group may be selected to ensure that various viewpoints are included. For example, if the group is going to discuss employee attitudes, one may wish the group to include young employees, older employees, employees from different departments, representatives of various minorities, and both men and women. (But one would probably not include people from widely different levels of management. Those of lower levels might be inclined to be silent or to defer to the opinions of higher level people.) A discussion leader keeps the group on the subject and encourages full participation so that a talkative person or one with strong feelings does not monopolize the discussion and lead the group to his personal conclusions. The discussion may be tape recorded, enabling those evaluating the focus group interview actually to hear the feeling in people's voices. The tape recording is done with the foreknowledge of the participants and does not inhibit the discussion.

Neither of these types of study provides any quantitative measure of attitudes or opinion, as the small number of people involved may not be representative of the public in general or of any particular public.

TESTS OF READABILITY AND INTEREST

Public relations management is vitally concerned with easy readability and whether written material is interestingly composed. A pioneer in devising ways of measuring these things was Rudolf Flesch, who devised what is called the Flesch test. Other people have since developed similar tests and measurements, but all are based on the same overall principles.

It is remarkable how much readability can be improved by using the simple methods suggested by Flesch and others who worked in the field. Yet a great deal of copy is written that would flunk a Flesch test. An example occurred in which copy for newspaper ads received from an advertising agency seemed overburdened with long sentences and multisyllabled, technical-sounding words. The client gave the ads Flesch tests and promptly fired them back to be rewritten.

Some of the ads were written in a way so that even people with Ph. D. degrees would not be interested in them. That does not mean that people with only high school educations could not read or understand them. It means that the ads were uninterestingly written and difficult to read. Most people simply will not bother to try to read copy if it is at all difficult to do so or is uninteresting.

The Flesch test is easy to apply and does not cost any out-of-pocket money. The test is in two parts. The first part concerns readability—the average number of words per sentence and the average number of syllables per hundred words. The idea is to keep sentences from having an average of too many words and from having too many syllables per hundred words. The second part of the test concerns human interest. The measure is the number of personal words per hundred words and the number of personal sentences. More personal words and personal sentences improve the score. Charts devised by Flesch and included in his book *How to Test Readability* are used to arrive at test scores.[6] It can pay dividends for public relations management to obtain copies of one of the books on testing readability and human interest. Then the methods may be applied to the written material they prepare.

SUBSCRIPTION TO RESEARCH REPORTS

Services providing reports on pertinent subjects applying to business and other organizations in general may be subscribed to. For example, one such service run by the Opinion Research Corporation prepares and mails out frequent reports. Subjects include such matters as the ethics of business, opinion about multinational corporations, and what the public is willing to do about the energy crisis.

ANALYSIS OF LETTERS FROM CUSTOMERS AND OTHERS

Aside from the kinds of research discussed so far, simpler forms may be used to help form a background for decisions. These may include analysis of letters and verbal comments received over a period of time. Any organi-

---

[6] New York: Harper, 1951.

zation should pay continuous and close attention to any communication it receives from the public. If it does not, it loses a potentially valuable source of information about itself, its services and products, and the environment in which it operates.

One large business took a defensive attitude about the many letters it received from customers and the public at large. On receiving a letter, it immediately dispatched a noncommittal reply to the effect that the letter had been received and sent to one of its divisions for investigation. Later a defensive reply was prepared and sent from the division. A tabulation was made each month and sent to the officers of the business concerning the number and kind of letters received, but no real analysis was made of the content and implications of individual letters. Furthermore, no overall analysis was made of customers' comments over a period of time. Thus the business lost a golden opportunity to take advantage of customers' comments.

An analysis of the comments in the newspapers (such as letters to the editor, column comments, and editorials), radio and television editorials, and magazines and books can uncover public relations problems or potential problems and changes in trends. Careful analysis not only of the individual press comments and their implications but also a composite analysis of all such comments over a period of time should be made.

MAKING BETTER USE OF RESEARCH DATA

We have available a great deal of information from research. We do not make nearly as effective use of it as we should, partly because it is spread over so many pages of various reports made by and to so many different people.

We need to do a great deal more in the use of the computer. One may not often associate the computer with the public relations function, yet think of the ways in which it may be used to analyze large volumes of data. Think of the ability it provides to determine the relationships between demographic and psychographic factors and attitudes. Consider its use in keeping track of trends, particularly when one conducts a continuous sampling of publics. The computer can make it possible more easily to determine relationships between attitudes and kinds of experiences—the interrelationships between attitudes on different subjects. The computer can be a tremendous boon just in the storage and easy retrieval of data of all kinds. Public relations management has been remiss in using the computer so little in most organizations.

Beyond the use of the computer, one of the needs of public relations management is to think more in terms of specifics in everything it does. Examples are problem analysis, measurement of results, and the acceptance of specific accountability.

Through the use of research public relations management should, whenever possible, determine potential public relations problems while they are still on the horizon so that corrective objectives may be set and action taken while the problems are still small.

Even when problems are well known and recognized, it is desirable to document them. Research provides the means of doing so. When there is no agreement on problems, the need to document is all the more essential. Important public relations recommendations should be documented by all the pertinent research findings and the other supporting evidence available. This is no different from what is expected of people in the other departments of well-managed organizations. Through the proper use of research, public relations management should make its communication function infinitely more effective. Research is one of the important tools for accomplishing the purposes of the public relations function through effective management.

SEVEN

Communication

Most people perceive the public relations function as being primarily concerned with communications. Generally they are thinking more of the tools of communicating, the media primarily, than the meaning we imply in our discussion of communication here—that of imparting information.

You sometimes hear it said that public relations people are the communication specialists. However, when you think of the vital importance of communication to getting anything done—in instructing, informing, supervising, and motivating workers, and students—you realize that communicative ability is a key to every part of any organization. The very essence of good management is efficient, effective use of information. The primary source of information is communication.

There are ways of communicating other than the use of words. And they can be very important. Think of the grimace, the smile, the wink, the frown, the blush, or simply ignoring a person, saying nothing at all. Those are all ways of communicating without words. The quality of performance communicates eloquently. Think of that for a moment. It is obvious that spoken or written words can be a key way of communicating, but people are much less apt to think of the quality of performance as an important communicator. The quality of performance communicates ability or lack of ability. It communicates interest or lack of interest in the quality of work and in the "customer." It communicates good management or poor management and a host of other things more eloquently than words can.

There are many kinds of performance besides those related to products or services. For example, performance communicates concern for the public interest or the lack of concern for the public interest. An organization's performance conveys its real interest or lack of real interest in its employees regardless of what it says or its "good intentions." The performance of

111

WHY GOOD COMMUNICATION IS SO

IMPORTANT

THE ESSENCE OF GOOD

MANAGEMENT IS EFFICIENT,

EFFECTIVE USE OF INFORMATION.

THE PRIMARY SOURCE OF

INFORMATION IS COMMUNICATION.

Figure 20

political parties and civic and religious organizations communicates interest or lack of interest in their members.

Words can be a key element in communication so long as we remember that they are really only symbols of something else more real. When words do not symbolize what people see or hear or what they sense, those words lose a large part of their ability to convey the desired communication. "Anything that conveys information is a kind of communication."[1]

Tremendous advances have been and are being made in communicative devices and tools—improved telephone systems, dataphones, television, picturephones, closed circuit television, newspapers, magazines, computers, and so on. *Public relations management in the past has tended to confuse the use of these communicative devices and tools with communication itself.* Relatively little real attention has been given to the communicative processes. Failure to give attention to communication per se has the effect of negating much of the value of the communicative tools and devices.

COMMUNICATION IS ANYTHING

THAT CONVEYS INFORMATION.

Figure 21

[1] Reprinted by permission of the publisher from *The New Face of Communication* by Glenn A. Bassett. © 1968 by American Management Association, Inc., p. 16.

THE COMMUNICATIVE PROCESS

One of the things that can lead to a better understanding of communication is to examine its process. In achieving communication from one person to another, first the initiator of a communication must have information of some kind to be conveyed. It may be just a simple message such as "General Airline flight number 123 to San Francisco has been delayed one hour in Chicago."

Second, for this information to be conveyed, it must be put into symbols, such as words, that are understood by both the initiator of the communication and the receiver. The initiator may decide to say "General Airlines flight number 123 from New York to San Francisco will arrive one hour late." Or he may decide merely to ask that the flight arrival board at the airport post the information as "one hour late" after the flight number.

Symbols need not necessarily be words. A factory whistle may signal starting and quitting time for the workers. A red traffic light means stop. An alarm clock bell may mean it is time to get up. The chime on a railroad dining care may mean it is breakfast time. Various codes used by the military express commands, and convey information. Bells indicate the end of school class periods.

As a third step in the communicative process, the symbols must be conveyed or transmitted. Thus an announcement over the loudspeaker in the airport can be used. The information can also be posted on the flight arrival board.

Fourth, the symbols (words, etc.) must be received. The man expecting his wife on a flight from Minneapolis pays no attention to the announcement about the New York flight, but Aunt Minnie who is waiting for her niece to arrive from New York receives the communication. She hears the message.

Fifth, the receiver must understand the symbols. Aunt Minnie hears the announcement and goes to look at the flight arrival board to confirm what she heard. Sure enough, she heard right. She understood the message. With a long face she sits down to wait another hour.

Some students of communication also include feedback as a step in the communicative process. However, although feedback is desirable, takes place frequently, and is essential over a period of time, it does not necessarily take place in all communications. For example, a person may hear an alarm clock bell and realize that it is time to get up. Later he may hear the chime that signals breakfast, but he may decide to stay in bed. Thus although messages have been conveyed and understood, there is no

STEPS IN COMMUNICATION

1. There must be a source of information--the
    initiator of the communication.

2. The initiator must put the information into
    symbols (words, etc.)

3. The symbols (words, etc.) must be conveyed
    or transmitted.

4. The symbols (words, etc.) must be received.

5. The symbols (words, etc.) must be understood
    by the receiver.

Figure 22

feedback. People may listen to the radio and understand the message conveyed, but there may be no feedback as a result.

Even in a simple situation such as the example of Aunt Minnie, there can be many barriers to communication. The information may be incomplete. The airline or the flight number may be omitted. The initiator of the communication may put the information into symbols not understood by Aunt Minnie, such as "General Airlines Flight 123 will arrive at 1900 hours." Aunt Minnie, not being acquainted with 24-hour time, probably does not understand the symbols "1900 hours."

The loudspeaker system may need repair, resulting in distorting the message so it cannot be understood easily. The person operating the flight arrival board may fail to post the information, or may post it in the wrong place so that it is not conveyed. At the time of the loudspeaker announcement, someone standing next to Aunt Minnie may cough loudly. Or she can be conversing with a friend and fail to receive the message. When Aunt Minnie hears the announcement that the flight will arrive at 1900 hours, she may not understand at all. She may think the plane is arriving at nine o'clock.

COMMUNICATION SHOULD BE IN TERMS OF THE AUDIENCES' INTERESTS

In communication, as in all other things, people consistently seek to serve what they believe to be their own best interests. Each person has his own belief as to what is in his best interest. For effective communication your message must be stated in terms of the interests of your audience. Effective communication requires a knowledge of what the other person wants to hear because this determines whether he will listen and what he will hear.

People generally read and listen to things that agree with their own viewpoints. Conversely, they are less apt to read or listen to viewpoints that do not agree with their own. With that fact in mind, one can see how difficult it is to change people's opinions and attitudes through communication.

How are we going to know whether we are communicating what we intended? We cannot tell unless we specifically set about to check in some way or another. Organizations of all kinds merrily go on their way talking to customers, to educators, to young people, to the various other publics, thoroughly convinced that they are communicating and that what they have said has merit. They do not realize that frequently their audience may not have the same comprehension, that he does not believe, or that he does not have the slightest interest in what is said. The message may not be getting through. Perhaps the organization is even creating unfavorable public relations with what it says.

In audience tests some years ago, the Bell Telephone System found, through the use of audience research, that some of their motion pictures actually had a negative effect concerning the attitudes the pictures were intended to improve. Yet they had employed what were supposed to be some of the best writers and producers to make the pictures.

BASIC FORM OF COMMUNICATION

As pointed out by Glenn A. Bassett, communication in its most basic form is an on–off, yes–no, present–absent process.[2] A light in the driveway at night tells us that someone is expected. Broken windshield glass on the highway tells us that someone has had an accident. Seeing suitcases being loaded into a car informs us that someone is going on a trip.

"Communication engineers call the amount of information that such a

[2] Reprinted by permission of the publisher from *The New Face of Communication* by Glenn A. Bassett. © 1968 by American Management Association, Inc., p. 17.

message possesses a 'bit.' A bit, however, is not necessarily a very small quantity of information. It may be a very small or a very large quantity since it is the amount of information needed to reduce the available alternative choices by exactly 50 percent by dividing all meaningful choices into two mutually exclusive ('yes' or 'no') categories."

"Everything from very simple to very complex options may be covered by bits." Bassett uses as an example the story of Paul Revere. "One or two lights were to be hung in the tower of the old North Church in Boston to advise Paul Revere that the British were coming. The absence of lights was to be the signal that the British were not coming. A single light meant that they were coming by land; two lights that the approach was by sea. Thus, by using lamps, three bits of information could be transmitted."[2]

BARRIERS TO COMMUNICATION

Ambiguous Word Meanings

Bassett points out that many of our day-to-day communication problems stem from the fact that our language has "progressed so far beyond the unambiguous simplicity of single bits of information that it is now only vaguely based on those bits."[3] Bassett uses as an example the word "moral." "An individual is 'moral' if he obeys the law, refrains from stealing the property of others, is faithful to his wife, charitable to the poor, and so on. Or is he? Must other requirements be met to achieve morality? Are there instances in which one or more of the previously mentioned requirements may not be met, yet the individual may be considered moral? Is it also necessary to refrain from drinking, smoking, dancing and swearing to be moral? To a large segment of the population, morality is the avoidance of such kinds of behavior."[4] To other groups, being involved in these activities is completely moral.

A great many of the words we use in day-to-day communication are like "moral" and are potentially ambiguous in meaning. Words as used by different people have different meanings. Some word symbols, such as automobile, bird, stick, and chair, are understood in the same way by nearly everyone. There can be no doubt what the initiator of a communication is talking about when he refers to them, but other words are not understood in the same way by everyone. They are abstract and are not the symbols for specific objects.

[3] and [4] Reprinted by permission of the publisher from *The New Face of Communication* by Glenn A. Bassett. © 1968 by American Management Association, Inc., p. 18.

For example, "democracy" may symbolize a different thing to some people from what it does to others. To many the word may be fuzzy. People may have a feeling of what is meant, but they would have difficulty explaining it. The same can be true of countless other words—"motivation," for example. In the technical world the same word or phrase may have completely different meanings to people working in different fields.

With the tremendous variety of experiences, attitudes, and viewpoints among the various publics, is it any wonder that abstract and ambiguous words can mean totally different things to different people? The fact that they do is one reason why it is frequently desirable to be redundant in communicating, using more than one symbol to mean the same thing. If the receivers of the communication do not get the meaning you wish to convey with one symbol, they may with the other. The two symbols work together to clarify the intended meaning. The use of examples is another way of helping to clarify meaning. Examples give a more complete idea of the meaning you wish to convey.

Often we express a thought, and it seems to us that we are being perfectly clear as to the meaning. However, we are likely to be thinking only in terms of our own interest, experience, knowledge, and background. The person we are trying to communicate with is likely not to have had the same interest, experience, knowledge, and background we have had. He is apt not to be able to form the same mental picture that we form. Although he may say "I see what you mean," in reality he may not. From that viewpoint, he is like a blind man. He cannot form the mental picture you do, so he cannot see what you mean. Or if his experiences are different from yours, he may get a completely different mental picture and he only thinks he sees what you mean. You too think he sees what you mean, but he does not.

Inability to Perceive

Differences in perception can be mountainous barriers to communication. People cannot perceive what is beyond the range of their comprehension. People cannot perceive something they cannot conceive of. Differences of perception and different concepts may result in different reception for communicative effort. These differences in perception are major causes of failure of communicative efforts.

In the sense we are discussing, perception concerns the capacity to comprehend, to discern, to understand. It concerns awareness. It is the way a person senses a situation or experience. Perception is influenced by a person's ability to sense or to be aware of a communication. It depends on his frame of reference. It concerns the way a person receives a communication. A person's reaction to communication depends to a great degree on how he sees and perceives things. His view depends on his biases, interpretations, and preferences.

In another meaning used elsewhere in this book (see Chapter 4), perception primarily concerns insight and the way a person senses a situation relative to his frame of reference. Thus good public relations perception is sensing a situation or experience correctly from a public relations viewpoint.

Differences in perception are one of the reasons political rhetoric often falls on deaf ears. Quantities of rhetoric will not convince a person with opposing perception. People from one culture or tradition may not understand the communicative efforts of those from another culture or tradition because of differences in perception. Business viewpoints may be perceived differently by management than by labor and vice versa. Differences in perception lead to different proposals with regard to economic problems and other social matters. One group of people may feel strongly that the key economic problem is inflation whereas another group feels it is recession. Perceptual differences may prevent effective communication between different groups in society, between business and government, faculty and students, and so on.

Effective managements require broad perception to see situations from many viewpoints. Effectiveness in education requires greatly broadening one's perception. Effective political activity in the public interest requires broad perception to be convincing to a range of viewpoints and to provide leadership.

A member of a family of business people remarked that her second husband viewed profit unfavorably and tended to be suspicious of business. She ascribed his feelings to the fact that he was the son of a preacher who was not favorably disposed toward profit. He had also spent his entire career as an engineer working for the state. The problem concerned his perception, which came from his background. His perception also resulted from his lack of information and knowledge that the money necessary to operate the church and for taxes to operate the state government originally had to come from the profit of business. (This was discussed in Chapter 3 and is discussed further in Chapter 11).

A vice president of a large service business was appointed to determine whether the business needed a marketing function. In reality the business was badly in need of it, but little of of the man's experience concerned marketing management. He did not have the perception or the knowledge and information necessary to do the job to which he had been appointed. Good problem analysis, followed by the formulation of specific objectives, could have led to the right answer, but perception based on prior experience, emotion, and organizational bias made this logical step more difficult.

Public relations managers should do all they can to understand differences in perception among people and groups. Communicative efforts can then be guided accordingly. Government foreign relations people and those working for multinational corporations should do all they can to understand the differences in perception between cultures and nations. In problem and opportunity analyses, all management people should also consider the gaps in their own perceptions and strive to fill the gaps.

PERCEPTION, ATTITUDES AND COMMUNICATION

There is a close relationship between perception and attitudes. One's perception is the key to his attitudes. Attitudes, in turn, are the primary concern of public relations management. Attitudes are a key element that biases a person's evaluation of any communicative effort. For businesses, attitudes are one of the key components of consumer reception of communication. Therefore, a study of attitudes is of great importance to anyone interested in communication. An individual's attitude toward your communication will determine how much attention he will pay to it or whether he will screen it out through his selective perception barrier, which we discuss in more detail later in this chapter. This fact accounts for some of the complexity we face in communication and in the problems of interpersonal relationships.

In Chapter 1 we made reference to a study by Pacific Telephone Company of what really determines customer attitudes. One part of the study showed the effect of attitudes toward the degree of favorableness toward that company's communicative efforts.

As shown in Figure 23, people with high (favorable) attitudes toward the company also felt more favorable toward its advertising. Thus 75 percent of those with high attitudes had very or quite favorable opinions of the advertising, as compared with only 55 percent for those with low attitudes toward the company. Of those with high (favorable) attitudes toward the company, only 3 percent had "not very favorable or only fairly favorable" opinions of its advertising. But 20 percent of those with low (unfavorable) attitudes toward the company had "not very favorable or only fairly favorable" opinions of its advertising. This shows the important relationship between performance and the reception and acceptance of communicative efforts. Of even greater importance, *it provides measured quantitative indication of the importance of good public relations*.

Over the years there has been a great deal of debate concerning the relationship between an organization's public relations and its advertising effort

Opinion of Company's Advertising	Respondents with High Attitudes	Respondents with Low Attitudes	Difference
Very or quite favorable	75%	55%	20%
Not very or only fairly favorable	3%	20%	17%
No opinion, no answer	22%	25%	3%

Figure 23.   Printed with permission of The Pacific Telephone and Telegraph Co., San Fransisco.[5]

and sales and thus its profitability. Figure 23 indicates mathematically that there is a definite relationship. It is reasonable to expect that on matters concerning which people have more intense feelings and stronger attitudes, the differences of opinion of advertising between those with high and low attitudes would be much greater.

COMMUNICATION AND ATTITUDES

The most important determinant of a person's views of the world, his behavior, his reception of communication, and his perception is his needs and thus his views of performance. When the initiators of communications and the receivers have completely different desires and needs, completely different backgrounds, experiences, and attitudes, it may be difficult or impossible to communicate. That is one reason why merely establishing communicative channels cannot solve the world's disagreements and conflicts.

As long as one merely communicates uncontroversial messages such as "It's a nice day," both initiator and receiver of the communication may agree. However, as soon as the communicative effort shifts to areas in which the parties have different needs, different self-interests and, therefore, different views of performance, communicative effort in itself will not solve the problem.

Let us again refer to the results of the study made by Pacific Telephone Company of what really determines attitudes. The results indicated that high incidence of unfavorable experiences (poor performance) was the most conspicuous characteristic of people with unfavorable (low) attitudes. As a part of the study, multiple regression (computer) analysis showed the relationships between various factors and the favorableness of attitudes. The higher the score, as shown in Figure 24, the greater the relationship. Scores of less than 0.20 reflect little or no meaningful relationship.

The results show the relatively low importance of communication by itself as a factor in determining attitudes. They indicate that roughly nine times out of ten, unfavorable attitudes are the result of unfavorable experiences (performance problems).

There must be a change or promised change in performance or an event that changes the performance that people desire in order to overcome the problems. For example, from an international point of view, an agreement to change a boundary, an agreement not to fish within 200 miles of a country's coast, or an agreement to lower a tariff may be necessary. When the receiver of a communication has completely different desires from those of the sender, agreement is unlikely regardless of the amount of communication.

Another barrier to communication is disruptive influence. Perhaps the simplest and most common disruptive influence is noise—the noise and interference of other people talking, of a blaring radio, or of traffic. Jamming another country's radio reception is an example of a barrier. Pain can be a barrier. The large number of advertising and "public relations" messages encountered by an individual is a disruptive barrier.

In discussing changing attitudes in Chapter 2 and earlier in this chapter, another barrier was mentioned. People generally listen to communications with which they agree or that express viewpoints concerned with their self-interest.

Selective perception is an important barrier to communication. For example, radio listeners and television viewers may pay attention to a program but disregard all or part of the advertising on it. They are using

Predictive Attributes

Unfavorable experiences (performance problems)	0.54
Advertising and publicity	0.18
Government control	0.14
Education	0.11
Cooperativeness	0.11
Employment status	0.11
Know employees	0.08
Age	0.07
Satisfaction with environment	0.05
Estimated score for all variables together	0.63

Figure 24.   The numbers associated with each attribute are called Beta scores. Printed with permission of The Pacific Telephone and Telegraph Co., San Francisco.[6]

selective perception. In our example earlier in this chapter, the man at the airport waiting for this wife to arrive from Minneapolis paid no attention to the announcement about the late plane from New York. His selective perception barrier screened out the announcement.

In looking through the mail one may throw out some of it after scarcely glancing at it. Some of it may be looked at more thoroughly to see if it is of any interest, and then discarded. The rest may be read. One is using selective perception.

What determines which advertising commercials on the radio or television you listen to? Suppose you were not interested in buying a refrigerator. Week after week you disregard the refrigerator commercial in your favorite program. Then one day your refrigerator breaks down. Next time the program comes on you are all ears. Now you want to know about refrigerators so that you can get a good one, and get the best price. The commercial is now in terms of your interests. The selective perception barrier has been removed until after you buy a refrigerator.

Proliferation of Communicative Efforts and Credibility

The number of communicative efforts of all kinds bombarding people has grown to a point that staggers the imagination. They include attempts to sell products and services, to put across political ideas, to request contributions. Even the news often becomes biased in favor of one viewpoint or another. One danger from proliferation of communicative effort is a loss of credibility for all.

Illiteracy

Worldwide, one of the greatest barriers to communication is illiteracy. Almost half the people of the world cannot read and write.[7] In some countries of Asia and Africa nine out of ten people are illiterate. Think of the effect this has on the world's cultural, political, and economic relationships. Think of it as a public relations consideration for multinational organizations and for governments. If a person cannot read or write the symbols we call words, he will not receive or understand the written communication they represent.

Beyond Literacy

In the "developed" countries of the world, including the United States, the percentage of technically literate people is high. But what percentage of the

---

[7] *The World Book Encyclopedia.* Chicago: Field Enterprises Educational Corp., 1968.

people are able to read only at the fourth or sixth grade levels? With the great increase in the amount and complexity of knowledge, the low level of literate ability is an important barrier to communication. *The mere technical ability to read and write may no longer be a good measure of true literacy in today's world.* The problem is an important barrier to communication that should be considered by public relations managers, by organizations of all kinds, and by government.

Other barriers that make communication difficult may be the ability of either the communicator or the receiver to organize thought.

Communication without feedback is not likely to be effective for very long. Receivers of communication may only nod or frown, but there must be feedback in due course.

For effective communication both parties involved must want to communicate. This is true of face-to-face communication between individuals and of efforts to communicate with employees or the general public, and it is true on an international basis.

FACTORS IMPORTANT TO EFFECTIVE COMMUNICATION

The first factor important to effective communication is getting attention. A great many more communicative stimuli come to us than we are willing or able to receive. There is a constant stream of information competing for attention. Therefore, getting the attention of a person or persons with whom we want to communicate is the first requirement of communication.

Second, the interest of those with whom we wish to communicate must be aroused and retained. We must somehow capture their interest in our idea or objective. And, of course, we must keep their interest. We should be careful that a written communication, for example, is not difficult to read or too long. What we say must be in terms of the interests of those with whom we wish to communicate. It must meet or offer to meet some need even if that need is only the pleasure of reading what we have written. Otherwise we will not get or keep interest. In oral communication such things as inflection, voice tone, loudness, and the speed with which we talk are all helpful in keeping interest.

The third important factor in communicating is comprehension. It is not unusual for a considerable part of the public to construe a message as meaning something entirely different from what was intended. People must understand what we are trying to tell them. Otherwise we have not communicated.

The fourth factor in communication is believability. It we are to communicate successfully, we must be believed. If we are to persuade—to change attitudes or sell a service or a product—people must believe what we say. One of the greatest barriers to believability can be summed up by the old saying, "Actions speak louder than words." One frequently hears references to an organization having lost its credibility. That means people do not believe the organization any longer. Those who have lost credibility find it difficult or impossible to communicate. Once lost, credibility is hard to restore.

Actions are the most important of all forms of communication. That is the foundation of our definition that good public relations is the result of "good performance, publicly acknowledged and appreciated." If we do not perform well from the public's viewpoint, all the talk in the world will do little good. This has been borne out many times in the research of newspaper ads built around messages that people did not believe reflected the organization's actions. Research has shown that such messages have low believability scores.

When an organization says one thing and does another, it destroys its credibility. Advertising copy that cannot be backed up, publicity and ballyhoo that stretch and embellish the truth, tricky wording, fine print paragraphs, and failure to live up to warranties and guarantees are all examples of the kind of thing that destroys credibility.

The fifth factor in communication is motivation. Communication has the task of getting people to do something or not to do something. For example, in a social conversation the aim might be to get someone to think favorably of us. Communication should impel people to act, to change their attitudes, or to buy a product or a service. As we have said, people usually are motivated to do what they believe is in their own best interest. In other words, in their mind there must be "something in it for them." For this reason, as well as for the reason of getting and keeping attention, successful communication must respond to the wants, needs, or lacks of people.

FACTORS IN COMMUNICATION

ATTENTION

INTEREST

COMPREHENSION

BELIEVABILITY

MOTIVATION

Figure 25

WAYS OF COMMUNICATING

Let us consider some of the ways of communicating. There is person-to-person communication—for example, face-to-face or by telephone. Face-to-face communication can be the most effective kind there is—or the least effective, depending on how well it is done. We not only use words; we also use our eyes, our gestures, our mood, and the inflections of our voice. All these things communicate.

Let us take an example of where a change in inflection changes the meaning completely and, therefore, what we communicate. Here is the same sentence with several different inflections as indicated by the underlined words:

"*Me* thinks the lady doth protest too much."
"Me *thinks* the lady doth protest too much."
"Me thinks *the* lady doth protest too much."
"Me thinks the *lady* doth protest too much."
"Me thinks the lady *doth* protest too much."
"Me thinks the lady doth *protest* too much."
"Me thinks the lady doth protest *too* much."
"Me thinks the lady doth protest too *much*."

The inflection emphasizing "me" in the first reading indicates that perhaps someone else does not think the lady protests too much, but the inflection in the second reading emphasizing "thinks" leads one to believe the speaker is not certain, and so forth.

Consider the receptionist in an office or the salesman who greets a visitor with a smile and a lilt in the voice asking, "May I help you?" Compare the public relations such a question brings with that of the receptionist who ignores the visitor and finally snaps, "Yes?" Or consider the salesman who stands behind the counter talking with another employee and ignores a customer as compared with one who greets the customer immediately and goes to help him as soon as possible.

The setting can be conducive to communication. A businessman who takes a customer from whom he wishes an order to lunch at his exclusive club may so flatter the customer by introducing him to these surroundings that the customer is more likely to place the order. A cheerful office is better for a conference than a corner of a cluttered and drafty warehouse.

Telephone communications can also be potentially quite effective or, on the contrary, very ineffective. We can have the voice with a smile over the phone or we can be the terrible tempered Mr. Bang. We can be disinterested or with no apparent knowledge of what we should show a great deal about.

We can be bureaucratic, quoting rules and regulations conveying to the customers that we "don't give a damn" over the phone.

Radio and television offer some of the same communicative advantages that face-to-face and telephone conversation offer except that they are one-way communication. Radio, of course, can bring the inflections of the voice and about the same favorable or unfavorable qualities that we might encounter in a telephone conversation. Television has the added advantage of offering visual impact as a part of the communicative effort.

Had you thought of the fact that on radio or television one is not really talking to an audience? Seldom is group dynamics involved. So often the delivery, replete with histrionics of one kind or another, fails to recognize the reality of one person talking to another person. In the 1930s in the radio soap opera days, studies made by the Procter and Gamble Company showed that advertising messages in which the announcer's tone and words were as if he were talking with only one person were more effective than those aimed at "the entire audience." The idea was advanced that such personalized copy written as though the announcer were talking to a single individual would sell more than the old so-called "hard-hitting" style of commercials aimed at the entire audience. The radio advertising people worked with a well-known announcer and with the copy people at the advertising agency to develop good personalized commercials. Different announcer and copy styles were tested in five reasonably sized but isolated markets. The personalized style sold up to 400 percent more than the hard-hitting style. Therefore, the air media commercials were converted to the personalized style.

This example relates to one of the problems of the environment discussed in Chapter 3—that the relationship between organizations and their customers has become impersonal. The example shows one other small step that can be taken to help overcome the problem.

Printed messages can have a mood that adds or detracts from communication, aside from the mere words. The words are important, but frequently so are the other qualities. For instance, the kind of paper used can set a mood or detract. Whether or not a leaflet or letter is businesslike, the proper use of color, appropriate layout, and so forth all communicate.

The choice of type face and illustrations is important from a public relations viewpoint when preparing a newspaper or magazine advertisement or a leaflet. The kind of handwriting or the excellence of the form and typing in a typewritten letter are important.

THE EFFECT OF THE COMPANY A MESSAGE KEEPS

The kind of company a message keeps is important, too. For example, some messages would be out of place in *Playboy Magazine*. It is not a magazine in which one would normally put a church message. A corporate story in a labor publication would probably not be in keeping and would run the risk of not communicating what it is intended to communicate.

The same is true with regard to television. The choice of the television show used to carry an organization's message is important. There can be disadvantages in including an organization's commercials in a television show that is in bad taste or undesirable in some other way. There have been many cancellations of shows because sponsorship might be misconstructed in view of the content of the show.

There is no reason unnecessarily to risk negative connotation because of association with material that is in bad taste or otherwise undesirable. Some may say that this has a censoring effect on the media. However, the network or station is at liberty to find some other sponsor. It would be foolish to spend an organization's money to sponsor questionable material or to advertise in association with questionable material merely because someone says unwillingness to do so will have a censoring effect. Some may feel that questionable material gets a larger audience. However, examination of audience size records show that such is not the case.

Another instance of the effect of the company a message keeps concerns becoming lost in a deluge of television commercials coming one right after another. The communicative ability of an advertising commercial that is sandwiched into a series of three or four others is questionable.

FACTS VERSUS INFERENCE

One of the things we quickly learn about communications is that no matter what the other person's intentions, he is presenting his personal point of view in giving us what he feels are facts. Whether we find that point of view acceptable depends to a large degree on how it ties in with our own experiences and convictions.

In *The New Face of Communication* Glenn Bassett points out that human beings "deal almost entirely in inferences, preferences, and personal points of view. They are sometimes more and sometimes less objective and unbiased. But people are almost totally unaccustomed to telling the hard, cold, bare facts in working out their problems."[8] We discussed differences between viewpoints derived from inference and those derived from observation in Chapter 4.

In recent years we have heard the expressions "We are not communicating" or "I can't communicate with him" used a great deal. These

---

[8] Reprinted by permission of the publisher from *The New Face of Communication* by Glenn A. Bassett. © 1968 by American Management Association, Inc., p. 25.

expressions refer in a popular way specifically to the problems we are discussing here. The failure to communicate can be one of the several causes of problems between individuals—or between a business and a customer, or between organizations and government.

BE CAREFUL OF OTHER MEANINGS FOR WORDS

An advertisement once used by the telephone company in promoting long-distance telephone calls was headlined "Talk is Cheap." Here the writer was using "cheap" in the sense of low cost, but the word "cheap" has other meanings or connotations making its use undesirable. For example, the word could mean "poor quality," "worthy of scorn," or "yielding small satisfaction."

Words and phrases may even have the opposite meaning in one place from what they do in another. In England, for example, a telephone operator may ask, "Are you through?" meaning, "Is your connection established?" In the United States the meaning would be, "Are you finished with your conversation?"

In communicating, "the symbols we call words have power only to the extent that people know their meaning."[9] Many businesses, the sciences, lawyers, and churches use words and expressions that are not understood by other people. One might call it "shop jargon." A large percentage of other people frequently do not even have an interest in understanding them.

Each of the various publics may require specific consideration to communicate with it best. It is frequently helpful to use the vernacular, sometimes the slang, of the group or public with which we wish to communicate. Think of the youth, for example. Of course, we should not demean our own language. We can use the language of the educated man or woman but in a way that the uneducated person may easily understand and accept.

IN COMMUNICATING, THE

SYMBOLS WE CALL WORDS HAVE POWER

ONLY TO THE EXTENT THAT PEOPLE

KNOW THEIR MEANINGS.

Figure 26

[9] Reprinted by permission of the publisher from *The New Face of Communication* by Glenn A. Bassett. © 1968 by American Management Association, Inc., p. 31.

ILLUSTRATIONS AND COMMUNICATION

What about illustrations for use in advertisements and for use in connection with publicity? It has been said that a picture is worth a thousand words. It truly may be. A picture or illustration is used to attract interest and to bolster and work with the copy in getting a message across. Creating interest should not be the sole purpose of an illustration. Sometimes an illustration can convey the message without many words.

At times the use of a picture or illustration may detract from the effectiveness of a communication. If the illustration has no bearing on what is said, it certainly cannot bolster it. It is more apt to detract by drawing attention away from the subject at hand.

One frequently sees a picture of a pretty girl used as an illustration in advertising. However, if the picture of the pretty girl does not specifically relate to the subject of the ad, it is not likely to improve the ad's communicative ability. People may be "captured" by the pretty illustration but not find out what the ad is about.

An illustration that is not understood may also detract from the ad's message. Think of communication on technical matters for which an engineer may provide a technical illustration. The public may not understand it.

Attempts at pictorial communication should help people quickly to visualize and understand what the ad is trying to tell them. When such attempts are successful, they clarify and intensify the message as well as getting interest.

The communicative power of illustrations is affected by many things—for example, size, color, position, clarity of reproduction, whether it has good contrasts. More is said about illustrations later in Chapter 8 on communicative tools.

GROUP DYNAMICS AND COMMUNICATION

The principles of group dynamics are important to communicating with groups of people and within groups of people. How is information shared within a group? Who are the opinion leaders of a group, (or a community)? It is probable that the best way of communicating with a group or within a group is through its opinion leaders. In turn, the opinion leaders communicate with their peers within the group. Opinion leaders influence the judgments and the actions of others in their groups through their attitudes, actions, and interpretation of events. They do so by participation within the group, community, state, and nation.

We have said that feedback is usually important to successful communication. Public relations management may obtain early and valuable feedback from opinion leaders because opinion leaders are apt to be aware of problems and potential issues while the problems are still in their infancy and only on the horizon.

It is fairly easy to get feedback from individuals, perhaps only by observing their frowns, their smiles—their total demeanor. It is more difficult to get feedback from large groups especially. Problems can develop and become important while one waits for attitudes to crystallize so that they may be determined through conventional opinion research, but it is frequently possible to get feedback earlier from opinion leaders.

Who are the opinion leaders? Unfortunately, most lists of opinion leaders rely to a large extent on titles. The lists mostly include business executives and elected officials. In reality opinion leaders may be members of any profession, trade, race, religion, degree of education, and so on. Some may be prominent. Others may seldom be visible. They are more apt than not to be without titles. Some remain leaders for long periods of time, others for only a short time.

Opinion leaders are people who are listened to and respected by others and whose judgment is likely to be followed by others. *Qualification as an opinion leader does not depend on position, title, or family name.* Different fields and activities have different opinion leaders. The person need not be popular. In fact, he or she may be unpopular or in the forefront of an unpopular cause. He or she may either attempt to maintain the status quo or advocate change. And he or she may appear in the press often or may never be in the public eye. In considering whether a person is an opinion leader, one must consider only current status, not past performance or potential. Determining which people are opinion leaders can only be done by those who are acquainted with the community, and may require considerable inquiry as well as good perception and judgment.

One may not only impart information by developing good communicative channels with opinion leaders, but one may also use them as an advance warning system to learn of changes in attitudes—changes in the organization's public environment.

If the majority of a group or the "in" people in the group have a certain viewpoint, it is apt to be unpopular for a member of the group even to listen to another viewpoint—be it right or wrong. Consider this as it applies to political matters, customs, or religious beliefs. It is one reason for the old adage that warns not to discuss politics or religion in polite society. People's feelings about those two subjects are apt to be strong.

We are unable to do more than lightly touch on one aspect of the subject of group dynamics in this book. It is a subject that should be profitably explored in greater detail by those with public relations management responsibilities.

SYMBOLS AND SYMBOLIC EVENTS IN COMMUNICATION

A communicative effect of considerable interest concerns the use of symbolic events to dramatically affect large numbers of people. As an example of a symbolic event, at the time of the student demonstrations at what is now San Francisco State University, S. I. Hayakawa, wearing the beret for which he was well known, dramatically pulled the wires from a sound truck the demonstrators were using. The effect brought about a positive reaction from as far away as the American troops in Vietnam. One of the greatest uses of symbols and symbolic events was by the Nazis and Adolf Hitler in getting control of Germany before World War II.

Symbolic events are used by terrorists. Through bombing, hijacking an airplane, or holding hostages, one terrorist or a small group of terrorists may gain worldwide attention for a cause. The terrorists usually have no interest in their hostages. They have no interest in who may be killed by their bombs. Their interest is in the dramatic communicative effect of their action, the quick and widespread attention it elicits. The only effective counter communicative action is to prevent the terrorists from achieving their planned objective.

Events may be and are staged to become communicative symbols, either favorable or unfavorable for a viewpoint or a cause. Dramatic symbols, such as Churchill's "V" for victory sign, can become valuable reminders of people, organizations, viewpoints, and causes.

LISTENING AND COMMUNICATION

There is another aspect to communication about which we have said nothing so far. In communicating more than half the job is in listening. To communicate effectively requires listening effectively. Yet relatively little attention is usually given to listening as an important communicative process. Listening concerns the public relations manager in two ways. First, he can arrange his oral communication so that it encourages others to listen better. Second, he can study ways of listening better and make it a point to use them. Listening helps him better perceive the environment.

As to the importance of listening to communication, think of the millions of radios in the United States and all over the world. Think of the millions of people viewing their television sets many hours a day. Think of the millions of elementary school, high school, and college students who must listen well to their instructors if they wish to learn and to get good grades.

The written word is slower to be assimilated than the spoken word. Thus given the information explosion and the fact that so much comes to us orally from conferences, meetings, radio, television, and over the telephone, listening effectively becomes more and more important. Yet how much oral communication gets through correctly? You will recall the game in which a message is passed from person to person. The message received by the last person is apt to the scarcely recognizable as the one given by the first person.

Unfortunately, many people do not know how to listen. Many disputes arise because one person insists he told someone something whereas the other person insists he did not. That is one reason why so often you hear, "Put it in writing." It is a good reason for taking extra care when attempting to communicate orally.

One of the problems in listening is that too often when one ought to be listening, he is thinking about something else, perhaps deciding on what he is going to say when it is his turn to talk. Perhaps he is deciding on his rebuttal to the speaker. The effective listener will refrain from planning his rebuttal and instead listen to learn what the speaker has to say.

Effective listening is hard work. It requires concentrating on what the other person is saying. It requires that there be no distractions. According to Ralph G. Nichols and Leonard A. Stevens, when we listen, concentration must be achieved despite the fact that we think much faster than people talk.[10]

The average rate of speech for most people is about 125 words per minute. This rate is slow for the human brain. Experiments in the fields of speech show that people can comprehend speech at more than 300 words per minute. The brain deals with words at lightning speed, but when we listen, it receives words at a slow speed. Thus a person can think about something else part of the time while he is listening.

A person should try to make good listeners of his audience through such devices as the pacing and inflections of his voice and the use of anecdotes. He should speak at as fast a pace as he can effectively do so.

In his book *Communication and Organizational Behavior*, William V. Haney points out that when people are listened to sensitively, with understanding and respect, they tend to listen to themselves with more care and to make clearer what they feel and think.[11] Group members tend to listen

---

[10] Ralph G. Nichols and Leonard A. Stevens, *Are You Listening?*. New York: McGraw-Hill, 1957.
[11] Homewood, Ill.: Richard D. Irwin, 1967.

more to one another and to become less argumentative. Being listened to reduces the threat of having one's ideas criticized. One is more likely to feel that his contributions are worthwhile.

Another important result of listening is the change that takes place in the listener himself. Besides the fact that listening provides more information than any other activity, it builds positive relationships and improves the attitudes of the listener.

Nonevaluative listening to a person who is offering resistance to a proposal may be helpful. Discontinue talking and listen, without argument and without passing judgment on what the other fellow is saying. Listen so that you may understand how the problem looks to the other person and why he may be against your viewpoint. Since he no longer faces the necessity of confronting you, he may relax his defenses. Both of you may be willing to listen to each other.

Books on the subject of listening and the benefits of being a good listener are available by specialists in the field, such as William V. Haney and Ralph G. Nichols. Public relations workers (people responsible for external relations) would do well to give the subject additional study.

COMMUNICATING WITH EMPLOYEES

Communication with employees has special significance because employees are the key to an organization's performance. In communicating with members of an organization, one may use formal or informal lines of communication or mass media. An example of formal communication is to send a letter or memorandum to an individual through organizational lines. An example of informal communication is a person communicating directly with another person in another department or at another level without going through lines of organization. Examples of mass communication include the organization's magazine for employees, newsletters, and newspapers. More informal communication takes place than formal, although there are managers who insist that every discussion be confirmed formally. The climate in some organizations requires formal communication in every instance.

Of course, important decisions, instructions, and information should always be formally transmitted or confirmed in writing so that one can be sure that everyone has the same understanding and the same access to the reference material. It is also necessary for future reference and for use after personnel shifts. It is vital, and may be a requirement, in legal matters or those involving legal processes.

Informal communication is quicker and allows for give and take. Effective decisions may be reached more rapidly taking into consideration the problems, opportunities, and viewpoints of several groups or people. Discussions may consider relevant related matters that may be omitted from formal communication. Informal communication may utilize the telephone, including people within the same building or thousands of miles apart. It is apt to provide for better rapport. Informal communication can cross lines of organization and can be between any two levels of the organization, thus ensuring less editing and censorship and a better upward flow of information.

All three kinds of communication, through lines of organization, across lines, and using mass communication, have important functions. One should recognize that effective lines of communications do not necessarily follow formal organizational lines.

Poor communication in an organization is frequently blamed on ineffective mass communication. In reality the true cause is more likely to be a failure to inform people properly through formal or informal lines of communication. *No matter how well done, mass communication is a poor substitute and cannot make up for ineffective communication by supervision.* For instance, an entire department may be uninformed or inadequately informed on important subjects because of a failure to cover the matter in correspondence sent through the proper communicative lines. Sometimes the boss may fail to inform his people of important matters. Another communication breakdown stems from failure to communicate to colleagues and employees the trends, viewpoints, reasons, and decisions brought out at important meetings.

Poor morale may frequently be attributed to unsatisfactory communication. It is greatest among workers when they do not receive the amount and kind of information they need. Research among employees, conducted by a leading research firm for one of the country's largest businesses, indicates that morale problems due to poor communication exists up to and including at least upper-middle management levels.

Particularly when a climate of distrust exists, employees may feel that communicative efforts are self-serving. One of the chief complaints about communication is that the information received is often out of date. Many say that the information provided is "only what top management wants me to know." Employees want to know what is back of the organization's policies.

There is a direct relationship between job satisfaction and how well informed employees feel. The relationship was measured in one large business. Here are the results:

	Employees with high job satisfaction	Employees with low job satisfaction
Information about the company is accurate.	78%	37%
Important information is often out of date	34%	71%
Information is only what top management wants me to know	51%	90%

The table shows that 78 percent of the employees with high job satisfaction felt that information provided about the company was accurate. Of those with low job satisfaction, only 37 percent felt so. Only 34 percent of those with high job satisfaction felt that information was often out of date. This compares with 71 percent who had low job satisfaction. Again 51 percent of those with high job satisfaction, as compared with 90 percent of those with low job satisfaction, said that information provided was only what top management wanted them to know.

One of the key problems in communication is the lack of upward communication. Although employee suggestion plans serve a useful purpose, they should not be considered as providing the necessary upward communication.

Upward communication is generally especially difficult. Yet upward communication can be an important source of innovation and of information. However, the very structure of most organizations make it difficult.

According to Glenn A. Bassett, three problems affect the communication climate in organizations:

1. Employees frequently believe it is safer not to communicate. (This is the reason for the old injunction "don't make waves.")
2. Because of the nature of organizations, upward communication can be summarily shut off by higher levels of management.
3. The person in authority can readily assume that it is his subordinate's responsibility to communicate effectively with him, rather than his to communicate effectively with the subordinate.[12]

A member of an organization whose communication is not interpreted correctly is likely to be held personally accountable and to be punished for

[12] Glenn A. Bassett, *The New Face of Communication*. New York: American Management Association, Inc., 1968.

having been ineffective in his efforts to communicate. This often results in a tendency to avoid becoming involved. Open, timely communication may be avoided simply because people are fully aware that the risks are unduly high as compared with the rewards.

Organizations are designed to amplify downward communication by penalizing people for failing to hear and heed messages, but the same authority that ensures that the manager is heard by his subordinates also grants him the right to refuse to hear them.

In effect upward communication can be and frequently is shut off or severely reduced because of the superior's unwillingness to listen or his readiness to punish people who communicate in ways that displease him. Any person who has authority over another person is in a position to write most of the rules of the relationship as he sees fit. It is easy for the boss to simplify his world by assuming that it is the employee's responsibility to communicate with him and that the inability to do so is the employee's tough luck.

In the process upward communication suffers greatly. That is why it is important that we make a special effort to improve upward communication and to reduce the risk and the problems involved in it.

True upward communication is absolutely vital to an organization. Upper level managers have little chance for knowledge of the environment in which the lower level—the first line between the organization and its customers—operates. Without upward communication, upper management will not have a knowledge of what is happening until perhaps they notice sales falling off or other symptoms of problems.

Another roadblock to effective communication between employees and higher levels of management is that their jobs and interests are apt to be completely different. The boss is primarily interested in management problems and information. He may have little knowledge of the technical aspects of the employee's job. The employee, on the other hand, is primarily interested in the technical side and has little interest in problems of management. Figure 27 explains some of the difficulties encountered in communication between lower and higher organizational levels.

As indicated in Figure 27, the higher one goes in the organization, the more management knowledge and interest are necessary and the less technical knowledge and interest are usually needed. Of course, generally speaking, the smaller the business and the more technical its work, the more technical interest and knowledge are needed by upper management.

The interest of nonmanagement people is almost 100 percent technical. Thus it may be difficult for people in upper levels to communicate effectively with lower level people in terms of their interests. For the same reason

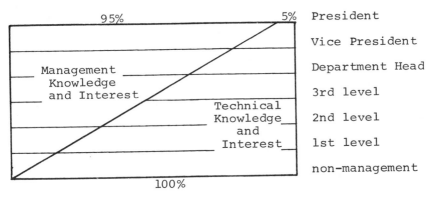

Figure 27[13]

it may be difficult for lower levels of communicate effectively with upper levels.

The problems that can be caused by poor communication, lack of communication, and the disregarding of upward communication are exemplified by a story told by Earl Brooks of the Cornell University Business School.[14] Brooks was a consultant for the New York Central Railroad before its merger with the Pennsylvania Railroad. He was in a tower in a switchyard of the railroad talking with the man who ran the "hump" used to segregate freight cars onto various tracks. The cars on the "hump" rolled down by gravity to make up trains going to various destinations. The "hump" was operated by using a large lever in the tower that was manually pulled back by the operator.

The lever activated retarders that pushed against the wheels of the freight cars to prevent them from going too fast and crashing against cars already coupled to the trains. Such a crash might derail cars and destroy the merchandise with which they were loaded.

It was observed that a tremendous strain was involved in pulling the lever. It did not look as though it would be effective in preventing cars from crashing and doing a great deal of damage. When asked whether the mechanism was operating properly, the operator said he had a problem of communication. He added that probably it was noticeable that he had to squint his eyes a great deal in doing his work. The switchyard tower had

---

[13] Adapted from the book, *Management by Objectives* by George S. Odiorne, Copyright, ©, 1965 by Pitman Publishing Corporation, New York.
[14] Class lecture.

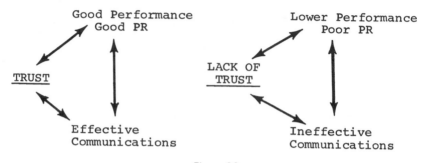

Figure 28

large windows on all sides so that the observation of the cars would be easy. One of the windows had a broken shutter that required replacement. The window allowed the sun to glare in, causing the operator to squint a great deal.

He said he had told the railroad three years earlier, two years earlier, one year earlier, and six months earlier about the broken shutter but that nothing had been done. So he said "I am not going to tell them the retarder is broken. Pretty soon we are going to lose a lot of freight cars when we can't stop them. But if the railroad is not interested in the broken shutter and my eyes, I'm not going to tell them about the broken retarder."

The kind of attitude on the part of the New York Central in disregarding the operator's communication about the shutter is probably one of the things that led to the eventual downfall of the Penn Central Railroad.

Among employees, good communication and performance are highly correlated. In his book, *New Patterns of Management,* Rensis Likert suggests that supervisors who are supportive, friendly, and helpful rather than hostile have the highest performance groups.[15]

William V. Haney says that the key is trust.[16] Trust develops a climate of openness in which there is effective two-way communication and, in turn, better performance, which results in better public relations.

Conversely, in a hostile climate, communications suffer. There is a tendency toward lack of communication or even miscommunication. Performance and public relations suffer. Figure 28 illustrates the point.

As Figure 28 indicates, trust leads to effective communication, good performance, and good public relations. And they in turn then lead to continued trust. On the other hand, lack of trust leads to ineffective communication, poor performance, and poor public relations, which in turn lead to continued lack of trust.

[15] New York: McGraw-Hill, 1961.
[16] *Communications and Organizational Behavior.* Homewood, Ill.: Richard D. Irwin, 1967.

One often hears discussions of the need for two-way communications and of the need for a program to develop them. Unfortunately, one usually hears the most about those needs within organizations where two-way communications are well nigh impossible because of impersonality and the lack of trust.

In such organizations management manifests less trust of employees by imposing detailed descriptions as to how employees are to carry out their tasks. Its approach is impersonal. Conversely, the employees have less trust of management. This results, among other things, in cutting off effective upward communications and in turn costly management errors based on erroneous information and misinformation.

Two-way communication is not likely to develop from a two-way communication program, but it will develop almost automatically in an atmosphere of mutual trust and openness.

CONCLUSION

It is apparent that the subject of communication is a very broad one. In the beginning of this chapter it was said that the very essence of good management is efficient, effective use of information. The primary source of information is communication. This is important to public relations management as a prerequisite to its management responsibilities. It is also important from the viewpoint of its public communication responsibilities.

Public relations management in the past has tended to confuse the use of communicative devices and tools with communication per se. For effective communication, a message must be in terms of the interest of its audience. And it must be couched in words and other symbols that are understood and accepted by the receivers of the communication. Language has progressed far beyond unambiguous simplicity. Many words are abstract and potentially ambiguous. In communicating the symbols we call words have power only to the extent that people know their meaning.

More than half the job of communicating is listening. Yet relatively little attention is usually given to listening as an important part of the communicative process.

Communication with employees is especially important. There is a direct relationship between job satisfaction and how well informed employees feel. Communication between levels is difficult because the primary interests of upper levels are management centered, whereas those of lower levels tend to be technically centered. For effective communication with employees, a climate of trust is essential.

There are tools we can use to measure whether we are communicating.

We have discussed comprehension and readership survey studies of newspaper and magazine ads and stories, for example. To determine how easily or difficult the language in our written or spoken communication is, we can also use the Flesch test or one of the other similar tests. These were discussed in Chapter 6. Such tests can help us to improve our ability as writers by making what we write both easier to read and more interesting.

EIGHT

Communicative
TOOLS OF
PUBLIC RELATIONS

In Chapter 1 we said that one should not confuse the purpose of the public relations function as being that of the publicist. In this chapter we discuss publicity, advertising, and other communicative tools in their relationship to the overall public relations function.

We have said that good public relations results from good performance, publicly acknowledged and appreciated. Using the communicative tools, the most important of which are usually advertising and publicity, to inform the publics effectively about the organization's performance develops acknowledgment and appreciation for it. The good performance would likely be taken for granted or go unnoticed if the organization failed to publicize it.

There are times when we may publicize matters that do not seem to concern performance. For example, we may announce an important appointment to a high post, call attention to special accomplishments of a valued employee, or announce a retirement. However, if one analyzes the objectives of those examples, and if they are effectively done, they are very much concerned with performance. Publicity related to appointments to high posts should concern the person's performance from the public's viewpoint. Announcing special accomplishments and retirements relates to the organization as an employer—a very important kind of performance.

When publicity does not, from the public's viewpoint, relate to performance in some way or another, it is apt to get scant attention from the press. Among other things, it is not news the public is likely to care about. As an example, a major business made a habit of issuing news stories about every major and sometimes minor appointment or promotion. However, the stories were not written from the public's viewpoint. They were designed merely to bolster the egos of the company people mentioned in them. When the city editor of one large metropolitan paper would see the company's representative, who was named Harvey Green, coming he was known to call out, "Stop the press—Harvey Green has an announcement." The business involved was known for its poor public relations.

There is nothing wrong with releasing stories concerning appointments or promotions of people within an organization. To the contrary, it is quite desirable. But the stories should be written with an objective of improving the organization's public relations in some specific way. For instance, they may call attention to promotions made for good performance within the business as viewed by the public. They may refer to civic interests and accomplishments. Or they may concern the up-from-the-ranks aspects of a promotion. Sometimes they may refer to the new improved performance and community objectives of the new appointee.

People in other departments or top management may suggest the use of advertising and publicity to develop an image or to overcome a problem when the organization's performance is contrary to that to be depicted. In such cases one may expect little or no effectiveness. We go back to our point that good public relations starts with good performance as viewed by the public. The function of advertising and publicity is to reflect the performance and get public acknowledgment and appreciation for it. Advertising and publicity that do not reflect good performance are likely merely to destroy credibility. In today's world advertising cannot be successfully used to cover an organization's dirty linen or to "sell" a viewpoint that the public feels is contrary to its best interests.

THE IMPORTANCE OF SPECIFIC OBJECTIVES

In Chapter 5 we discussed objectives. Specific objectives should be set before using any of the forms of publicity and advertising (including exhibits, talks, demonstrations, direct mail, etc.) They should contain a clear definition of the audience (publics) to be reached. Included should be the locations where the advertising should be seen or heard and the demographic groups to be covered (sex, age, education, occupations, income groups, races, ethnic groups, etc.)

Sometimes a specific race, ethnic or other demographic group may be reached satisfactorily through media of general circulation or audience, but real effectiveness may require the use of media aimed specifically at the group. For example, one may wish to use newspaper, magazine, radio, or television advertising aimed particularly at women, doctors, blacks, young people, educated people, people with high income, and so on.

The objectives should be specific as to' what is to be accomplished and by what time. These objectives must be written communicative objectives, not sales or other objectives. Plans should be specific as to exactly what is to be done, the specific messages to be used, including the conclusion one expects the audience to reach, and the schedules of use. It is usually more effective to state specifically in publicity or advertising the conclusion to be reached by the listener or reader than to leave it to inference. People may not take the trouble of drawing conclusions, or they may draw conclusions that were not intended.

SPECIAL SOURCES TO WHICH ADVERTISING AND PUBLICITY MAY BE CREDITED

Publicity frequently has an advantage over advertising in that the public is usually more apt to consider the newspaper, radio, or television station to be the "neutral" source and originator of the message than the organization that actually released it. In contrast advertising messages may sometimes be discounted by the public because they may be considered to be too much involved with the self-interest of the advertiser. The advertiser naturally tries to make himself look good.

Having a well-known, well-liked and thus usually believed spokesman can help to gain acceptance for a message. The audience may partially attribute the message to the spokesman. A person who is considered to be an expert on a subject may be a source who provides extra credibility for an organization's message. Sometimes sources such as well-known television actors or actresses are used merely to get attention when a better source may be available also to help lend credibility to the message.

Special communicative "sources" may be desirable to provide acceptability for a message. A good example is "Smokey the Bear" who cautions people about forest fires. Straightforward messages without the use of such "sources" might be considered didactic, preachy, or even dictatorial by the public.

Over the years the telephone companies have used cartoon characters such as "Bugs Bunny" and "Rosie the Elephant" to be the spokesman and "source" of messages concerning mass changeovers of telephone numbers or dialing procedures in large metropolitan areas. The carton characters were used to prevent the appearance of a large corporation preaching and instructing the public. Television commercials built around an animated character named "Mr. Bumble" were used to provide dialing instructions in a more palatable way than would be possible with a straightforward message. Mr. Bumble made dialing and other errors in using the telephone. His butler, Smythe, pointed out how he could avoid them and the trouble they caused him. Thus the telephone company was able to get the point across without being preachy.

Sometimes the medium can be a disinterested source that helps to provide credibility. For example, the Good Housekeeping Seal of Approval is accepted by many women as providing credibility for advertising messages.

The meaning of a message can depend not only on what is said but also on who says it.

PUBLICITY

One of the most generally used ways of reaching the public is through news releases. News stories have the advantage that with their use there is no cost for space or time. News stories may have better credibility than advertising. They may receive greater attention and readership than advertising, provided the subject is of public interest. Stories can also be prepared, released, and shown in the media more rapidly than advertising. When dealing with important news, time is valuable.

COVERING IMPORTANT FACTS EARLY

Sometimes a newspaper may give us little space or none at all, which is one of the reasons why news releases are usually written with the most important things first—the detail and less important things following. Then if the paper wishes to cut the story, it can do so without much rewriting and still give its readers the essential facts.

In preparing releases, as good publicists know, it is the newsworthy facts that count. Newspapers worth their salt will seldom use an organization's releases that editorialize or amount to free advertising. However, they are anxious for news of anything of interest to the publics they serve. Of course, they must be the judges of what is news and what is of interest. One of the worst things an organization can do is to get into an argument with the media about a news story. News releases should be provided to television and radio stations as well as to newspapers. Sometimes television stations may accept well-made 16 MM film footage to go with a release.

One must remember that the media are businesses. They must sell their papers or get listeners and viewers in order to stay in business. Sometimes they may use a lengthy release, or they may give it very little space or none at all. They may rewrite it completely. One thing is certain—if we have good relations with a paper's editorial staff or with a radio or television station's news people, they are much more inclined to give us a fair shake in what they are doing. They are only human. They are a special public.

A cardinal rule is to avoid asking a paper or a station to withhold news. Yet one frequently hears management people suggest that it be done. Sometimes people take issue with stories as published. One hears requests that the media be "given the facts" and requested to "make a correction." It may be desirable to be sure a paper, for example, has correct information, but requesting a correction is almost always undesirable. Even if a correction is printed, it is likely only to call further attention to some matter that would better be dropped.

Many years ago management hired press agents who had three primary jobs to do. One was to get names and pictures in the paper. A second was to keep unfavorable matters out of the paper. The third was to get the papers to publicize stories extolling the virtues of the company's products or viewpoints, right or wrong.

Although the press agents were able to get the names and pictures in the paper, and sometimes could even get the company's "boiler plate" (advertising disguised as news) published, even in those days they had difficulty keeping a story out of the paper. Our reference is to reputable papers. In the case of some smaller papers, public relations management may occasionally get the editor to go their way, particularly if their organization is an advertiser. However, such papers rarely have much credibility with their readers.

Quite often newspapers or radio and television stations may approach the organization for information concerning a matter they feel is of public interest. The questions may involve personnel matters such as strikes, financial statements, regulatory agency investigations, future plans, or statements made by consumer groups. The information should always be furnished if at all possible. If the organization withholds the information, provides only partial answers, or hedges, the media will undoubtedly get information elsewhere, and that information may be one-sided, incorrect, or exaggerated. The story as published or aired may not be factual or favorable.

DOUBLE CHECK THE FACTS—KEEP RECORDS OF INFORMATION SOURCES

One of the key rules in preparing news releases, advertisements, or any other communicative materials is always to double check the facts that are used to be sure they are 100 percent correct. Another publication, except an official government data publication, should not be considered as a source. It is clearly necessary to check every point of a news release with the place, the information, and data originated.

The source of any information used in publicity or advertising should be the same as it would be if the data were to be used in connection with regulatory agency questions or hearings, and the data should be as carefully checked. Otherwise, the publicity may rebound to the embarrassment of the organization. In addition to the need for maintaining credibility with the public, one may be asked by the Federal Trade Commission or other government agencies and commissions to verify and justify statements made. Official requests may be received for backup data concerning statements made in advertising and publicity.

Penalties for using data or making statements that cannot be backed up may be severe. For example, the Federal Trade Commission may require the organization to advertise that its statements were false. Businesses may be required to sign cease and desist orders that in the future they will not use false statements or those that cannot be verified. Even more stringent penalties may be imposed. The Federal Food and Drug Administration ordered a million dollars worth of birth control pills seized because their manufacturer repeatedly made statements about them that could not be backed up. Actions by regulatory agencies of the government are given wide publicity throughout the United States and sometimes throughout the world.

A written record of every source and what information the source provided or checked is desirable for all publicity or advertising whether it be a newspaper story, a television spot, a lecture, or a poster. This written record should be preserved as backup along with a copy of the material as used. Such a written record should also be kept relative to important policy decisions and actions taken, along with the reasons for the decisions.

ILLUSTRATIONS FOR USE WITH PUBLICITY

Newspapers will accept captioned, newsworthy photographs to illustrate stories. These should generally include people but preferably not large groups. Photographs with high contrasts print well, and conversely those with low contrasts print poorly in most newspapers. Action pictures get much more reader interest and are more apt to be used. Newspapers sometimes use captioned photographs that tell the story in themselves, without additional copy. Good eight-by-ten inch, glossy, black and white photographs are preferred.

MAGAZINE ARTICLES

In addition to the newspapers, magazine articles and news releases can be extremely effective when done properly. Publicity may be obtained from trade publications, for example, through the use of news releases. Feature articles on subjects of public interest written for the organization by well-known writers and with prior arrangement with a magazine are effective in reaching not only the public in general but frequently special publics. For instance, the Bell Telephone System employed nationally known writers to prepare important magazine feature articles on the Bell Telephone Laboratories and other subjects. The articles appeared in the *Readers Digest* and the *Saturday Evening Post* among others.

In addition to the magazine feature articles, newspapers on occasion may use special feature articles. Of course, the subjects covered in such articles concerning an organization's facets and accomplishments must be of more than ordinary interest to the public.

PRESS INTERVIEWS

Press interviews on controversial matters are almost unavoidable. Both the person interviewed and the organization can come to grief if the interview is not done well. Interviews by newspaper and magazine reporters, air media people, and the writers of books and magazine articles should be given very special attention and special preparation.

Interviews are generally with the top people of the organization and are often made by very able reporters and writers. The person being interviewed should be fully aware that frequently the questions and the interview in general may be probing and seem to have a critical tone. If the person or his organization has something to hide, it is wise to assume that the reporter or writer knows about it.

One is not usually able to evade questions or to give generalized evasive answers to them. Attempts at evasiveness will likely result not only in magnifying small problems (or large ones) out of all proportion but also in the destruction of credibility.

It is important that the person being interviewed be well prepared. Answers should be on hand for all possible important questions and on all important matters. They should be prepared for even the most unexpected questions on matters supposedly unknown by the public. The interview should be carefully rehearsed, using an able "devil's advocate" in lieu of the real interviewer. Remember, there will be no opportunity later to retract or change misstatements or undesirable statements. During the interviews, care should be taken that important matters are not undesirably played down.

The person being interviewed should be careful to answer the specific questions asked. In answering questions, he should avoid changing the subject and discussing other matters that may be of special interest to the organization or concerning his special responsibilities or interests.

The reporter's or writer's objective in making the interview should be determined in advance. What are his special fields and interests? What are his special biases? How does he generally write up interviews?

The person being interviewed should provide up-to-date information that has been thoroughly checked for accuracy and completeness, recognizing that the media are in the news business. What is said should be *news*.

When asked questions that for truly competitive or security reasons should not be answered, the interviewee should point out that he cannot discuss them and give the reasons why. The interview should always remain polite and appear to be friendly.

ADVERTISING

Advertising is another tool for keeping the public informed. Advertising differs from publicity in that its sponsor pays for the space in newspapers and magazines or time on the air. Advertising has an advantage over publicity in that the media cannot change what an ad says. Public relations management has complete control in advertising over what actually appears, except for the quality of the reproduction. Of course, the media may not accept an ad. For example, the publication may not accept any advertising, or may not have space. Some do not accept advertising felt to be immoral.

The cost of space in newspapers and magazines and of time on the air for radio and television is high. One should make the most of it by ensuring that the advertising used is as effective as possible.

Most mass media advertising is prepared for the client and placed in the media by advertising agencies. Agencies have account executives whose duties consist of most of the contact work with the client, learning his desires, obtaining information, getting approval for the advertising prepared, and discussing billing and advertising schedules. Agencies also have copy people, art directors, media time and space buyers, and sometimes research people. Generally, though, one should not depend on agency research. It tends to be self-serving. Agencies are paid a commission by the client on the expenses incurred for production of print and air media advertising. They also receive compensation from the media based on the dollar amount of print advertising space or air time purchased for the client.

Advertising and advertising decision making are broad subjects. Our discussion of them cannot be in depth in a book of this kind. Following are brief discussions of some of the highlights important to public relations management.

NEWSPAPER AND MAGAZINE ADVERTISING

Newspaper advertising has certain advantages over some of the other media. Newspaper (and magazine) advertising as a whole has an established circulation or "audience" of people who subscribe to the papers (or magazines). Radio and television, on the other hand, have "roving" audiences—people who switch from program to program and station to station.

Newspaper advertising permits the use of many more words, which may be necessary when one wishes to be explicit and give detail. Degrees of emphasis may be given by various uses of type and illustrations. Newspaper advertising remains available for later reading or rereading and reference. It provides a record of what has been said. For example, newspaper advertising is desirable for mass legal notifications concerning large numbers of people, such as notices of hearings before regulatory agencies. In a newspaper a person can see an entire ad at one time, which is sometimes an advantage, whereas in the air media only part of a commercial can be seen or heard at any given moment in time. Sometimes certain parts of an ad may be of particular interest to a reader. With a newspaper ad, he may give those parts preferred attention and reading.

Magazine advertising has these same advantages, but since magazines are published much less frequently, their use does not permit the flexibility of advertising offered by newspapers. In addition, magazine pages are smaller than newspaper pages. Magazine advertising does not permit the large illustrations, headlines, and space available for use on a newspaper page. One may give more relative importance to a subject in newspaper advertising when it is desirable. Newspaper advertising may be arranged to appear on a specific date, whereas the magazine advertising appears only on the date the magazine is delivered or purchased.

In many magazines advertisements may reach a more selective audience than most newspaper ads. For example, one may use ads in garden magazines, business magazines, travel magazines, woman's magazines, scientific magazines, and innumerable trade and professional magazines.

Print advertising (newspapers, magazines, and direct mail) allows people to read and assimilate messages at their own rate and at the time they wish. This is important because there is a great difference in the speed with which people may receive, comprehend, and assimilate messages either by reading or listening. Print advertising is also an advantage in reaching those people whose schedules require them to get their information by reading on the commuter train, for example. On the other hand, many people dislike to or simply cannot or will not bother to read. Messages in print are easier to avoid than those on radio or television. People with better educations are more apt to receive communications by means of the print media than those with poorer educations.

Since a person must voluntarily read print messages, the print media will usually be read by those already agreeing with the message. On the other hand, broadcast media may be involuntarily seen and heard, at least for a time until the channel or station is changed, by those who do not agree with a message.

ILLUSTRATIONS

Illustrations can add a great deal to the effectiveness of advertising. Sometimes a picture is really worth a thousand words, as the old adage indicates, but it is not necessary or even desirable that all advertisements be illustrated. For example, illustrations would not be appropriate in most legal advertisements, financial advertisements, or announcements.

Besides helping to create and hold interest, illustrations should always relate to and work with the copy in helping to create a mental image and an understanding of the desired message. In addition illustrations help to set the mood of advertisements. Mood can be likened to flavor—it can be the salt, the pepper, the vinegar, the sugar, or the spice of the ad. It can be perfunctory, sweet, sour, bright, full of zest, gloomy, or cold, and thus help or hinder an ad's effectiveness.

Most newspaper printing and the paper stock used do not permit quality reproduction of photographs. It is important for illustrations in newspaper advertising to be prepared with this in view. Such illustrations should have high contrasts. As discussed in Chapter 7 on communication, illustrations with low contrast frequently print as just a smudge on the newspaper page. Photographs with insufficient contrast should be retouched to add contrast, or one should use line drawings. As was true of illustrations for publicity, action illustrations are likely to get more reader interest and attention than passive ones.

A good many magazines use paper and methods of printing that permit better quality illustrations than is possible in the average newspaper.

PREPARATION TIME FOR ADVERTISING

If really need be, newspaper advertisements, including layout copy and illustrations, may be prepared for use in just a few days. Magazine advertisements, however, generally require a long lead time because magazines close for printing a good while before actual publication dates.

READERSHIP

Unless a message is of unusual interest for some reason, we cannot expect a tremendous percentage of the public to read any given advertisement (or news stories either). Which page an ad or the news story appears on, what other ads or stories are around it, how newsworthy we have made the copy and whether it is written from the reader's viewpoint all have a decided effect on how much the ad or the publicity will be read. Generally speaking, the more pages in a newspaper or magazine, the poorer the readership, especially if there is a large number of advertisements.

Anyone who arranges for advertising is almost certain to be asked to advertise in special editions of newspapers that are published to tie in with events ranging anywhere from the opening of baseball season to the fiftieth anniversary of the founding of a paper, or the centennial anniversary of the establishment of the city. However, advertising in special editions is probably less effective than that used in regular editions. With the maze of advertisements published, readership is generally lower. The cost per thousand readers is higher. Knowledgeable advertising people generally try to steer clear of special editions.

THE AIR MEDIA

Radio and television advertising are both effective advertising media when properly used. Radio can be heard while the listener goes about other matters and as he drives down the highway. This is not true for television. Both radio and television can make effective use of the persuasiveness of the voice. They reach people automatically when a station is tuned in, without the need to subscribe.

On the other hand, all that is needed to cut off a broadcast and eliminate the advertising is a flick of a switch. One's selective perception barrier may "tune out" commercials. Or people may take the opportunity to visit the bathroom or kitchen while the commercials are on. Radio can reach people in remote places, but it is the only medium that cannot provide picture illustrations. Television has most of the same advantages as radio. In addition it provides moving visuals and the opportunity to demonstrate. Its entertainment and informational abilities are so great that it may attract huge audiences. Because both radio and television stations operate continuously over all or a considerable part of the day and night, advertising messages may be broadcast more than once, at various times, on any given station.

OUTDOOR ADVERTISING

Outdoor advertising is used a great deal in marketing, in political campaigns, and in connection with charitable appeals of Community Chests, United Giving campaigns, and so on. In the latter case, outdoor advertising firms are frequently solicited for free space, which they usually contribute as a public relations gesture.

Outdoor advertising has been effectively used in connection with some public relations activity. At one time the telephone company was having trouble getting people in the Los Angeles basin to use area codes when dialing out-of-town telephone numbers to and from Los Angeles. As a part of a corrective program, it purchased outdoor advertising near the boundaries of the Los Angeles numbering plan area, which had the number 213. The message read, "You are now entering the 213 numbering plan area." The unique advertising was commented on favorably by the press and received considerable attention from the public. Outdoor advertising messages may be seen by large numbers of people in locations where there is considerable traffic. They must be brief enough to be read at a glance.

Nonetheless, outdoor advertising is controversial. A large enough percentage of the public is opposed to it so that its users run the risk of negative reactions. Many people feel it is harmful to the scenery and environment. Legislative action has been taken to restrict it. Public relations management should consider the pros and cons well before deciding to use it.

BASIS FOR PURCHASING ADVERTISING

Generally, advertising in newspapers and magazines should be purchased on the basis of buying the lowest cost per thousand readers of the kind one wishes to reach. For example, if one wishes to reach central city readers but not those in surrounding suburban areas, circulation in the suburban areas would be discounted. If one wishes to reach only a sector of a suburban area, he would not purchase central city media. The same considerations apply to other demographic characteristics.

In the purchase of newspaper advertising, the tendency is to use larger advertisements than is necessary for effectiveness. For example, full page advertisements may be used when smaller ones may be as effective. The difference in cost is large. Readership surveys over the years have shown that the largest ads seldom get the best readership. Advertisements in which copy, layout, illustrations and the signature are carefully thought out seldom require full page space for maximum effectiveness.

There are advantages in having news on the page along with one's newspaper ad. More people are attracted to read the page, including your ad, instead of skipping over it for lack of interest.

When it is desirable to quickly get people to remember an important message, several small size ads (for example, two columns by five inches or three columns by seven inches) may sometimes be effectively used on different pages of the same issue of a newspaper. Since larger sized advertisements may be needed to give importance to a message, they may be used on days when "flights" of the smaller ads are not used.

One may save a good deal of money by using care not to purchase unnecessary duplicate coverage of newspaper advertising. In communicating many kinds of messages, for example, when one uses metropolitan newspapers of large circulation, it may serve no useful purpose to purchase space in smaller newspapers in suburban areas. For some kinds of messages, of course, there are important advantages in using the smaller suburban newspapers. For example, you can reach people in individual communities or areas more economically, avoiding advertising to areas where there is no purpose.

In considering radio and television, one should recognize that the cost per thousand listeners or viewers delivered at any given time depends on the programming on the stations in the area and varies greatly. Of course, it also depends on the coverage of the stations. Demographic differences may be large depending on time of day and kind of programming. For example, more women than men may be reached through the air media during the day. In some areas radio may be effective in reaching commuters who travel by automobile during the commuting hours. National rating services provide audience data. One should not rely on audience data supplied by the media, as discussed in Chapter 6.

The cost per thousand persons reached by one medium should not be compared with that of another medium without careful consideration of all the factors. Media vary in effectiveness depending on the purpose and the kind of message delivered.

It is sometimes suggested that studies be made of the effectiveness of various media and that the most effective one be used to the exclusion of the others. This may be desirable in certain situations, particularly in some marketing efforts. However, in many situations it is desirable to use a variety of media to get across one's message effectively. Properly used, the different media can add to one another's effectiveness and compound the communicative impact. Also, as said earlier in this chapter, one medium may have greater impact on a certain group of people, whereas a different medium may be most effective with another. The effectiveness of public relations advertising can be stretched a great deal by careful and prudent purchase of time and space.

CONTINUITY OF ADVERTISING

Advertising is not something that can be turned on and off effectively. Its effectiveness is cumulative. Assuming that the advertising used is good, effective results may depend on use over a period of time and in reasonable concentration.

OTHER CONSIDERATIONS

Suggestions are sometimes made to cover more than one subject in the same advertisement or other communicative effort. The result of such a procedure is loss of effectiveness. Consider the problems of getting and keeping interest, of the number of words and amount of space needed to cover each subject effectively, of bridging the copy for two or more subjects, or illustrations suitable for more than one subject, and so on. Getting the necessary public comprehension and retention of information on more than one subject would be asking a great deal.

Sometimes one may be tempted to use advertising and publicity on a number of different subjects during the same period of time, none of them getting a large enough coverage and budget for effectiveness. The problem is one of having too many objectives, as discussed in Chapter 5. One needs to determine which subjects are most important and discard the others.

Closely allied is the practice by some organizations of changing public relations advertising and publicity programs, objectives, and approaches each year. This usually is the result when public relations management caters to the changing managements and viewpoints of dominant other departments. It may also result when people within the organization have seen advertising on a particular theme for a year and have become tired of it. In reality, however, the advertising may have been used so short a time that it has barely begun to be effective. One should remember that the public is not as interested in or knowledgeable about the advertising being used as those within the organization. Therefore, the public will usually not notice that it has been used for a considerable length of time. Establishing and changing communicative themes used in advertising and publicity should be done on the basis of objectives established as a result of problem analysis and the feedback of results from the publics.

OTHER COMMUNICATIVE TOOLS

In addition to publicity and advertising, there are many other communicative tools of public relations. One that lends itself admirably to getting a message before organizations is the speaker. Speakers usually do not affect the budget much because there is little out-of-pocket cost, except for props. The speaker should always prepare his material so that it is of interest to the particular group to whom he is talking. Otherwise he may not be listened to or understood. The truth of the matter is that he will probably not be invited to talk again.

One of the advantages of the speaker is that he may develop rapport with the members of the audience. The speaker may become the source of the information included in the talk, rather than the organization he represents. This adds a great deal to credibility and acceptance of the information presented.

Great care must be taken in the use of talks prepared for speakers' bureaus that the speakers do not become merely presenters of pitches prepared by someone else. From the audience viewpoint the speaker should always be the source of the information presented. Many a speaker who has memorized his talk well and presented it flawlessly has by the manner used betrayed the fact that he was not the source of the information. Thus much of the benefit of the talk has been lost.

The vice president for public relations of an organization known for a great deal of public relations activity was requested to speak on public relations before the local chapter of the Public Relations Society. One of the vice president's staff suggested sending a member of the speakers' bureau instead and was unhappy that the program chairman would not agree. The program chairman wanted the person who would be considered the source to do the speaking even if the talk might actually be prepared by a staff writer. During the inevitable question and answer period, questions would undoubtedly come up that someone from the speakers' bureau could not answer well.

It is frequently advantageous for organization executives to talk before important groups. This can be an effective way to develop rapport and to authoritatively convey important messages, and also contributes to good community relations.

As in every other public relations activity, development and adherence to specific objectives is an important key to effectiveness in speaking before groups.

MOTION PICTURES

Motion pictures are an excellent way to get to groups. They may be used by insurance businesses and automobile and tool manufacturers, for example, to promote safety. Pictures may be produced on safe driving, safe use of bicycles, safe use of tools, and so on. The Red Cross and other organizations may make pictures on water safety and swimming, boat safety, and life saving.

Industrial and other businesses use pictures to tell dramatic stories of innovativeness in the public interest—for example, by depicting what has been done in the interest of national defense, in improving the way of life, and the invention of important new devices such as transistors, solar batteries, computers, and telephones. Charitable organizations such as the Community Chest or United Fund use motion pictures to show how effectively money contributions are spent. Motion pictures can be helpful in telling people how to use a common product or service properly. They can be used to show the public services performed by organizations.

Motion pictures permit greater exploration of subjects than most other media while providing moving visuals and the persuasiveness of the voice. They make possible the use of a story line, thus adding interest and greater palatability to the message. Many motion pictures are suitable for use on television provided that television rights have been secured and proper talent payments made to those who appear in the pictures.

Firms specialize in getting motion pictures used on television and arranging for distribution of motion pictures for showings before all manner of audiences such as school classrooms, service clubs, social clubs, and women's organizations. These firms maintain libraries of films of the organizations who subscribe to their distribution services. They prepare and distribute film catalogs of the various films available. They have staffs to receive orders for films. They handle shipping, receiving the films being returned, and film maintenance. They provide complete records of showings to their clients.

Motion pictures are generally expensive to produce. Once they have been made and the prints are on hand, it is prudent to make the greatest possible use of them.

Motion pictures have some of the same advantages as company speakers except that films do not provide the personal contact and the development of rapport that is possible with a good speaker. On the other hand, films provide the extra advantage of a much wider use of visual presentation and of interest-holding action and scenery. In most cases the prints may be used for several years.

PLACARDS, DISPLAYS, EXHIBITS

Placards and displays of one kind or another are good ways to get across short messages. To be quickly read, the number of words used must be kept to an extreme minimum. Displays are frequently used in windows and lobbies. They may be designed to give three-dimensional impact, frequently using moving parts that help to gain attention. Placards may be used on vehicles, in windows, in offices, on bulletin boards, and many other places.

Exhibits used to meet specific objectives can be an effective tool. Exhibits may range all the way from the very elaborate ones found at Disneyland, for example, to those used at county fairs, conventions, annual meetings, and conferences. The effectiveness of exhibits depends on visitor traffic to see them. They can be designed to provide demonstrations of how equipment works or what happens under various circumstances. For example, demonstrations can show how business machines work or what happens when one misdials a telephone call.

Exhibits may be manned or unmanned. They are designed to provide information about an organization or its activities or products and are an excellent way to reach special audiences. For example, book publishers often have exhibits at important conferences and other events attended by college professors. One or more people are on hand to answer questions and promote new textbooks. An organization may have exhibits on several different themes, shipping the appropriate ones to the various events where it is desirable to reach specialized audiences.

Some exhibits are very expensive and include intricate operating parts. They may cost large sums of money to build and considerable amounts to ship, set up, and dismantle. Many such exhibits may be found at scientific, engineering, and other similar conferences, conventions, and trade shows. Advance promotion, especially of elaborate exhibits, is desirable to get as many people as possible to come to see the exhibits.

There are businesses that specialize in designing and constructing exhibits. Display houses also specialize in this work.

OPEN HOUSES AND TOURS

Open houses and tours are a fine way of letting people know more about the organization. As is discussed in Chapter 9, they are an excellent community relations tool. They can be open to the general public or to any of the many special publics. Tours are effective in informing VIPs, politicians, student groups, and so on. Family nights for employees and their families enable a very important group to come to an open house or tour at which they are the special guests.

The amount of knowledge most people have about an organization can be likened to the part of an iceberg that is above the water. Open houses and tours help to explore the parts of the iceberg below the water.

BOOKLETS, LEAFLETS, DIRECT MAIL, BILL ENCLOSURES

Booklets and leaflets are an excellent way to communicate with specific groups of people. They may be distributed at exhibits and displays, in business and other offices, over the counter, by direct mail, or on request in response to other advertising and publicity. They may be merely a sheet of paper printed on one side or both, or they may contain many pages. Preparation of booklets and leaflets should be done by people knowledgeable in the field. Such work is out of the realm of many large advertising agencies, whose specialties are primarily mass media advertising.

In the preparation of booklets and leaflets, careful attention should be given to layout and to choices of type that attract interest, place emphasis where it belongs, and make for easy reading and comprehension of the message. Booklets and leaflets should be designed with proper dimensions to fit envelopes for easy mailing.

Direct mail may use booklets or leaflets. In addition, letters, formal announcements, and postcards are commonly used. Direct mail can be an effective way to deliver your message to specific customers. The message can be personalized if desirable. Direct mail offers the advantage of timeliness. It can be arranged to arrive at the best time for effectiveness—for example, just prior to an open house or plant visit, or to tie in with a special event. Examples of direct mail are a film catalog or an invitation to an open house.

Postage costs for direct mail can be very large. For direct mail to be economical as a communicative medium, great care must be taken with layout, color, type, and message to get and keep the interest of the potential reader. Otherwise it may end up in the wastebasket with no more than a glance.

Many businesses specialize in the distribution of direct mail. Organizations not having mailing lists of their own can purchase a variety of lists designed to reach people with an assortment of interests.

Bill enclosures are a form of direct mail. They are used mostly by utilities and retail businesses that have considerable numbers of customers who are billed directly by mail. Distribution of bill enclosures along with the bills can be made with no extra cost, provided they are designed with care not to increase the mailing weight beyond the minimum first class rate. The only cost is for writing, layout, art work, and printing. Readership of bill enclosures varies a great deal. Good layout and appropriate type and color are important to getting and holding interest.

Bill enclosures are effective primarily as messages going to customers' homes. They are not usually effective in reaching business customers because the enclosures rarely reach the right person since bills are normally opened by bookkeepers and other clerical people.

COMMUNICATIVE TOOLS FOR INFORMING EMPLOYEES

Keeping employees well informed about opportunities, problems, objectives, plans, and results may use several kinds of communicative tools. Being sure they are informed is important for motivating them and making them feel they are part of the team.

It is generally recognized that one of the greatest problems in industry today is poor motivation of employees. Poor motivation may have a tremendous bearing on public relations. Among other things, it can show up in the way employees treat customers and in the way they do their job.

Keeping employees informed about what is happening is important because it is vital to their feeling involved and a part of the organization. Employee information can be given by word of mouth—for example, by the employee's supervisor. In matters concerning the employee's work and work group word of mouth is undoubtedly the best way, and there is a great need for manager and supervisor commitment to it. The need applies not only to business but to all other kinds of organizations as well. It cannot be merely the effort of one part of the organization, such as the public relations department. Top management must be committed to public relations objectives that stress, among other things, the importance of employees and employee groups.

In larger organizations employee newspapers and printed bulletins may be mailed to the employees' homes or distributed at work locations. Magazines for employees are another way of letting them and their families know about subjects of more general interest. Letters from the head of the organization, a vice president, or department head may be used to inform employees about especially important matters, to thank them for special action they may have taken, and so on. Employee get-togethers for talks by key members of the organization and others are also an effective way to cover important matters.

Leaflets and booklets may be especially prepared for employees. For example, indoctrination booklets tell new employees about such things as the company's structure, its history, vacations, sickness benefits, and holidays. Other booklets may inform them exclusively about sickness and accident benefits and retirement plans.

Films produced for employee audiences are effective in getting messages across dramatically. Safety films are an example. Public films frequently meet a dual purpose of also informing employees on such things as new discoveries and inventions and interesting technical advances.

Seminars, workshops, and conferences run by the organization or by outside organizations are helpful in reaching special groups of employees on important technical subjects. Seminars, workshops, courses, and conferences sponsored by outside professional and business groups are especially desirable. They can bring out the views and experiences of many other organizations and can help prevent employees from becoming "ingrown" and resistant to change. They may permit rubbing elbows and developing friendships and working relationships with people from other business and organizations. Thus they are a particularly effective communications medium for educating employees.

The great importance of continuing employee education can be illustrated by the estimate that the half-life of an education in some fields today is three years. Thus it is vital that the employees in all parts of the organization be continually reeducated. Reeducation of employees is important as related to those working in the public relations function as well, although over the years it has been largely neglected.

Receiving information from employees is as necessary as providing information to them, and many organizations do not give it enough attention. As discussed in chapter 7, success in upward communication depends to a considerable extent on a climate of trust that encourages two-way communication.

Employee suggestion plans properly administered are a good way of receiving some kinds of information from employees, but they cannot substitute for good communication between the employee and his boss.

NINE

Special Kinds of Public Relations

In this chapter we discuss four important specialized subdivisions of the public relations function—public affairs, community relations, contributions, and financial public relations. All are important to an organization's public relations. Community relations is often included as a part of the general public relations function in many organizations. Public affairs, contributions, and financial public relations may be handled separately from the mainstream of public relations.

PUBLIC AFFAIRS

Public affairs means different things to different people. In some organizations the term applies generally to political and governmental relationships and matters closely allied to them. In other organizations public affairs activity is considered to be much broader in scope and refers to all the public relations functions, including community relations, political relations, and financial relations. In this chapter we discuss public affairs as being restricted to political and governmental relations and allied matters.

The political world is an important special public. Therefore, in many organizations a separate person or department is set up to deal with it. However, public affairs activity should still be considered as an integral part of the overall public relations function. It would be foolish to expect that important public affairs activity can be successful without the acceptance and support of the general public. And to get the acceptance and support of the public requires public relations objectives and action much beyond the narrow scope of public affairs activity. Conversely, no amount of public affairs activity will long prevent what the public desires from being fulfilled. It is axiomatic that those in public office listen to the voters or lose their offices.

THE EFFECT OF "UNDER THE TABLE" ACTIVITY

The old time lobbyist is held in ill repute by the public. Public affairs activity has had a generally undesirable reputation. Many people think of it as having to do with skullduggery and "under the table" manipulation of political matters. Unfortunately a good deal of the undesirable reputation has been earned. The recent wave of disclosures, both domestic and international, of hidden payments for political and business favor shows the problem to be a continuing one. Although many of the disclosures did not concern political lobbyists, they had much the same effect on public confidence in lobbyists.

Over the years more and more regulation has come to control the activities of lobbyists. With hearings of government agencies, boards, commissions, committees, and so on required to be open to the public in most states, "under the table" activity is more hazardous. Stricter accounting requirements by the Securities and Exchange Commission and new political contribution laws are noteworthy. "Under the table" activity is seldom very successful over the long pull. Good communication and close scrutiny of legislation at all levels, as well as of government agencies and commissions, are the order of the day.

Some commissions set up to regulate businesses or professions are actually made up largely of the people they are expected to regulate. Thus regulation may be ineffective. Such situations almost always rebound eventually, causing loss of credibility and public acceptance of the businesses and professions involved.

PUBLIC AFFAIRS WORK IS MORE IMPORTANT TODAY

Without using "under the table" activity, professional public affairs work is more important today than ever before. It can accomplish more for the organization while operating in the public interest than the old time lobbyist could.

In today's complex world government has expanded its regulatory powers and controls in every direction in most parts of the world. This has been brought about by a number of factors, the most important being the increasing dependency of people on forces outside their control. The population explosion and urbanization are factors. Failure of organizations to give proper recognition to the public interest, to meet their social responsibilities, centralization and concentration of governmental power on a national level, and the trend toward statism are other factors. These factors have been abetted by a technology in which the majority of individuals have become cogs in one of the vast machines that produce automobiles and canned foods or supplies water or electric power, for example.

Government has become coordinator-adjudicator of a complex economy and society in which the majority of individuals by themselves tend to be relatively powerless. Yet government reacts and sometimes overreacts to what it feels is the citizens' desires. An example is the emphasis put on some consumer issues both in Congress and in state legislatures without sufficient study and without much needed information from knowledgeable organizations.

Through the years overregulation and poor regulation have become problems stifling entire industries and unnecessarily adding greatly to the costs to the consumer. Development of desirable new products and services may be held back for years by unnecessary slowness or failure to act by government agencies. Management's ability to make necessary and logical decisions to meet changing situations becomes hampered and hemmed in. Laws piled one on another are devised by well-meaning legislators, many of whom have schooling, training, and knowledge only in the area of the law.

However, the laws are seldom repealed. They remain in force long after their usefulness and the need for them is past. Sometimes regulation of one industry may conflict with regulation of others. For example, the rationale of the railroad rate structure was that railroads would carry heavy bulky items at relatively low rates per ton and other items at higher rates. The low rates and high rates would balance and allow a profit. This did not work out well because the railroads carried the heavy, bulky low rate items (the sand and gravel), and trucks and airlines carried the profitable high rate business.[1]

Railroad rates have become so complicated that some companies find it profitable to audit all freight bills. More than 150,000 rate changes are made annually, and the basic rate books do not show cross references to all new rates.

PUBLIC AFFAIRS PROBLEMS AND FUNCTIONS

Organizations experience three primary kinds of problems requiring public affairs activity. The first is to ensure that relative to the governmental co-

[1] E. Jerome McCarthy, *Basic Marketing,* 4th ed. Homewood, Ill.: Richard D. Irwin, 1971.

ordination process, the proper parts of government know about and consider the problems of the organization that would otherwise remain unknown. This lack of knowledge could result in curtailment of the organization's ability to compete and to contribute to society as it should.

It is in the public interest and not an evil thing to be sure that people in government know the organization's viewpoints. Society is so complex that it is impossible for those in government, either the legislative or executive branch, to formulate logical plans without extensive information from the various businesses and other organizations that have the knowledge required. One of the public affairs management's duties is to learn about the various committee and agency hearings and arrange for competent testimony and data to be supplied by the proper departments of the organization.

This is far from being an altruistic matter. Supplying competent testimony and data can result in enactment of laws and regulations based on facts and at the same time more favorable to the organization. It can help to avoid undesirable laws and regulations. Failure to be properly represented in hearings often results in the adoption of rulings and regulations that are favored primarily by pressure groups and that are not truly in the interest of the public or desirable for the organization.

With the ever-increasing role that government is playing in the activities of almost all organizations, it is imperative that organizations be aware of possible future actions and what is said in hearings. It is imperative that organizations take proper measures so that their viewpoints are known and their arguments are strongly presented, so that they can take responsible steps to ensure that the environment in which they operate will be as favorable as it properly should be. This is so important to business organizations that it should not be left primarily as the responsibility of trade groups and associations. The need concerns not only areas involving the particular competences of the organization but also some of the more general areas concerning the social climate. Inflation and other matters of national economic importance are examples.

In earlier chapters we discussed the importance of the public interest. The organization may find that something it is doing should be changed from the standpoint of the public interest. The change should be made before a conflict develops that may result in regulation or legislation that not only controls the problem but is also punitive to the organizations involved.

The change may cause problems in competing with other businesses that continue the undesirable practices. The organization then has the responsibility to work with government to establish regulation in the best interest both of the businesses involved and society as a whole. Failure to do so will only redound against the organization in the long run. Peter Drucker points out in his book *Management: Tasks, Responsibilities, Practices* that organizations have shunned this responsibility with the traditional viewpoint that "no regulation is the best regulation."[2] However, in the kind of circumstance described, regulation is in the interest of responsible business. When legislation or regulation is inevitable, it is in the organization's interest to see that it is the best that can be achieved, which can be done only by good representation by knowledgeable and responsible people at hearings of regulatory bodies and legislative committees.

Meetings held by the Commonwealth Club of The California Study Section on Consumerism provide commentary by regulatory agencies. Representatives of Federal regulatory agencies such as the Food and Drug Administration and the Consumer Products Safety Commission brought out that when hearings are conducted to determine what regulations should cover and to write the regulations, businesses that should have great interest in them have been conspicuous by their absence. The organizations that are the most knowledgeable and have the biggest stake in the outcome allow people with only superficial knowledge and biased or radical views to have the loudest voices in the creation of regulations and legislation.

Problems can be created by people of zeal who are well meaning but without sufficient understanding or knowledge of the facts. These people seek to impose the viewpoints of their self-appointed benevolent groups on the rest of society. Their manner may be carefully planned to gain maximum press coverage. Their viewpoints can be contrary to the interests of business and other organizations. Sometimes they may be people who favor special interests of business or other organizations. Government agencies and legislative committees sometimes take the course of least resistance and give way entirely to such pressure groups when affected business organizations are not effectively represented at hearings.

Recognizing the importance of matters of this kind and taking appropriate action is needed to make the public relations function effective. Failure by the organization and by the management of the public relations function to recognize the need for effective action in this area is not only a major disregard of the public interest but also one of the causes of the lack of public confidence in business.

Since government does react to the expressed will of the people, it is of great importance that the people be informed. Frequently, the organizations concerned are the only source of valid information for either government or the public. Unless this information is provided, poor government decisions may come about as a result of pressures from an uninformed or misinformed public.

[2] New York: Harper and Row, 1974.

Government agencies and legislatures frequently attempt to cater to each successive pressure group, sometimes going to extremes and creating unwarranted problems, particularly for business, education, and other governmental departments. In recent years a few organizations have made minor attempts to inform the public on matters of concern to them. For example, nuclear generators of electricity are opposed by some groups. A few electric utilities have attempted to provide the public with some information about such generators. An organization to inform key individuals and the public about nuclear generators has been set up by manufacturers and others.

Too frequently information may be provided on a one-time basis with the idea that the public has then been informed. This course disregards the small percentage of readers of most advertisements and publicity and the short memory of most people. Information that is interestingly presented must be provided with reasonable frequency.

On the whole, information provided the public on most issues is sketchy, incomplete, and sometimes self-serving. Or no information is provided at all.

If the democratic process is to work at all, the public must be better informed. To be effective, information must be in terms of the publics' self-interest. Unless organizations that are involved can make their cases strongly, both to government and to the general public, pressure groups, splinter groups, and others can take command of the situation. This is not in either the organization's interest or in the public interest. Because informing the public is a key public relations function, good coordination between those responsible for public affairs activity and the rest of the public relations function is required.

The second problem calling for public affairs activity is the need to protect the organization and society from the waste imposed by government, which draws from the economy to support countless endeavors by taxes. For example, many different federal regulatory agencies and commissions are set up to accomplish parts of the same overall purposes. Many have overlapping duties. National, state, and local agencies are created with the same or overlapping responsibilities. Government has entered into the printing business in a big way. A large number of booklets, free for the asking, include titles such as *Floor Polish and Floor Care,* a consumer publication from the General Services Administration of the federal government. In the education field many adult courses are of great value, but many others, such as courses in *Folk Dancing, Great Museums of Europe,* and *Sail Boating* may be questionable use of tax money during times when schools have difficulty obtaining enough money for the fundamentals. Federal government revenue sharing and financing of local projects of all manner and value have reached vast proportions. Loans to foreign governments, at interest rates a small fraction of what the federal government must pay to get the money, are common. As said earlier, by 1974 government in the United States was spending 41 percent of the national income. Deficit spending for the eight years prior to 1974 came to $119 billion. During the three years from 1974 to 1976, federal deficit spending was budgeted at a net additional $90 billion more than income, making a gross federal debt of $453 billion.[3] However, counting the amount of Social Security trust funds, used by the federal government to finance its deficit spending, the gross federal deficit budgeted for the years 1974, 1975, and 1976 alone came to $137 billion, instead of the net amount of $90 billion.

The amount of money used by government is so large that business is no longer able to finance needed increased capacity and modernization reasonably. Increase in capacity and modernization are vital to increasing the production of goods and services necessary to restrict inflation and to provide employment. Thus it is important for the organization (business or nonbusiness) to effectively present the need for government responsibility in fiscal matters.

The task of government and political institutions revolves around balancing two basic principles. The first is to establish the equity and order necessary to protect one person from another. The second is the need to limit government power to protect the people from the state.

In *The Age of Discontinuity* Peter Drucker calls attention to the growing disparity between apparent power and the lack of control in government.[4] He adds that we are good at creating administrative agencies, but no sooner are they created than they became ends in themselves. They defy public will and public policy.

The third problem requiring public affairs activity is the need to be well informed concerning the political world. This need ties in directly with the two problems we have just discussed. The public affairs function includes that of a listening post to keep track of the countless proposed new laws being introduced in legislatures, city councils, and other government bodies. Copies of these proposals should be reviewed frequently by one or more parts of the organization to determine what effect the proposals may have. Public affairs management has the responsibility for keeping tabs on proposed and pending legislation and seeing that knowledgeable people in the competences involved examine its effect on the organization and the public.

---

[3] Figures derived from the *Budget of the U.S. Government,* Fiscal Year 1976, Office of the President of the United States, Washington, D.C.

[4] New York: Harper and Row, 1969.

SPECIAL KINDS OF KNOWLEDGE NEEDED

Dealing with the government in public affairs matters takes special knowledge of government organization and procedure and the special ability to deal effectively with the government people involved. The government people include elected officials, members of agencies and commissions, and employees of government departments. They range all the way from the local level, where one may deal with city councils and planning commissions and their members, to the national level and congressmen, congressional committees, and people in federal government departments. It may be necessary or desirable to take part and provide information or arguments in public hearings on a local, state, or national level.

In public hearings business representatives especially may expect sometimes to be severely challenged as to the information or arguments they present and their credibility. One reason for this is that the past record of business has been blemished so many times. One example is the lobbying efforts on behalf of the International Telephone and Telegraph Company a few years ago, which received a great deal of attention and coverage in the news. The problems of the dairy industry and milk price control boards and the unfavorable publicity they received is another example. Some of the real estate land developers and oil companies have fallen into the same situation.

Business has a very serious need to present its case in hearings. To do so effectively, however, requires credibility. There is a need for a much more positive approach in the public affairs practice. Ethics, integrity, and the public interest must be emphasized in deed as well as in word.

In public affairs activity on a national level more and more activity involves requests for information or hearings by such government groups as the Federal Trade Commission, the Food and Drug Administration, the Federal Communications Commission, the Internal Revenue Service, and the Securities and Exchange Commission.

Many large businesses daily exchange information and viewpoints with certain of the agencies and commissions. Some businesses have separate departments whose only function is dealing with a particular regulatory agency on a day-to-day basis as well as in connection with important hearings. The ability of people in those departments to develop rapport and deal effectively with agency and commission staffs, as well as with the commissioners, is of prime importance. It cannot be emphasized too much that their credibility must be good. They must be able to see and understand the government staff viewpoints as well as those of their own organization. What applies on a national level also applies on a state level, although for most organizations less activity is required.

Public affairs people must not only be knowledgeable of government organization and able to deal effectively with people in government but they must also be cognizant of and able to deal effectively with other political organizations and the people who influence political and governmental decisions. These include opinion leaders (discussed in Chapter 6) as well as the leaders of county, state, and national political party organizations, for those people should also be informed about matters of interest to the organization. In turn the organization should know their attitudes.

To carry out their work effectively, it is axiomatic that those in public affairs management must be knowledgeable about all parts of their own organization in order to be cognizant of what political proposals may affect the organization and to know what knowledge is available in the organization and where to obtain it.

There may be no single area of public relations activity in which well-thought-out specific objectives and plans are more important than in public affairs, and no area has greater need for constant review of plans and objectives than in public affairs.

COMMUNITY RELATIONS

Community relations is a close partner of public affairs. Good community relations start with good performance with regard to the organization's products and services. Good service and products are fundamental. If they are not what they should be, other community relations activities will not help much in maintaining good relationships.

What is the purpose of community relations activity? The community relations function's purpose is to keep on good terms with the community as a whole and with the key individuals in the community. It includes being a good corporate citizen.

The Importance of Community Relations

Good community relations is important and pays off in dollars and cents. An example concerns a long and violent strike against a small telephone company in the Midwest. Supervisory employees attempting to maintain service were attacked, and their homes were damaged. Numerous telephone cables were cut, disrupting service. A bomb was exploded at one of the central office buildings. Local police would take little action. In spite of the extensive violence, a considerable part of the local citizenry sided with the strikers. Over the years the company had been aloof and had done nothing to establish good community relations. It was a costly oversight.

Good community relations are important to success in recruiting employees, in maintaining the morale of the organization's employees, and in obtaining cooperation of the city government, including the police department. Good community relations consists of recognizing and fulfilling the organization's responsibilities in and to the communities in which it operates.

Community Relations and the Organization's Employees

To the organization its own employees should be among the most important people in the community. How well the employees think of their employer and their esprit de corps can have a great influence on the quality of community relations. This is doubly true because good esprit de corps can also lead to good performance, which is vital to good community relations. Impersonality in relations with employees can be a negative factor in community relations. Management policy and the employees' supervisors will be key factors in overcoming impersonality. Over a period of time such things as family nights and work group events can also help to reduce impersonality.

Knowing the Community and Vice Versa

Community relations is a two-way matter. It is important for the people of the community to know the organization, just as it is important for the people of the organization to know the community. Steps should be taken as a part of the public relations program to make this possible. Aside from publicity and advertising, open houses, plant and office visits for the general public, for key groups and for key individuals and opinion leaders are excellent ways to accomplish this. Perhaps the most effective way is for management people to become really interested in the community and thus get to know its people.

Visits by junior high school, high school, and when appropriate, college students can pay big dividends if properly handled. These people may include future employees. They will include the educators, the elected officials, and the voters of tomorrow.

Working Through Individuals and Small Groups

Work in community relations is most effectively done through individuals or small groups of people in person-to-person relationships. It must always take into consideration the community's social system. Every community has people in social, educational, professional, and special interest groups with personal relationships important to communications in the community. The discussion of opinion leaders in Chapter 6 provides clues for identifying such people. Paying close attention to the people mentioned in the loca newspapers will sometimes help to reveal the social system. If you know who these people are, you will probably know where to go for informatior and help when necessary. The social system always has thought leaders whc pass judgment on community projects, usually informally. These are the decision makers.

As brought out in Chapter 6, by social system and thought leaders we are not necessarily referring to the economic elite or to people with important titles in the usual run of business, civic, and political organizations. Special interest groups and minority groups, for example, are frequently important parts of the social system and include important thought leaders.

Keeping a Notebook of Facts

In community relations work it is helpful to have all the important facts about the community in an up-to-date notebook or in a file of five-by-three inch cards. This file should include the names of all the political leaders and other key individuals, along with information about their interests and their business, political, and social connections. It should include information on the various organizations in the community including those such as civic, business, agricultural, conservation, fraternal, racial, religious, labor, minority, and others, along with their purpose, membership size, and their leaders. This file or notebook should also include information on the demographic characteristics of the community—such things as the national origins and religions of the predominant groups and the various special events and festivals they may sponsor or participate in regularly.

Helpful information includes key dates in the community history, predominant businesses, industries, and crops, the names of all the newspapers and magazines and radio and television stations in the community, along with the names and titles of their key people.

An important item for the notebook is a recap of social problems in the community, such as minority group problems. It should include a record of the specific objectives for the organization's community relations activity, the problems they were designed to overcome, the plans used to reach them, and the results.

A chronology of all of the organization's activities in the community, regularly kept up-to-date, is a key item.

Community relations includes such things as taking part in community affairs—for example, in connection with organized community money drives such as the community chest. It includes helping to solve the minority relations problems. One of the primary functions of community relations is to recognize and carry out the company's social responsibilities in the community.

WHAT IS SOCIAL RESPONSIBILITY?

It is important to be sure we understand what is meant by social responsibility. Although urban problems, minority relations, and air and water pollution may sometimes be in the limelight, we are not referring only to them but rather to the whole broad spectrum of social responsibility.

Let us take an example of the lack of social responsibility. Driving down the road through Monument Valley in Arizona a few years ago, one could observe trucks unloading telephone poles for a new telephone line along the side of the road. Monument Valley is one of the most scenic parts of the country. The view of the scenery for the visitors and their pictures should not be cluttered by an aerial telephone line. But it was, even in this day and age of underground construction know-how.

Two examples of well-intentioned but misdirected activity may be of interest. A business's local community relations committee in a large city decided to carry out activity in favor of busing school students. Since a majority of the citizenry of the city did not favor busing, this resulted in a controversy that had a negative affect on community relations. In another instance a community relations committee of a utility became involved in the transportation, at company expense, of senior citizens for such things as medical appointments. This resulted in complaints concerning the expenditures of money by the utility for such a purpose.

A key aspect of social responsibility includes avoiding actions that may have undesirable effects on the community. In *The Age of Discontinuity* Peter Drucker points out that it is the job of the organization to look ahead and to think through which of its impacts are likely to become or cause social problems. And it is the duty of the organization to try to prevent those undesirable side results.[5] This is a public relations function. Drucker says that it is in the self-interest of the organization. Failure leads only to more regulations, punitive laws, and outside interference.

What are some of the impacts an organization can have on a community that may become social problems? An example that is easy to visualize is releasing undesirable pollutants into the air. Another is discharging undesirable waste into rivers, bays, or the ocean—or into a municipal sewage system not equipped to handle it.

[5] New York: Harper and Row, 1969.

The whole area of solid waste production is one that should be explored. The amount of solid waste produced increased from about 2.5 pounds per day per person in 1920 to some 6.5 to 8 pounds per day in 1970, according to a 1974 study by the Commonwealth Club of California.[6] The character of the waste had also changed to include a much larger fraction of non-biodegradable materials. Two of the causes are (1) utilization of the package as a marketing tool in lieu of its traditional function in storage and shipping, and (2) the growth of a convenience-oriented, throwaway society and the onetime use of vast quantities of merchandise.

The results of solid waste include degradation of the physical environment and a physical blight of the land. Of great importance is the depletion of finite natural resources, including mineral and fossil fuel. Solid waste results in the reduction of the quality of life through expanding consumption of open space and causes the misallocation of limited economic resources.

One of the most undesirable impacts on society is caused by the underuse of misuse of human resources. The discharge or layoff of workers is an example. Although sometimes discharges or layoffs are necessary, care should be taken to avoid creating social problems as much as possible. Pay and promotion not based on performance and ability are also examples of the misuse of human resources.

Other impacts on society with undesirable side effects include the failure to take into consideration traffic or the need for parking facilities, which causes inconvenience and hazards to the area involved. Things that may cause a blight or scar on the land, such as undesirable grading, dumping, unsightly power or telephone lines, strip mining, destruction of a watershed, and stripping the land of its trees, all have undesirable side effects. Undesirable noise, eyesore buildings, and the unnecessary use, misallocation, or destruction of natural resources are other examples.

We are realizing that the world's resources of space, finite material, and beauty are limited. We can no longer move out to a fresh landscape to escape the impacts of organizations and people that become problems. Public relations management should keep that realization constantly in mind.

DOING THE ORGANIZATION'S PART

In the area of industry and commerce, people today expect more from business than simply economic performance. They expect business to use its power to help solve broader problems when it can. It is no longer enough merely to "lend an executive" to assist in the local community chest drive.

---

[6] *Incentives or Penalties for Solid Waste Producers,* San Francisco.

Business has a large stake in the society in which it operates. It can flourish only when it operates in a healthy, orderly society. It has a responsibility to its shareholders to make profit, but it also has a responsibility as a corporate citizen with special abilities, resources, and power. Good community relations go beyond the open houses; they include helping concrete things to happen in important areas.

What are some of the things business can do in taking a more active role in the community?

1. It can work for better government.
2. It can help to improve education, not merely by providing scholarships and contributions for colleges and universities. The entire field of education should have specific objectives and be accountable for specific results. Business can help educators by showing the benefits of more specific objectives and how they may be set.
3. It can set an example of good citizenship.
4. It can provide the leadership in raising moral standards.
5. It can take a leadership role in helping to combat crime.
6. It can do more in leading the way toward alleviating social problems.
7. It can help, in addition to contributions, in connection with desirable community cultural events.
8. It can help to train and employ the disadvantaged so that they may become self-sufficient members of the community.

There is much debate and controversy as to what responsibilities a business has in field of social responsibility. How far should it go? It would be unwise to suggest that the management or owners of a business should neglect the business to accomplish social goals. In addition sometimes communities do not want a business to emphasize social matters for fear of the company's becoming overly paternalistic or dominant.

Business must be careful not to overextend itself or to dominate, but it has a stake in the society in which in operates. It is of interest to take another look at the eight community activities, just discussed, in which a business might take a more active role.

1. Business certainly has as much to gain from better government as any other institution or group of people.
2. Business benefits greatly through better output from education and the schools. Its employees and its executives (as well as its suppliers, stockholders, customers, regulators, etc.) are products of the education system.

3. Business is apt to be the greatest loser as a result of poor citizenship on the part of the people of a community.
4. Business has the most to lose from poor moral standards.
5. The aggregate harm to business and industry as a result of crime is as great or greater than any other institution.
6. Business and industry lose more because of social problems—not only through higher taxes but also because of resultant crime and other societal ills.
7. By helping with desirable cultural events, business can help to bind the community together, improve its communication, and strengthen the environment in which it operates.
8. Helping to train and employ the disadvantaged reduces costs of government (a considerable part of which is borne by business), makes the disadvantaged producing members of society, and can add able and loyal employees.

An organization's community relations may also include taking part in such worthy community projects as centennial celebrations, civic or community preparations for important events, participation on committees to study such things as transportation, streets, streetlighting, maintaining law and order, and fire prevention, and providing fireworks on an important holiday. As a citizen of the community, every organization has to participate in such affairs or otherwise suffer poor public relations—or perhaps pay more taxes to have the government try to do the job.

On the other hand, the amount of money that the organization can budget for such purposes is limited. If management is not careful, it can find itself spending an inordinate amount of money. It is necessary that specific community relations objectives be spelled out and that those charged with community relations strictly adhere to those objectives. In that way the money will be used prudently and effectively. Having specific objectives and guidelines that are uniform throughout the organization so that a united front can be presented is crucially important to maintaining a good public relations climate.

CONTRIBUTIONS

Community relations and contributions are closely related. Contributions is another area in which everyone concerned must be fully aware of the specific objectives and to what groups and under what conditions contributions will be made. Prudent management is vital. Requests for contributions should always be received in writing. Agreement or refusal to contribute should also be in writing.

The kind of information needed in order to consider a request for a contribution from an institution includes determining how much real need there is for the institution and how important to the community are the institution's functions. It should also be determined what other institutions, if any, provide similar services. Where does the institution get its funds? What are its administrative expenses? What other businesses give to the institution? How much do they give? What do they think of the institution? Informal organizations of businesses and foundations such as Contributions Round Tables exist in most larger cities to exchange information concerning requests for contributions. Other considerations include what is given to similar institutions elsewhere and the use or benefits the organization's own people receive from the institution requesting a contribution.

There will always be more requests for contributions than can be prudently met. Many are worthy, but some are self-serving groups with no valid claim to a charitable contribution. Sometimes, however, these groups are extremely tenacious, demanding, and almost threatening. They refuse to take "no" for an answer. Although requests for contributions should normally be answered, when tenacious groups become demanding, the only way out is to not reply to their requests.

A good rule is to be sure that all contributions go to institutions in the community or communities in which the donor organization operates. Contributions are usually not made to tax-supported causes or institutions. The organization is already contributing heavily to them through the taxes it pays. On the other hand, contributions designated for specific purposes or for specific studies are made to tax-supported colleges and universities. Contributions should not be made to any cause that investigation indicates is contrary to the best interest of the donor organization or to the communities in which it operates.

Normally it is wise to make capital contributions to institutions such as hospitals for buildings or equipment but not for operating funds. Operating revenues of such institutions should cover operating expenses, especially when buildings and equipment have been obtained through contributions.

It is wise for publicly owned businesses not to contribute to religious organizations since both stockholders and employees are probably of many different faiths, sects, and creeds. It would not be in the public interest for the organization to favor one religious group with contributions but not all the others.

Great care should be taken in making political contributions to be sure that the organization abides by all the current state and national laws and regulations, and that the contributions are in the public interest. However, it should be recognized that it is in the public interest and the best interest of the organization lawfully to support or oppose political measures affecting the management's or the community's interests. Some public groups attack businesses that lawfully support or oppose political measures. Such groups should be actively opposed.

To safeguard the organization's budget for contributions, formal recommendations, including reasons for each separate contribution, a history of past contributions to the receiving institution, and a summary of other pertinent information should always be provided. Recommendations should be approved and endorsed by the person knowledgeable about and with responsibility for contributions for the organization as a whole. He should then obtain department head approval for each contribution.

Because contributions are in reality made by the owners of the business, all contributions and commitments for contributions of any size should be specifically approved by the board of directors. The contributions budget as a whole, showing the amounts given to specific kinds of institutions should also be approved by the board. In addition board approval should be received before any contributions concerning political measures are made. Explicit requirement for board approval may help to prevent bribery by "contribution," much publicized in the last few years.

FINANCIAL PUBLIC RELATIONS

Another special kind of public relations is financial public relations. Financial public relations is specialized, and its management requires a knowledge of the rules laid down by the Securities and Exchange Commission (SEC). One of the purposes of this special type of public relations is to develop good financial public relations both for the present and for the future. The future is especially important; those in the financial world have long memories. Another important purpose includes the provision of public information required by laws and regulations.

Financial public relations people usually work with legal firms who specialize in SEC work and with investment bankers, as well as with their own managements. Because of the importance to the organization of having an investment banker who recognizes the need for good public relations, public relations management should be involved in the choice of the banker.

Financial public relations people should be well acquainted both with what may be said and what should not be said in connection with the organization's finances and financial arrangements. Regulations, laid down primarily by the SEC, change frequently. Therefore, it would serve no purpose to list them here. Suffice it to say, great care is necessary in the areas of ethics, integrity, and the public interest. It is particularly important not to imply anything in statements that may concern finances or financing if those implications cannot be backed up completely.

Whenever the chief executive or other officers of an organization plan to make public talks that involve finance, financial public relations people should see that are well prepared with all the necessary information and data.

Some years ago the president of a large organization met with security analysts in Dallas, Texas. After his talk he was asked about plans for expansion in the Dallas-Fort Worth area. These expansion plans were substantial and would require large expenditures of capital. Unfortunately, public relations management had not properly prepared the president, and he was not acquainted with the expansion plans in the area. He was unable to answer any of the questions of a local nature that he was asked and naturally left an undesirable impression as a result of his appearance.

One of the means sometimes used to judge a chief executive is to review annual reports for the past few years to learn what problems or opportunities were discussed. A look at the record will indicate how effectively the organization has acted on the opportunities foreseen or the problems enumerated in the reports. If after a suitable time nothing has been accomplished toward reaching the opportunities or overcoming the problems, it is apt to reflect badly on the management.

Getting out the annual report and the quarterly statements are important duties of financial public relations management, as are any other public statements concerning finances and financial arrangements.

Before concluding this discussion of financial public relations, two problems concerning boards of directors should be brought out. Matters related to boards of directors are important to public relations in general and are not specifically the concern of financial public relations people. However, matters regarding them are usually most visible at the time of annual meetings of stockholders, which do concern financial public relations. Also, matters regarding boards are frequently administered by the financial department of business organizations.

Public relations problems can arise because most boards have no real function. They are often viewed by management as merely legal necessities that act primarily to rubber-stamp decisions previously arrived at by management. One problem concerns rubber-stamp action by boards that may later be challenged by stockholders or others as not being in the best interest of the organization or the stockholders.

Boards should be well informed about the business and should review management's proposals and decisions. They should be the final watchdogs of the organization. Recent court decisions have held boards and board members accountable for their actions or lack of actions. Such court actions can result in quite undesirable public relations problems.

With top management concurrence, public relations management can help to ensure that boards are informed about the business so that they can better meet their responsibilities. Planned programs developed by public relations managements have been used in some businesses for this purpose. In addition the public relations manager can help to make certain that top management is aware of the potential problems and liabilities related to the action or lack of action on the part of boards and board members.

Another problem concerns continuing efforts to force the addition of representatives of special interests and various minority groups to some boards of directors through proxy solicitation and in discussion during annual meetings. The inclusion of representatives of special interests or of special groups would defeat the proper purpose of the boards, which should be one of management rather than representation of special viewpoints. The requirement for membership on boards of directors should be knowledge and the ability needed in managing the business. It should include the ability to add knowledgeable outside viewpoints free from organizational bias and internal politics. The addition of board members who represent particular groups or viewpoints would lead to diversion of valuable time and resources from the management of the business to unproductive controversy not in the best interest of the business or society. Perhaps the best answer to the problem is to ensure that Boards function effectively as an important part of management.

SUMMARY

Three specialized kinds of public relations activity—public affairs, community relations, and contributions—are all closely related.

Public affairs is concerned with political and governmental relations and allied matters. However, it should be considered an integral part of the overall public relations function. Because of the "under the table" activity of lobbyists in the past, lobbying has a poor reputation for skullduggery and manipulation. In spite of this public affairs is more important today than ever before. It can accomplish more while operating in the public interest than the old-time lobbyist could. It is in the public interest to be sure that people in government know an organization's viewpoint. Business has a serious need to present its case. It would not be possible for government to formulate logical plans, laws, and regulations without the extensive information that various businesses and other organizations can supply. In addition it is imperative that organizations be aware of the possible future actions, laws, and regulations of government and of what is said in hearings concerning them.

Good community relations pays off in dollars and cents. It is important to success in recruiting employees, in maintaining their morale, and in obtaining cooperation of the city government. It is important in being a good "corporate citizen." Community relations is a two-way matter. It is desirable for people of the community to know the organization and for the people of the organization to know the community. In community relations work is most effectively done through individuals and small groups in person-to-person relationships—through community leaders.

The organization should look ahead and think through which of its impacts are likely to become or lead to social problems. It is in the interest of the organization to try to prevent those undesirable side results. Failure leads only to more regulation, punitive laws, and outside interference.

People expect more of business than economic performance solely. Business has a large stake in the society in which it operates. It can flourish only when it operates in a healthy, orderly society. It has a responsibility to its owners to make a profit, but it also has a responsibility as a corporate citizen with special abilities, resources, and power.

Contributions should go to the community or communities in which the donor organization operates, but not normally to tax-supported institutions. Contributions should not be made to any cause that investigation indicates is contrary to the best interests of the donor. Capital contributions for buildings and equipment, but not for operating funds, should be made to institutions such as hospitals. It is unwise for publicly owned businesses to make contributions to religious organizations. Great care should be taken that political contributions always conform to the law and that they are in the public interest. The contributions budget and all contributions of any size should be approved by the board of directors. *All* political contributions should have its approval.

The management of financial public relations, the fourth type of specialized public relations, requires a knowledge of the rules laid down by the Securities and Exchange Commission. Its purpose includes developing and maintaining good financial relations both for the present and for the future. It also provides public information required by laws and regulations. People in financial public relations normally work with legal firms who specialize in SEC work and with investment bankers, as well as their own managements.

Financial public relations people should be responsible for the annual report and the quarterly statements. One of the means used to judge a chief executive is to review annual reports for past years to learn what problems and opportunities were discussed. A look at the record will indicate how effectively the organization has acted on the opportunities foreseen and the problems enumerated.

TEN

DEVELOPING AND
IMPLEMENTING
PUBLIC RELATIONS
(OR EXTERNAL RELATIONS)
Plans

One of the most common problems in the management of the public relations function is the failure to have real plans of action based on specific objectives. There is a tendency in many organizations for public relations management to carry out requests for publicity that may come from other departments, from the media, or from government commissions and to fail to recognize or neglect important problems. The tendency is to go from day-to-day, carrying out demand work, without consideration of specific objectives or regard for the relative importance of various functions. At the end of the year, the organization finds itself no better off from the standpoint of public relations, than it was at the beginning of the year as a result of its failure to manage the public relations function effectively.

Certainly there will be demand work that must be done, but good planning will greatly reduce the amount. Demand work must not prevent the achievement of specific objectives.

BENEFITS OF SPECIFIC PLANS

Specific plans help to ensure that efforts are directed toward reaching objectives. They provide a written reference that lets each part of the organization and each person involved know exactly what is to be done, who is responsible for doing it, and when it is to be done. Otherwise, many of those involved may not know exactly what is expected of them. Too frequently the manager keeps the plans in his head, and those lower on the management scale are frustrated because they do not know or are not sure of the plans.

Good planning can be of primary importance in developing the esprit de corps that is essential to any organization's real effectiveness. *Esprit de corps, results from harmony, unity, and a desire for organizational achievement, together with good leadership in working toward specific organizational objectives.*

Since good planning focuses on specific objectives and specific plans for reaching them, both effectively communicated, it fosters unity of purpose. As objectives are reached, good planning may result in unity of accomplishment and the mutual appreciation that is a requirement of harmony. When many people in all levels of an organization have a part in setting objectives and in developing plans to reach them, agreement, harmony, and a desire for organizational achievement are also promoted.

Good Planning Helps to Coordinate and Integrate

A good description of problems or opportunities, written specific objectives, and well-conceived plans for carrying them out are especially important because they let everyone know where the organization is going and why. Everyone can pull in the same direction and at the proper time—with a realization of just exactly what they are trying to accomplish. Good plans can help to make sure that all the various public relations efforts can be coordinated and integrated. Coordination and integration require careful direction in carrying out the plans. This is discussed later.

Sometimes people in public relations work write news stories about this or that all year long and measure their results by the number of column inches of newspaper clippings they obtain, all without any real objectives for their writing. There may be little or no attempt to coordinate and integrate efforts with what is being done in other public relations activity or by other departments. Those column inches of news clippings may have very little influence on the organization's public relations. In the office next to the news writer, there may be a person with responsibility for audiovisual public relations work whose only objective is to count the number of talks and film showings made. He may have no idea as to how they should fit into the total scheme of things—no real objectives or plans. There may be little thought given to the need for coordinating and integrating efforts with the rest of the public relations function. The talks and film showings may have little effect on people's attitudes toward the organization. The audiovisual person is not likely to have much of an idea of what the news writer is doing, and vice versa. No one may be coordinating and integrating their efforts. Clearly defined objectives and specific plans can make it easier to coordinate and integrate the efforts of all the people in the organization.

Without a specific plan the results can be somewhat like those of the proverbial 20-mule teams of early California days, but with each mule pulling at a different time and in a different direction. Under such conditions, the wagon does not move. It may go to pieces. All the mules must pull at the same time and in the same direction. We should make sure that every item in the plan is being or has been carried out at the proper time. To complete the analogy of the 20-mule team, there can only be one driver for the mule team, one head responsible for the overall effort in the entire organization.

Having specific plans makes easier the analysis and evaluation of results that is essential to effective management. Feedback of the results to those involved may also help promote unity, harmony, and "esprit de corps."

TYING PUBLIC RELATIONS PLANS TO THE ORGANIZATION'S PLANS

One of the first considerations in developing plans for the public relations function is to be fully aware of and to take into consideration the objectives and plans for the organization as a whole. Public relation's objectives and plans should relate specifically to those of the entire organization, as was discussed in Chapter 5. It is desirable to reemphasize it here, both as to objectives and the plans for carrying them out.

Sometimes an organization may not have agreed on objectives and plans. Public relations management may be able to assist in giving impetus to their development. An example of this involved one of the large telephone companies. Consideration was being given to charging for the calls to "Information" that had been provided without extra charge for many years. It was known that imposition of the charge would be unpopular unless a plan could be developed that was logical and equitable. Timing and the relation of the imposition of the charge to other events was also an important consideration. Public relations management was active in the interdepartmental discussion of various ideas in order to come up with a plan acceptable to both the company and its customers. Word of a similar proposal by other telephone companies to make such a charge reached the press and resulted in inquiries that had to be answered. Because the timing of the proposed charge was poor, public relations management obtained agreement to defer the charge in that company.

BARRIERS TO IMPLEMENTING THE PUBLIC RELATIONS PLANS

The best of plans and suggestions have no value if the planner is unable to get approval for them. Many excellent plans fail to get acceptance because those responsible for making them first fail to recognize the barriers to getting acceptance. Second, they fail to develop plans for overcoming those barriers.

Suppose you were in the position of the department head, vice president, or president who is asked to approve a plan. What would you ask of those submitting it? As a prudent manager, you would undoubtedly want to know specifically what problem the plan was supposed to overcome. You would also want to know the problem causes and then specific objectives of the plan. In terms of hard reality what would be the purpose of carrying out the plan? You could also usefully ask:

- Why are the objectives important to the organization?
- What will be the specific long- and short-range benefits in carrying out the plan?
- How much will it cost?
- What department will pay the bill?
- Why do the benefits warrant the cost?
- Will the plan really do effectively the job that it is intended to do?
- What will happen if it is not carried out?
- What departments will be involved?
- How will the plan affect their staffs and their need for people?
- How will it affect the other jobs that they are charged with carrying out?
- Do the other groups and departments involved agree with the plan? Why?
- If some oppose the plan, why?
- How long will it take to carry out the plan?
- What are the alternatives to carrying out the plan?
- Have other plans with the same objectives been tried before?
- What were their results?

One can readily see from this list of possible questions that plans should be prepared from their very inception with the idea of overcoming barriers to their acceptance and implementation. Effectively answering any questions that may arise is one of the key ways of overcoming barriers.

One of the first rules in developing a plan is to consider its acceptance by higher management while it is being prepared and when it is complete, to be certain that it is the kind of plan higher management is likely to approve. Can one answer satisfactorily questions such as those just posed? Careful and complete documentation of the problem, the problem causes, the choice of specific objectives, and the kind of plan proposed is essential.

Barriers to approval are frequently caused by what people perceive as threats to their views and desires. They may also arise because plans do not conform with traditions. Plans should be presented as much as possible in terms of what those in higher management consider to be in their own best interests. For example, you may find that a certain person is primarily interested in saving money. In such a case the presentation of your plan might put a little more emphasis on the money savings benefits. Or you may find the person you are dealing with spent a good deal of his career in personnel type work. The presentation of your plan could give a little extra emphasis to the personnel aspects.

As brought out in our discussion of communication, nonevaluative listening may be helpful in getting your ideas across. Slow down on trying to sell your ideas and listen without argument or passing judgment. Listen in order to understand better how the problem looks to the other person and why the barriers in his mind to your plan make sense to him. No longer needing to confront your arguments, he may relax. Then you both may be more willing to listen to each other. In addition you will probably find that you have a much better concept of the objectives which may make it easier for you to reach them. When you listen, you and the ideas you are presenting may no longer seem to be a threat to the other person's views and desires. You may find ways and places to compromise, removing his objections.

You may find what aspect of the cost bothers the other person. Or you may be able to broaden the objectives and plans to include his desires. You may find out what is not clear about the purpose of the plan. You may understand why the other person wonders whether the benefits warrant the cost. You may be better able to explain how the plan will affect other departments' staffs in a way that overcomes their objections.

Barriers may be set up by other departments that do not understand public relations and believe public relations problems can be cured by "good publicity." These barriers should also be recognized in the planning stage. Clearance and active support should be obtained from each of the departments involved. Good answers to questions from the standpoint of the interests of the other departments is vital. Overcoming barriers to acceptance and approval of plans is of vital importance in managing the public relations function. Top management clearance of important plans and the expenditure of money is essential, but its involvement is also the first requirement in successfully and effectively carrying out your plans.

DEVELOPING THE PLAN

Description and Analysis of the Opportunity or Problem

In the development and implementation of plans, one should try to achieve the best possible public relations for the organization with the most prudent expenditure of money. If plans are for a business organization, the planners should also keep in mind that profit must always be the first requirement of every business. Profit finances not only the business itself and its survival; the composite profit of all businesses also finances all the nonbusiness activities of the world.

In the preparation of specific plans to meet opportunities or problems, one should start out with a description, analysis, and definition of the problem to be solved or the opportunity to be met, as well as primary evidence of the problem. Research findings, observations, and perception of symptoms and their underlying causes should be studied. Salient observations of the overall situation should be included.

In defining problems a great deal of care should be taken not to confuse symptoms with the real problems. Public relations managers and workers sometimes make plans and recommendations with insufficient real knowledge of a situation. The plans may then turn out to be unrealistic and unworkable, which does not enhance their makers' credibility and standing with people in other parts of the organization. To understand a problem and the overall situation one needs to get away from his or her desk and preconceived viewpoints to observe firsthand.

As an example of making recommendations without sufficient knowledge, consider the public relations manager for a telephone company engaged in making a major change in the method of placing certain kinds of long distance calls. The change had been scheduled by the technical people for a Saturday midnight. The time and date had been chosen so that the change would take place when the volume of calls was lowest. The company would be less likely to run into technical problems, and the public would be least inconvenienced. At the suggestion of the company's advertising agency, the public relations manager pushed hard for another date and time relating to catchy advertising wording proposed by the agency. Had he gone out to discuss the matter with knowledgeable people in other parts of the organization, he would have been better informed and would not have made the recommendation he did. Credibility of the public relations function would not have been jeopardized. This example illustrates the importance of perception and complete information. The public relations manager failed to inform himself fully and therefore could not be aware of the overall situation. Understanding a situation cannot be replaced by opinion and media research findings. Rather, research findings enhance perception.

A knowledge of the situation as a whole is vital. Success in the management of the public relations function can be achieved only with a reasonable knowledge of the work, viewpoints, and problems of the other departments and the interrelationships between all parts of the organization.

SETTING OBJECTIVES AND PLANS FOR MEASURING RESULTS

After the problems or opportunities have been defined and analyzed, tentative specific objectives for meeting them should be clearly stated, including a timetable for reaching milestones so that progress may be determined, and so that one may finally arrive at the objectives. Since setting objectives was discussed in detail in Chapter 5, we will not cover it in detail here. Objectives are the conclusions to be reached. The conclusions must always be worked out and decided on before any activities are planned because all the activities must work toward the conclusions.

Plans for measuring results should be prepared at the time tentative objectives are set. It is important to be sure one will be able to measure results in working toward an objective. Otherwise, the objective should be changed. It also is important to keep in mind what kind of objective may be set for a particular activity. For instance, only communicative objectives should be set for communicative functions. This is true whether one is attempting to change attitudes or to sell products. We would not be able to measure results of activity designed to reach generalized objectives such as "to be a good place to work." No criteria have been set as to what a good place to work might be. Therefore, one could not tell whether he had reached such an objective. If criteria are set, then they become the bases of the objectives to be used. Suppose Company X sets a communicative objective to increase the percentage of people having a favorable attitude about the company relative to water pollution. However, if Company X continues to empty plant waste into the river, the communicative activity will not change attitudes for long. Communicative activity can be expected to reach only communicative objectives involving such things as interest, comprehension, and believability.

To borrow an easily understood example from marketing, suppose a business decides to advertise to get people to buy product X. The business may be tempted to have as an objective increasing retail sales by, say, 10 percent. However, advertising is only one of the many elements in the marketing mix that affects sales. The quality of the product, the packaging, the effectiveness of the sales force in getting good displays, the availability of the product in stores, special promotions such as contests that get people to buy, competitive or uncompetitive pricing, and so on, all determine what will be sold. However, if the company's salesmen do not call on the stores' buyers and the stores do not stock the product, it will make no difference what kind of advertising is used. None of the product will be sold.

Advertising is a communicative medium. As such, it must have communicative objectives rather than sales objectives. Measured against communicative objectives, the advertising for product X in the example may have been very effective despite the fact that the salesmen were derelict and no product X was sold. The same principle holds true of communicative objectives for public relations. Performance is the chief other element in the public relations mix. If performance is not good, communications will not make public relations good.

Suppose a railroad must increase passenger fares on its commuter trains. It may set as a communicative objective that by X date Y percent of the commuters will be informed about the need to increase fares and the reasons why. But one should not expect to have as an objective that Z percent of the people will have a favorable attitude toward the fare increase unless it can be shown that the increase is in the self-interest of the commuters.

To measure the communicative ability of advertising or publicity one should check the effectiveness of the message, perhaps using comprehension and readership studies. (This was discussed in Chapter 6 on research.) Measurement of any kind of objective is important. Knowing the results of activity is of primary importance to management by objectives. The best planning is of little value unless management knows how well objectives are being met, which can be learned only by having visible, reliable measurements that are easily understood.

THE PUBLIC RELATIONS PLAN OR PROGRAM

A specific plan or program may now be prepared. It should list in chronological order specifically what things are to be done and specifically who is responsible for each of them. It should be as specific as possible as to the date each item will be started and completed. Plans should make clear who is responsible for seeing that each item is executed in the proper sequence and at the proper time.

In preparing plans consideration should be given to the relative importance of projects, and greater attention should be given to the more important ones. The relative importance of projects may sometimes be determined by opinion research. Otherwise, determination may depend on problem analysis and good perception.

Only a certain total amount of time, money, energy, and media usage is available for all the various public relations activities combined. Therefore, be careful to include in each plan all those things that are necessary for proper effectiveness but no more. The prudent use of resources is synonymous with prudent management.

UNDESIRABLE SIDE EFFECTS—ALTERNATIVE PLANS

The plan or program should be reviewed for undesirable side effects, and alternative plans should be considered. Care should be taken to minimize the risk of causing less favorable attitudes of one group while improving the attitudes of another. Taking into consideration all possibilities, the most suitable plan may then be chosen.

Examining alternative plans is like considering different routes for getting to a distant city. There may be several different possible routes one can take, taking into consideration the distance over each route, the kind and condition of the road, the amount of traffic, and possible weather conditions. Trains, planes, or even boats may be alternatives to driving.

In choosing a plan of action to carry out an organization's objectives, the various alternatives should be considered before any plan is settled on. *In the discussion all viewpoints, including viewpoints as to what the problem really is, should be explored. Every group that will have a hand in implementing the plan should be included.*

Beware of unanimity of opinion. It may mean that not enough thought has been expended by some of those involved or that some are not expressing themselves for "political" reasons. Watch out for the "party line" and organizational doctrinaire. They can lead to dangerous conformity. *It is management's job to bring out opposing viewpoints and to be sure all viewpoints and problems are fully exposed.* Be careful that problem analysis and the choice of alternatives are not based on the results someone thinks top management wants.

COORDINATING COMMITTEES

Important plans may frequently be coordinated and integrated by committees. Such committees may represent various parts of the organization and the various competences necessary to carry out the tasks. The committee meetings may ensure that the various parts of the organization are able to bring problems and opportunities they encounter, as well as their needs and viewpoints, to the attention of all departments for discussion in light of the interests of all those involved. Thus two-way (or multiple-way) communication may be made quick, easy, and reasonably complete.

Coordinating committees may also ensure that each part of the organization is proceeding properly and on schedule with its part of the overall plan. Meetings of coordinating committees are an excellent way to uncover pitfalls preventing the performance of tasks and to learn of matters that may call for help from various parts of the organization to solve.

A secretary may be appointed to record the completion of tasks as provided in the plan and to prepare minutes of committee meetings. The minutes, including lists of tasks completed and the status of those not completed, should be distributed to all those responsible for any parts of the plan. Minutes may also be used to keep higher management advised of progress and of the need for follow-up and supervisory action.

PLAN FORMAT

An excellent format, as shown in Figure 29, has been found to help in organizing plans effectively. Included are headings under which are listed (1) all the tasks in the plan chronologically, (2) the person responsible for the task being performed properly and on time, (3) the person responsible for ensuring that matters relative to the activity are properly coordinated both within the department and interdepartmentally, (4) the time when work on the task is to commence, (5) the date before which the task is to be completed, and (6) the date when the task is actually completed.

For better organization and easy understanding, such a plan may be divided into sections for each of the various departments or functional activities. Each department or function then lists chronologically the items for which it is responsible. Sometimes responsibility for an item may be shared by more than one department or person. When such is the case, the person with primary responsibility may be listed first with others following. If desired, the departments responsible may be shown as well as or in lieu of the names of individuals.

Figure 29 shows five possible parts of a plan for conducting an opinion research project. Jones, the coordinator of the project, also has responsibility for arranging for the research, which he has already completed. As an important part of the plan, he provided the objectives for the research to the field research people at the time he arranged for it on October 18, which was two days ahead of schedule.

Field work plans will be arranged later. Field work should be started by November 10 and completed no later than November 15. Local managers

Suggested Plan Format

Task	Responsibility	Coordinator	Start Date	Complete Date	Completed
1 Arrange for attitude research	Jones	Jones	10/5/76	10/20/76	10/18/76
2 Provide objectives to field research people	Jones	Jones	10/5/76	10/20/76	10/18/76
3 Review research field work plans	Neal	Jones	11/10/76	11/15/76	
4 Notify local managers of interviewing plans	Neal	Jones	12/20/76	12/28/76	
5 Commence research field work	Baker	Jones	1/5/77	1/15/77	

Figure 29

will be notified about the interviews to be conducted in their territory just before the field work starts. This is an important step and is the responsibility of Neal who must complete it by December 28.

Actual field work, the responsibility of Baker, should commence on January 5 and be completed by January 15. The full plan, of course, would show all the steps needed for completing the research project and reporting the results.

Another plan format is the PERT chart, which uses systems of boxes or circles, each one showing a task to be performed. These can be put into chronological sequence with arrows connecting them. Next to the arrow from each box or circle one may delineate who is responsible for the task and the time to be taken in reaching the next box or circle which indicates completion of the task.

Of special importance in PERT charts is the critical path, which is the longest trail that must be completed through the boxes or circles. The amount of time (and money) that must be budgeted to get from the starting point to the finishing point of the chart is vital. When many departments and competences are involved in lengthy multitask projects, PERT charts can become very large and complicated.

PRICING OUT THE PLAN

When the tentative plan and alternatives have been completed showing all the activities to be completed, they may then be priced out. If the tentative costs are not prudent, plans should be reviewed to determine where they may be best reduced. Perhaps objectives will need to be changed.

GETTING CLEARANCE AND SUPPORT

In our earlier discussion of barriers to implementing plans, we said that getting upper management clearance and support for the plan and the expenditure of money is essential. Complete top-level agreement with both the objectives and the plan as a whole is needed. Top-level association with the plan, top-level insistence that everyone in the organization puts forth the proper effort in carrying out the plan, and top-level review of the results are needed.

Much of what is necessary to implement public relations plans must be done by other departments. On matters involving other departments, their clearance should be obtained.

There should be feedback to upper management and to the other departments of action that has taken place and of the results obtained.

THE SEVEN STEPS IN PREPARING PLANS

Let us review the seven steps of preparing a plan, as shown in Figure 30.

First comes the determination and analysis of the underlying problem and a review of the situation as a whole.

Second is the determination of specific written objectives to overcome the problem (or to achieve the opportunity).

Third, the plans for determining effectiveness and measuring results are made.

Fourth comes the chronological detail showing what things are to be done to reach the objectives, who will do them, and when they should be completed. It should also make clear who will be responsible for coordinating the efforts of the various people.

PREPARING PUBLIC RELATIONS PLANS

1.   Determine and analyze the problem.

2.   Set specific written objectives for overcoming the problem.

3.   Plan results measurement.

4.   Chronologically detail

- What things are to be done

- Who will do them

- When they should be completed

- Who is responsible for coordinating the efforts of various people.

5.   Examine for undesirable side effects, - consider alternatives.

6.   Price the plans out.

7.   Get topside and other department clearance and support for the plan chosen and for expenditures,

and

Keep good records.

Figure 30

Fifth, examine the plans for undesirable side effects and consider alternatives.

Sixth, the plans should be priced out. Since cost is an important factor, it should be considered for both the proposed plan and possible alternatives.

Seventh, get clearance and support from top management and from other departments for the plan chosen and for the expenditure of money.

KEEPING RECORDS

It is important—not as a part of the program or plan but as a part of good management—to keep suitable records of the plan, its results, and the details of carrying it out in order to help in analysis if the plan does not turn out to be as effective as it should be or if some part should go wrong. These records should also be kept so that you can draw on past experience in the future.

SIMPLE AND COMPLEX PLANS

An organization will probably need a general overall master public relations plan with regard to the key opportunities and problems of the operation in general. In addition specific subplans to cover specific parts of the master plan will frequently be needed. Suppose community relations is a part of the overall public relations plan. Specific community relations objectives and plans will be prepared. One part of the plan may include helping with the Community Chest, for instance. Therefore, one will prepare objectives and a plan for that. Another part may involve holding open houses. What will be their specific objective? A plan showing all the details necessary to reach the objectives, including planning, arranging, publicizing, and holding the open houses, will be made.

The plan will include such things as disposition of exhibits or displays that may be used at the conclusion of each open house. It will also include determining the results of the open houses and their review, reporting the events and their results up the line to higher management. Every task should be spelled out, including the date, the time it is to be completed, and by whom.

The use of subplans to cover the parts of overall master plans is desirable to prevent the master plans from becoming so massive and complicated that they are hard to follow. By giving separate treatment to the subplans, it is easier to ensure that nothing important is left out. It also helps to delineate the work of various levels of the organization.

The overall plan and the task of managing it should be the responsibility of the top management level involved in the project. Subplans may then be prepared and managed by the appropriate lower level people.

When all the subplans are complete, they may then be assembled and reviewed to be sure that they are properly integrated and coordinated with the master plan. They may be reviewed to be sure that subobjectives all work toward the common main objectives, that proposed costs are prudent and correct, that personnel requirements, workability, completeness, desirability, and so on have been considered. Public relations plans can vary a great deal in their complexity and in the detail with which problems, objectives, and so forth, must be shown.

Some plans may be completed in a few days or a few months. Other plans may require many years to complete, depending on the obstacles to be overcome. For example, suppose the plan requires a change in a state constitution. Also assume that the political parties are unfavorably disposed to the change. A plan to accomplish such a change may take years to carry out.

A plan requiring the change of a state constitution may be questionable. However, the fate of countless businesses is wrapped up in problems equally complex. For example, federal regulation of the railroads is bogged down in an archaic government agency and rules that would require a great deal of effort to change. Nevertheless, it is the duty of the railroad managements to determine specific objectives for the needed changes and to develop specific plans for carrying out those objectives.

CARRYING OUT THE PLANS

We are now ready to carry out the plan or program. We have already discussed how essential top-level management involvement can be to success. Managers give emphasis to what they think their bosses want. Therefore, it is important beginning right at the start that the top level be involved and let people know they are. Top-level insistence on performance is important. Feedback to top-level people of important actions taken and of results achieved should be standard practice.

KEEPING PEOPLE INFORMED

Another important step in carrying out the plan is to make sure that all the people involved have been properly informed about the plan and what is specifically expected of them. Communication is a primary element in all aspects of the organization's life.

There are several more reasons for making certain that all those involved are informed. First, people must know what is expected of them. Explicit steps to ensure that everyone is informed must be taken. An organization cannot rely on osmosis to get the word around, nor can it depend on word of mouth. Experience demonstrates how word-of-mouth messages can be distorted or forgotten.

Second, the very act of informing people thoroughly gives emphasis to the program. People tend to think that the things they know considerably about are the important ones. If they do not know very much about something, or if they do not understand it, they may tend to assign less importance to it.

Third, if some of the people are left out and not informed, they may feel that they are not well accepted, that they have no importance to the organization, and that their work in unimportant. Since this is one of the most negative experiences a person can have, he may be less motivated and performance-minded. Loyalty will be undermined. It is important for everyone at all connected with the plan, or having any part in carrying it out, to know about it and understand it.

To inform people in the public relations, marketing, and sales departments about a matter, do not have the public relations manager sign the letter to people in all the departments. Suggest that heads of the other departments write their people. Many times letters on important subjects that are meant to affect several departments of an organization may be signed by the head of only one department, with copies for other departments. Communications handled in such a manner cannot be expected to achieve more than perfunctory acceptance and involvement by the other departments. Yet knowledge of the subject and vital action on it may be required of several departments.

Involvement of the head of each department is necessary. Of equal importance, personnel in lower levels of management in departments that receive only copies of other department's letters may not become particularly interested or involved. Jealously between departments or between the personnel in different departments may be accentuated and may add to the lack of interest and cooperation. Specific communication and authority from the manager of each department are needed.

Sometimes department heads may add their endorsement of another department head's letter—a sort of "I agree" or "me too," or "we're involved." However, this does not have the weight or receive the attention and cooperation that a letter signed by all the department heads or separate appropriate letters from each head would receive. Another problem with a letter affecting several departments but signed by only one department head is that it tends to emphasize and help cause impersonal relationships.

Communications affecting several departments but signed by only one department head are apt to lead to lack of integration and coordination of the effort and to insufficient overall management of the project. They may result in incomplete supervision to see that action is timely and effective. Even when proper communication is carried out, overcoming jealously between people and departments requires special consideration in many organizations.

Make certain that communication is effective and develops interest. Communication must be understood and believed. It should help to provide the necessary motivation to do what needs to be done.

Remember that people in organizations have short memories and that they have other interests, but on important subjects that involve them people desire continuing information. Employees may move to other work, and their replacements need to be informed. Thus there is a need constantly to reinform and to report new developments. Matters of importance should not be forgotten and allowed to die on the vine just because they have already been covered. Interest and motivation must be kept alive and active if plans are to be successfully implemented.

Public relations management should be kept informed of the plans and activities of the other parts of the organization. What the other parts do can greatly affect public relations plans and actions. Also, as said earlier, one of the public relations department's responsibilities is to counsel the other parts of the organization with regard to potential public relations opportunities and problems. If public relations management does not know about other department's plans, it cannot counsel them.

Public relations management should be ready to answer questions and provide information as requested by the press, radio, and television on the plans of the organization and its departments. It should coordinate and integrate public relations activity in connection with plans and activities throughout the organization. When communication failures occur, public relations management should take the initiative in getting them straightened out.

TWO-WAY INFORMATION

Another element important to the successful completion of a plan is a two-way information flow to ensure getting communications from, as well as to, other locations. It will also help to ensure getting communication from lower levels of the organization to headquarters and upper levels. Plans are frequently not as successful as they should be because distant locations just do not or are unable to communicate well with headquarters and because upper management people are apt to be insulated from the rest of the organization.

We have previously discussed the importance of two-way communication between employees and higher levels of management. Two-way communication between almost any kind of organization and its members is important for effective development and execution of plans.

Public relations management should arrange for appropriate channels and stimulation to ensure receiving information from other locations and lower levels. Inquiry by mail, discussion by telephone, visits and meetings at both nearby and distant locations can be helpful. However, most important are good rapport and a climate of trust, as was discussed in Chapter 7 on communication.

COORDINATION AND INTEGRATION OF THE WORK

On pages 183 and 184 we discussed the importance of coordination and integration in the formulation of plans. A plan format that helps ensure coordination and integration was presented on pages 191 and 192. But excellent plans can be made ineffective if they are not carefully coordinated and integrated when they are carried out.

Timing, which is a part of the coordinating effort, is important in carrying out the plan. Every part of the plan should be carried out at the time indicated, and everything that is done should help to reach the objectives that have been agreed on. Otherwise, effectiveness may be lost or curtailed. Some of the people involved in the program should not be allowed to decide that they will carry out an item in February that is scheduled for January— or perhaps omit a part of the plan altogether. With such a situation, the various parts of the plan will not mesh, and its effectiveness will be seriously damaged.

GOOD DIRECTION, SUPERVISION, AND LEADERSHIP

In Chapter 4 we discussed elements important to effective management. Among them were good direction, good supervision, and good leadership. Much of the earlier pages of this chapter concern direction and supervision as well as planning because need for them cannot be stressed too much. Good direction ensures that elements of the plan are performed effectively when they should be. It ensures good supervision. Good supervision makes certain that the work of implementing the plan is properly and efficiently done.

All those involved should understand that they are accountable for the results in the areas for which they are responsible. Regular review of progress in completing tasks in the allotted time and evaluation of results are important. Results should be reported to those responsible for the work as well as to upper management.

One of the primary functions of a good supervisor consists of training, coaching, and assisting the people who report to him. This does not mean, of course, that supervisors should "take over" or "get in the hair" of their people. When training, coaching, and assisting are not necessary, the supervisor should let his people carry out their jobs without interference.

In addition to good direction and good supervision, good leadership is important. Good leadership works to stimulate and motivate all those concerned with the plan to want to do a good job and to achieve good results. It works to develop esprit de corps—to develop harmony and unity.

A final requirement for effectively directing, supervising, and leading is properly to reward performance, both good and bad.

REVIEW OF RESULTS—INNOVATION

We have previously discussed the need for feedback and for review and evaluation of results. The public relations plan and its parts should never be considered unchangeable. If improvements can be found or if conditions suggest a change in plan, thorough consideration should be given to making the change.

Innovation is vital to any well-run business or group, including public relations. Public relations management would be remiss if it failed to find better ways and to improve. Much can be learned from a good look at the results of action taken in carrying out a plan and considering the reasons

REQUIREMENTS FOR EFFECTIVELY CARRYING OUT P/R PROGRAMS

1. TOP LEVEL INVOLVEMENT.
   TOP LEVEL INSISTENCE ON PERFORMANCE. FEEDBACK TO TOP LEVEL OF ACTION AND RESULTS.

2. INFORMED MANAGEMENT PEOPLE AND WORKERS IN ALL PARTS OF THE COMPANY INVOLVED.

3. EFFECTIVE TWO-WAY COMMUNICATION FLOW FOR PROPER EVALUATION OF THE PROGRAM'S PROGRESS AND RESULTS.

4. PROPER TIMING, WITH EACH PART OF THE PROGRAM CARRIED OUT AT THE TIME INDICATED.

5. GOOD MANAGEMENT AND SUPERVISION FOR EFFECTIVE PERFORMANCE.

6. REGULAR EVALUATION OF RESULTS.

7. PROPER REWARDS FOR GOOD AND BAD PERFORMANCE.

Figure 31

for those results, whether good or bad. One may learn much and make desirable improvements through analysis of opinion and media research. This is particularly true when research has been used before the inception of a plan to determine bench marks from which to measure results. Information about the findings, innovations, and new conditions should be provided to all those concerned, along with word about any changes that may be made in objectives. Figure 31 summarizes the requirements for effectively carrying out public relations programs.

SUMMARY

One of the most common problems in the management of the public relations function is the failure to have real plans based on specific objectives. The tendency is to go from day to day carrying out demand work without the consideration of objectives or plans for reaching them. Specific plans help to ensure that efforts are directed toward reaching objectives and are properly coordinated and integrated. They provide a written reference that lets each part of the organization and each person involved know what is to be done, who is to do it, and when it is to be done. Plans can lead to better esprit de corps.

In developing plans for the public relations function one of the first considerations is the objectives and the plans of the organization as a whole. Sometimes organizations may not have agreed on objectives and plans. Public relations management may assist in giving impetus to the development of plans.

The need for getting higher management acceptance of a plan should be considered while the plan is being prepared. Failure to get acceptance is one of the greatest barriers to implementation. The need for approval and active support of other parts of the organization should also be considered in the planning stage.

Top management clearance of important plans is essential. Its active involvement is also the first requirement in successfully and effectively carrying out plans. One needs more than tolerance and token acceptance from top management.

Public relations managers should get away from their desks and preconceived viewpoints in developing plans. Too much time spent in offices and the failure to get out and tap the viewpoints and knowledge of other parts of the organization can lead to unrealistic, unworkable, and ineffective plans. Getting the knowledge and viewpoints of others can broaden perception.

After describing problems or opportunities, the next step in planning should be setting tentative objectives. Means for measuring results should be planned at the same time. One should keep in mind what kind of objectives should be set for an activity. For example, only communicative objectives should be set for communicative functions.

After objectives have been set, specific plans for reaching them may be made. A plan or program lists specifically what things are to be done in chronological order, who is to do each of them, and when. Alternative plans should be considered. The most suitable plan, taking into consideration all the possibilities, should be chosen. When tentative plans have been completed, showing all the activities to be carried out, they should then be priced out. If tentative costs are not prudent, plans and alternatives should be reviewed to determine where they may best be reduced. The objectives may need to be changed.

Coordination committees, representing the various functional parts of an organization and the various competences, may be set up to ensure that all parts can express their viewpoints and needs. These committees also make it possible to understand better the responsibilities and viewpoints of others. They help to ensure that each part of a plan is proceeding properly and on schedule.

Organizations may need an overall master public relations plan and specific subplans to cover the various parts of the main plan. The use of subplans is desirable to prevent the master plan from being so massive and complicated that it is hard to follow. Subplans also help to delineate the work of various levels of the organization.

In carrying out the plan it is important from the start that top-level management be involved. One should make sure that all the people involved are properly informed about the plans and specifically as to what is expected of them. Communication must be effective.

Timing is important in carrying out a plan. Each step of a plan should be performed at the time indicated. Otherwise, effectiveness may be lost or seriously curtailed.

Good direction, supervision, and leadership are necessary for the plan to succeed. All those involved should realize that they are accountable for the results in the areas for which they are responsible. Good leadership works to stimulate and motivate those involved to want to do a good job and to achieve good results, which results in harmony and unity.

Feedback and the review and evaluation of results are essential. Much can be learned from a good look at the results of action taken in effecting a plan and considering the reasons for those results.

Public relations plans should never be considered to be unchangeable.

ELEVEN

The Management
of Change

The management of change is of particular importance because management is primarily concerned with results in the future—the future being from a few hours to many years away. The only certain thing about the future is change. Yet the future is based on today, and today cannot be neglected in favor of the future.

The management of change cannot be based on the premise that one can forecast the future. The past 60 years amply demonstrate that there is simply no way of forecasting the future. The future is not predictable. *The management of change is not concerned with decisions in the future. It is concerned with decisions for the present that will affect the future.* Although most or all of a change may take place in the future, the management of change requires planning and action now—in the present.

In the management of change one should not only consider the results of the change during the time needed to consummate it and immediately afterward but also during the entire period its results are may be felt. Failure to manage change will greatly affect the future and the changes that it will bring. The effect of such failure may last for many years or, for all practical purposes, permanently.

Good planning must be an important part of the management of change. Once one has considered what changes are desirable or necessary and also what changes owing to outside forces are inevitable, then one must plan for them. One needs to consider how these changes can be made most advantageous or least harmful by using the problem analysis, objectives, programs, and actions that have been discussed throughout this book.

In the management of the change of any given factor, one should not assume that other factors will remain the same in the future. The change itself will usually cause further change. Change is caused by reactions to actions. In turn reactions cause change and further actions, which bring even more change.

Changes in the culture of a country bring about change in its political and economic systems, which in turn cause more change in the culture. Cultural, social, political, and economic changes greatly affect the environment in which organizations exist and operate. Therefore, changes should be of great concern to public relations management. As said in Chapter 4, a key responsibility of public relations management is correctly to perceive and advise the rest of management on the environment in which the organization is operating and to use this information to help set organization objectives, policies, and plans.

Peter Drucker calls this "the age of discontinuity." In his book by that name he discusses the great changes taking place in previously held economic, social, and political beliefs, assumptions and values.[1] Our time, he says, is a time of momentous changes in politics, science, world views, mores, and the arts. We face an age of discontinuity in world economy and technology.

Enormous changes have already occurred in the culture of the United States during the 200 years that it has existed. In *The Evolution of Management Thought,* Daniel A. Wren says that the United States "was founded on the premise of limited government, private property, freedom of economic opportunity, stress on individual initiative, and a government which should keep its hands off of business."[2]

There were imbalances and imperfections between the ideals of economic "democracy" and its practice. Instead of laissez-faire capitalism perpetrating itself, as Adam Smith envisioned, many businessmen took collective action to ration and monopolize the market. Organized labor took on economic and political objectives. Special interest groups fought to expand their opportunities at the expense of other groups. With a large percentage of individuals feeling powerless, collective action became more and more prevalent.

This major change in culture is still underway. Many do not realize its magnitude and the effect it has on business, government, education, other organizations of all kinds, and the professions and the lives of people. One frequently hears references to the early culture as though it were still dominant. Many of those who are now only middle-aged were brought up and educated concerning economic, political, and social matters and customs that have since changed a great deal.

[1] Peter F. Drucker, *The Age of Discontinuity.* New York: Harper and Row, 1969.
[2] Daniel A. Wren, *The Evolution of Management Thought.* New York: Ronald Press, 1972.

Many in upper management are unable to perceive and understand the impact of the changes that have been and are taking place. Thus they are unable correctly to perceive the environment in which they operate. And they are unwilling to accept its reality, the restrictions it imposes, or what needs to be done about it. This can make the work of public relations management more difficult.

As brought out by Daniel Wren, there has been a change from the gospel of production efficiency to the gospel of consumption with stress on sales.[3] The Horatio Alger ethic of getting ahead by self-reliance, perseverance, thrift, and hard work is now held by relatively few. Our society has changed from its emphasis on the individual to stressing the importance of social relations. Affiliation needs and "contacts" have become a trade-off for achievement needs. Self-help has given way to government help.

At the time of the Great Depression of the 1930s, President Franklin D. Roosevelt adopted some of the economic viewpoints of John Maynard Keynes, who disagreed with the American ethic of thrift.[4] In addition the financial crash, which was both economic and intensely psychological in its impact, played a major part in destroying the positive attitudes toward the value of thrift and hard work. The disaster of the Depression struck the energetic as well as the lazy. It destroyed the thrifty as well as the thriftless. Thirty percent of the workers in the United States were without jobs. People learned from bitter experience to seek security. The depression compounded the desire for group affinity. The key emphasis became one of "getting along." Being accepted by others opened the door to accomplishment. Confidence in inner self-direction and individual self-interest gave way a great deal to confidence in the group.

During the Renaissance and the early days of the Industrial Revolution, the state had lost its role of economic planner with the growth of laissez-faire economic philosophy. The market was felt to provide the best way of economic control. Starting with the Roosevelt administration, and continuing since, economic policy control has passed to a considerable extent away from the hands of business management and into those of politicians and government.

The causes and results of change interact, bringing further reactions that interact with what has gone before. For example, the growth of population and urbanization contribute to a need for government help as compared with self-help. Government help then contributes to a reduction in self-reliance.

We have changed from the premise of limited government. Economic policy control has been shifted to politicians with government-made

[3] Ibid.
[4] Ibid.

economic policy dominating in even the most complex matters. Economic policy is subject to the votes of a public little informed or not informed at all in such matters, and of legislators who are scarcely better informed. Yet the choice is either that or having special interest groups and unscrupulous businesses control economic policy in a manner not in the public interest.

The increase in the role of government in economic matters during the Franklin Roosevelt administration was intended to shift power from "Wall Street" to the farmers, laborers, and "little man." It resulted in legislation such as the Social Security Act of 1935 and the Fair Labor Standards Act of 1938, which provided for minimum hourly wages for many kinds of workers. Charity became largely a public rather than a private concern.[5]

During the same period, growth made business and other organizations less personal and contributed to the problems of impersonality that were discussed in earlier chapters. In management, to a large extent, social competence, logic, and the ability to reason assumed greater importance. The ability to manipulate people took precedence over technical competence in the areas being managed. Many advocate that management ability at any organizational level is totally transferable to any field.

This has become the age of the organization and the institution. Peter Drucker points out that "every single social task of importance today is entrusted to a large institution organized for perpetuity and run by managers."[6] He adds that we have neither the political nor the social theory for such a "society of organizations." It is incompatible with the political and social theories that dominate our society and our approach to political and social issues. He postulates that new theory to fit the new situation will be a long time coming but that we cannot wait. We must use the little we know now.

Drucker believes that management is the answer. In discussing management he comments that only a short time ago people were fixed in their opportunities and jobs by class and birth. The provision of further opportunity has been the result of business management. Management is the force that reduced the privilege and class structure in Europe. Management in communist countries promises to be a major political and social force against their bureaucracies and is being opposed and resisted by the Soviet bureaucracy.[7]

Yet Drucker believes that the more management can use the traditions, values, and beliefs of a society, the more it will accomplish. However, management cannot be simply a craft, he says. It must recognize that all

---

[5] Ibid.

[6] Peter F. Drucker, *The Age of Discontinuity.* New York: Harper and Row, 1969.

[7] Peter F. Drucker, *Management: Tasks, Responsibilities, Practices.* New York: Harper and Row, 1974.

organizations exist for the sake of society, and therefore it has the duty to do what is in the interests of society. It has the duty to provide leadership in society. Drucker says that management is an organ of the institution or organization, and the organization, whether a business or a public service, is in turn an organ of society, existing to make specific contributions and to discharge specific social functions.[8]

Another change that has occurred with considerable political, economic, and social impact concerns the relative importance and power of business institutions. Although many large business institutions still have a great deal of power, their relative importance and their power have diminished. Organizations other than business have grown so that today the amount of the gross national product in the United States that goes to or through nonbusiness organizations is more than 50 percent.

Business and all other institutions have in varying degrees fallen from their pedestals. Daniel Wren puts it well in discussing business management. Businessmen, he said, have been closely identified with the city, but the city is deemed to be degrading by many. Inner cities are decaying. Yet it is business that has the resources, the ability and knowledge needed to rebuild them.[9]

A large percentage of youth are disenchanted with business. Yet business has the resources and the know-how needed to provide jobs and housing, to reduce pollution, and to solve other cultural problems.

Profitability is suspect, but it is the key to research, development, investment, prosperity, and the growth of the economy. Production and efficiency are no longer the cultural goals that they once were. Yet it is productivity that produces higher wages and lower costs.

There have been many other changes that have and are having their impact on the social environment and culture and thus on public relations, either directly or indirectly: the advent of the automobile and the airplane, which made the people of the developed world mobile and led to the establishment of enormous oil, automobile, airplane, airline, hotel and motel businesses, as well as great growth of many others; the growth of vast urban areas; the everchanging confrontations between Western countries, the Soviet Union, and China; the assertiveness of the Arabian and African countries; the disappearance of the open west of North America; the growth of equal employment opportunity pressures and regulations; the advent of the Environmental Protection Agency and the growth of government regulation in general; the growth of multinational business corporations.

The increase in mobility of people and the development of large business organizations have both led to a tendency to a rootless mode of life that has

[8] *Management: Tasks, Responsibilities, Practices.* New York: Harper and Row, 1974.
[9] *The Evolution of Management Thought.* New York: Ronald Press, 1972.

affected personal and family relationship and the mores of individuals, communities, and countries.

The past is a prologue to and the foundation of the future. It is desirable for management people to know about and recognize the major changes that have and are taking place, because a knowledge of where we are and how we got there is essential in correctly perceiving the present and in planning change for the future.

The changes listed have presented opportunities and problems to organizations in the past. Some of the undesirable changes could have been managed to alleviate or avoid problems. The opportunity today is to manage change so that as much as possible it will have favorable and more beneficial results for the organization and society and fewer unfavorable and harmful ones.

In a general way what can be predicted about the future? Earlier we said that this has become the age of the organization. Peter Drucker has predicted that we are approaching the turning point in the trend to entrusting everything to large organizations.[10] There is a disenchantment, he says, with the biggest and fastest growing of these institutions—modern government—as well as cynicism regarding its ability to perform. The revolt is occurring simultaneously in the Catholic Church and the big universities. It involves business and other institutions. The future concern will be to make organizations fully effective as major instruments and tools of man and central organs of human society.

In relation to the changing view toward entrusting everything to large organizations, Daniel Wren suggests that today self-actualization seems to be moving toward the forefront.[11] Affiliation, although still important, seems to have diminished in importance.

Drucker predicts that we can expect a rapidly changing technology and a new concern for production and productivity.[12] He comments that no matter how perceptive a reporter may be, he is no more capable than the next person of predicting the great events of tomorrow, whether catastrophe or blessing. Drucker suggests that today there is a split between two cultures in business and industry. The split is between the world of the scientifically trained person and the world of the humanistically trained person. "We cannot tolerate such a split anymore," he says. "We will have to demand of the scientifically trained person that he again become a humanist. Otherwise, he will lack the knowledge and perception needed to make his science effective, indeed to make it truly scientific."[13] On the

---

[10] Peter F. Drucker, *The Age of Discontinuity*. New York: Harper and Row, 1969.
[11] Daniel A. Wren, *The Evolution of Management Thought*. New York: Ronald Press, 1972.
[12] Peter F. Drucker, *The Age of Discontinuity*. New York: Harper and Row, 1969.
[13] Ibid.

other hand, "we will have to demand of the humanist that he acquire an understanding of science, or the humanities will be irrelevant and ineffectual." This observation applies to people in public relations management. It also has important broad implications in the management of change.

Public relations managers should be much concerned with the management of change. In reality a large number of public relations opportunities are lost and problems arise because of the failure correctly to perceive what is happening or what may happen and to take effective steps to do something about it. Examples of this occur constantly. Think of the energy crisis, a primary example of the failure to manage change. When warning signals of energy shortages went up, automobile manufacturers went merrily along building bigger and more powerful cars, with no regard for the diminishing supply and increasing demand for energy. They confused the public pleasure that comes from owning and driving big cars with the public interest that requires conservation of energy supplies. The failure to perceive the public interest and take the leadership in making necessary changes was a failure of public relations management and cost the automobile business a great deal. It resulted in loss of credibility for business in general and cost the country wasted petroleum that it could not affort to waste.

Consider the oil companies who found themselves in the same boat, preoccupied with tradition and habit. Repercussions in the oil business will last for many years. Among other things, they lost public confidence and goodwill.

Government was caught unaware and suffered many difficulties including monetary problems, greatly worsened inflation, and the loss of credibility. The reason was that those in key places did not manage change. Rather, they were managed by it. Instead of acting, they reacted or failed to do anything.

All were engrossed with the day-to-day functional operation and its demands. They looked within when they should have been looking outside of their organizations. No one did the looking ahead and broad planning that are so necessary. No one considered the public interest.

Needless to say, the public relations climate created by such problems can have the most serious effect on long-term profitability for business, on the effectiveness of government, and the economic and political welfare of the people. The underlying causes of such problems may lie in four areas. The first, as mentioned, is ineffective broad long-range planning. Too many public relations managers are preoccupied with today's and next week's problems. They are looking within but seldom look outside their organizations. They are creatures of habit and tradition, reacting instead of acting. They forget that they operate in a world that is increasingly interdependent. They may not understand what is actually taking place because their interests and education have been focused too narrowly on some one discipline or competence. Thus they may be afflicted with a kind tunnel vision.

The second cause is the lack of proper balance between the important need for profit (votes, power, peer group approbation, ego, etc.) on the one hand and the equally important public interest on the other. The importance of such a balance has been discussed earlier in Chapters 1 and 4.

The third cause is the desire to preserve the status quo, frequently to protect entrenched interests, and an unwillingness to recognize when change is ripe and necessary. An example concerned a large nationally known civic organization whose expressed object is to "get the facts." After over a year of hearings by one of its study groups, a report was prepared that raised questions concerning one of the professions. The report review committee, which included an unusually large number from that profession, promptly eliminated negative viewpoints brought out by some of the speakers. The result was loss of credibility by the organization, which was accused of representing only conservative political and entrenched business interests.

The fourth cause is the failure to act. The signs that change is needed go unheeded. The organization may be preoccupied with the past and past success, unwilling to make difficult decisions or to act on them. Sometimes this is caused by a lack of leadership. Many organizations have placed their faith in carefully outlined procedures and instructions and unwittingly substituted them for leadership. As a result, rule-encumbered inefficiency and ineffectiveness are prevalent in many organizations.

To paraphrase Jerome Hardy, former publisher of *Life Magazine,* in a speech delivered to the Commonwealth Club of California in San Francisco, "the great need in today's world is to have institutions capable of continual renewal and the great question is whether we can achieve this.[14] Parts of our society have spun webs of vested interest that resist change unto death. We love our institutions in an embrace of death, but love without criticism brings stagnation. Conversely, criticism without love brings destruction."

Failure continually to renew institutions and the way in which they operate can cause social pressures that eventually bring explosive changes, some of which are not desirable either to society or to the vested interests.

However, many times the status quo should be preserved. Change for the sake of change is not necessarily right. The conservative political and business interests that some believe to be undesirably entrenched may be the best possible ones and should be supported.

Business is a symbol that can be conveniently attacked. People with strong antibusiness and antiestablishment feelings are constantly on the

[14] July 19, 1968.

attack and would entrench their own institutions, viewpoints, and interests if given the opportunity. Those with little knowledge or understanding would make business institutions the whipping boy for every price increase, however justified, and for every economic misfortune and social ill. One should not accept change simply for the sake of change. Change should be accepted only when it best meets organizational or social needs. Each situation should be carefully examined on the basis of merit.

In most things it is usually not possible to look ahead as far as the year 1990 or 2000. Generally speaking, valid predictions cannot be made that far in advance. However, in matters such as energy shortages or population growth, for example, long-term predictions are frequently possible and necessary.

The need for change and the management of change revolve around many fundamental and interrelated factors. Some of them are listed below. Then we discuss them in more detail.

1. The social aspects of the Industrial Revolution.
2. Changes in social beliefs and customs of the country.
3. Growth and centralization of government.
4. Growth of population and urbanization.
5. The political and economic effect of the growing number of knowledge workers.
6. Consumerism.
7. The negative attitude toward profit and business.
8. The capital requirements crisis.
9. The energy crisis.
10. Concern for the physical environment.
11. Equal opportunity and equal treatment.
12. The shift in emphasis from technology to the quality of life.
13. The need for desirable motivation.
14. The information explosion.

THE SOCIAL ASPECTS OF THE INDUSTRIAL REVOLUTION

Although we think of the technological aspects of the Industrial Revolution as fairly complete, some of its social aspects have only now gotten underway. During the past century, rapid technological changes tremendously increased agricultural productivity and made obsolete the family farm, making millions of farm workers available for jobs in industry in cities. Where it once took 20 farm workers to feed one city man, it now takes only one farm worker to feed 10 city men. This change transformed the nation, greatly changing its problems, its outlook, and its viewpoints. The labor supply released from the farms made possible the transformation from an underdeveloped rural country to a developed industrial complex.

Industrialization contributes to a better world in countless ways. All one has to do is to look at the nonindustrial parts of the world to be able to count the overall blessings of industrialization. It vastly improves the lot of the majority of people. It provides for comfort, security, and infinitely better health. It can provide opportunity. However, it causes problems that require social changes paralleling and relating to the technical changes.

The social aspects of the Industrial Revolution involve such things as the motivation of people, which was not of much concern in the preindustrial society. They involve the problems brought about by urbanization—local transportation, police, recreation facilities, waste disposal, clean air and water supply, and so on. They are concerned with the argument as to what is relevant in education. They involve the problems of impersonality. They necessitate better communication.

The study and management of change necessary to complete the social phases of the Industrial Revolution present many opportunities as well as problems. Public relations managers can assist their organizations by giving careful attention to the management of change in this area, helping to make sure that it is prudently guided.

CHANGES IN SOCIAL BELIEFS AND CUSTOMS—THE CULTURE

Changes in social beliefs and customs have included the change from the premise of limited government that had a policy of keeping its hands off business. Antitrust laws were passed. "Trust busting" during Theodore Roosevelt's administration heralded government's entry into the regulation of business. Regulation was strengthened by the Clayton and the Federal Trade Commission Acts in 1914. A long series of new laws that established additional means of regulating business followed. More are being enacted today. These laws in effect attempt to increase opportunity for those with little capital and to protect the consumer in the marketplace.

Individual initiative gave way a great deal to collective action and dependence on government. Workers, farmers, and businessmen alike organized for collective action.[15] Producers joined to control the conditions under which they would sell their products. Distributors combined to con-

---

[15] Daniel A. Wren, *The Evolution of Management Thought*. New York: Ronald Press, 1972.

trol marketing and transportation. Laborers joined unions to bargain with management. This organizational revolution revealed the degree to which industrialization had shifted the context of economic decisions from personal relationships among individuals to a struggle for power among well-organized groups. The trend toward collective action continues. Reaction follows action and action follows reaction as various groups seek to protect themselves from the consequences.

Change in personal and family relationships and mores occurred and are still occurring. Generally, the family is not the unifying force it once was.

The growth of collective action is undoubtedly partly due to such things as the growth of population and urbanization. More care and better leadership, particularly by government, in reacting to the demands of special interest groups can help to curb abuses.

Concerning many facets of a broad subject such as the culture of a country, one cannot recommend in advance what action would help to manage change so that it is in the public interest and the interest of the organization. Trained perception, ethics, and integrity are needed in considering situations and arriving at decisions concerning particular matters.

GROWTH AND CENTRALIZATION OF GOVERNMENT

The growth and centralization of government come about partly because of urbanization and the problems it creates. An urbanized area sometimes encompass several counties or two or more states. Large business and other organizations also cross community, state, and frequently national boundaries. Individual communities and even whole states are no longer able to carry out regulatory and police functions. For example, the development and enforcement of clean air and water laws are beyond the power of most individual cities. Large rivers may flow through or adjoin many states. Transportation facilities and police authority may require regional, state, or national management. Activities of regulatory agencies such as the Environmental Protection Agency, the Federal Trade Commission, and the Food and Drug Administration, must be nationwide. Unfortunately, national agencies are frequently duplicated on a state and sometimes even on a city level with overlapping responsibilities and added expense.

Part of the problem of large government comes from failure of organizations to be responsive to the public interest and needs. Whenever this happens, pressures develop for government to step in. It is in the organization's self-interest continually to reassess the public interest. As pointed out by Peter Drucker, "it is the job of the organization to look ahead and to think

THE KEY SOCIAL RESPONSIBILITY

TO USE THE ORGANIZATION'S

RESOURCES, INCLUDING ITS HUMAN

RESOURCES, IN THE BEST INTEREST

OF SOCIETY.

Figure 32

through which of its impacts are likely to become or cause social problems.[16] And it is the duty of the organization to try to prevent those undesirable side results." Such social problems and their prevention are in the province of public relations management.

As Drucker points out, the automobile industry pioneered safe driving instruction and was instrumental in helping to design safe highways, but it failed to make accidents less dangerous. However, no one feels sorry for the automobile industry. It has "not lived up to the demands of leadership. It is the task of the leader to anticipate."[17] It is not sufficient to claim the crowd went wrong.

One hears a great deal about social responsibility. Much of this chapter is concerned with it. To paraphrase Drucker, they key social responsibility is the use of the organization's resources, including its human resources, in the best interests of society.

Contrary to the views of some, there is a limit to the responsibility of an organization. Drucker makes the important point that organizations do not act in a socially responsible way when they take on problems outside their sphere of competence and action.[18] They are socially responsible when they satisfy society's needs through concentration on specific jobs within their competences and when they convert public need into their own achievements.

With responsibility goes accountability. An organization that accepts social responsibility (or any other kind of responsibility) must also accept accountability for the results of what it does.[19]

The question is sometimes raised as to whether the assumption of social responsibility does not conflict with the need for profit. This goes back to our discussion in earlier chapters of the need for a proper balance between

[16] Peter F. Drucker, *The Age of Discontinuity.* New York: Harper and Row, 1969.
[17] Peter F. Drucker, *The Age of Discontinuity.* New York: Harper and Row, 1969.
[18] Ibid.
[19] Peter F. Drucker, *The Age of Discontinuity.* New York: Harper and Row, 1969.

ORGANIZATIONS ARE SOCIALLY RESPONSIBLE
WHEN THEY SATISFY SOCIETY'S NEED THROUGH
CONCENTRATION ON SPECIFIC JOBS WITHIN THEIR
SPHERE OF COMPETENCE--WHEN THEY CONVERT
PUBLIC NEED INTO THEIR OWN ACHIEVEMENT.

Figure 33

profit on the one hand and the public interest on the other. Profit is of primary importance. As brought out in earlier chapters, profit both for the present and long term must always be the first consideration and first requirement of every business. Profits and savings from past profits not only finance every business, but they also finance all nonbusiness institutions and activities. Without profit a business will be unable to assume any kind of responsibility. However, consideration of the public interest and social responsibility are part of the expense of doing business.

As Drucker said, business enterprises are organs of society and of the community.[20] No organ can survive independently of the body of which it is a part. Businesses, as well as other organizations, have an important stake in the communities in which they exist and operate. They reap the benefits of the communities. Their employees, customers, suppliers, members, contributors, competitors, and neighbors are there. As powerful and resourceful corporate and other organizations, they have the duties of citizens to the community and to the public. The failure of business to consider the public interest and social responsibility is one cause of the growth and centralization of government. In today's world business organizations are accountable not only for the goods and services they produce, but also for the quality of life in their areas of competence. Failure will only bring government intervention.

SOCIAL RESPONSIBILITY, AUTHORITY AND ACCOUNTABILITY

"Whoever assumes responsibility, asserts authority. Conversely one is responsible for whatever one has authority over.
With responsibility goes accountability."

Figure 34[21]

---

[20] *Management: Tasks, Responsibilities, Practices*, New York: Harper and Row, 1974.
[21] Peter F. Drucker, *The Age of Discontinuity*. New York: Harper and Row, 1969.

In reality social responsibility is not any more for the benefit of society than it is for the benefit of the organization. A business that is not profitable enough to meet the demands of its social responsibilities and what ought to be its public relations objectives is a business in trouble and one that is usually poorly managed.

As another aspect of the growth and centralization of government, there is a great tendency for the tentacles of government to reach out unnecessarily into every nook, cranny, and activity of the land with rules, regulations, advice, assistance, and regimentation. Business, local government, and pressure groups may clamor for intervention, assistance, and funding. However, since government resources are limited to the taxes it collects or deficit financing (which amounts to a tax on savings) undesirable and unnecessary government involvement should be avoided and opposed.

Pressures of all kinds call for government to solve every human problem and to expand in every direction. To paraphrase Drucker, vast multitudes of bureaucratic agencies become ends in themselves, defying public will and public policy.[22] Dozens of government agencies have different parts of overlapping tasks. The tremendous government expense fuels the fires of inflation, which should be of great concern to public relations management in business, political, educational, religious, and other organizations.

GROWTH OF POPULATION AND URBANIZATION

The growth of population and urbanization bring great changes in society and its problems. These changes, unless properly managed, can have undesirable effects on organizations of all kinds. Large parts of the United States have been or are becoming urbanized. Much of the area from Boston to Washington, D.C., the Los Angeles Basin with all of Los Angeles and a considerable are of San Bernardino and Orange Counties, the San Francisco Bay Area, and the Chicago Area are examples of highly urbanized areas.

Urbanization can bring the problems of rundown business buildings and dwellings—urban blight. In many areas no trees or other natural greenery are to be found in the "asphalt jungle." Urbanization presents problems of waste disposal and transportation. It requires special attention to recreational facilities. It brings increased crime and adds to police and fire protection problems. At the same time, many cities in urban areas have a

<hr>

[22] Peter F. Drucker, *The Age of Discontinuity.* New York: Harper and Row, 1969.

preponderance of poor and have difficulty in financing themselves through taxing their citizens.

For their own benefit, as well as those of the community, organizations can take an active hand in helping to reduce the problems of urbanization. Adequate parking space and staggered business hours can help with transportation and congestion. New types of transportation arrangements to meet the needs of the 1980s and 1990s can be proposed and installed. Planting trees and landscaping plants, industrial areas, and office buildings can provide better aesthetic values. Buildings can be kept in repair and properly painted. Areas can be kept clean and free of discarded material. Organizations can work for and abide by the requirements of adequate zoning laws and green belt areas. Business organizations particularly can resolve not to create or increase urban problems.

After a visit to America in the early nineteenth century, Alexis de Tocqueville, a French writer, commented that when a United States citizen conceived of a community need, a committee came into existence on behalf of the need. The need was met without the intercession of bureaucracy. Undoubtedly we can borrow from the past in taking needed action concerning urbanization. Urbanization contributes to the growth and centralization of government. The same public relations considerations of the public interest and social responsibility apply to both.

The great growth of population into thousands of communities has created another problem by adding greatly to the complexity of marketing channels and distribution, thus adding to the cost of consumer goods. This is discussed further on pages 219 and 220.

THE POLITICAL AND ECONOMIC EFFECT OF THE GROWING NUMBER OF KNOWLEDGE WORKERS

In Chapter 3 we called attention to the fact that more and more people are better educated. There has been a tremendous growth in the number of "knowledge workers" and that number will probably continue to grow. Knowledge workers are those using knowledge in the performance of their duties, as contrasted with manual workers. Drucker says that whatever the social programs of the last twenty-five years were meant to achieve, the first result was a growth of middle-class knowledge workers.[23] Relatively speaking, the number and political importance of bluecollar workers—primarily

---

[23] *Management: Tasks, Reponsibilities, Practices,* New York: Harper and Row, 1974.

less educated manual workers—is diminishing, and the relative political importance of the knowledge workers is increasing. This change can have a great effect on both political and economic decisions and on political and business organizations. It may greatly influence the makeup of political organizations and their platforms, and the political environment of business and of other nonpolitical organizations will change materially.

Knowledge workers may have quite different motivations from those of bluecollar workers, and this can lead to different demands on business and other organizations, including government. Yet these demands may frequently not bring more desirable or better decisions. Unfortunately, although people may be better educated, frequently their knowledge may be relatively superficial or narrowly focused on a given area without knowledge of important interrelationships with other areas. Situations and solutions that may seem infinitely simple to them may in fact be tremendously complex.

The increase in the political and economic power of knowledge workers and the better educated brings demands for better performance by all organizations—not only business organizations. Such demands may particularly concern the areas having to do with the quality of life—such as the physical environment.

Consumerism will be fostered. The impact of consumerism will undoubtedly spread from business as the chief target to other targets such as the professions, the courts, the education system, the legislative and executive branches of government, and to other nonbusiness institutions. (It may be known by names other than consumerism but its intent will be the same.)

Many knowledge workers, particularly those who work in nonbusiness organizations, have little understanding or interest in profit or profitability, which can cause important problems to society in general and to business in particular, and may lead to unrealistic consumer demands.

Business organizations may need different kinds of leadership and supervision, different working conditions, and perhaps different fringe benefits for knowledge workers. These things can lead to better motivation and reduced employee turnover.

The changes in performance requirements (political, economic, and other) resulting from the growth in the number and importance of knowledge workers and better educated people will affect public relations a great deal. Public relations management can help to provide the leadership to manage change in this area so that it is most advantageous both to society and to the organization.

CONSUMERISM

Consumerism is an area in which the management of change is especially important to public relations management. *The basic objective of our economic system is to meet consumers' needs as the consumers see them.* Furthermore, the business (or other organization) that ignores or fails to recognize this fact does so at its own peril.[24] *Consumerism concerns the balance of the rights and powers of buyers in relation to those of sellers.*

Since the turn of the century there have been three distinct consumer movements. The first occurred in the early 1900s at the time of Theodore Roosevelt and the Muckrakers. It brought the passage of the Pure Food and Drug Act of 1906, the Meat Inspection Act of the same year, and the creation of the Federal Trade Commission in 1914. The second came in the 1930s during the Great Depression of that era. With it came such things as the enlargement of the power of the Federal Trade Commission. The third and latest began in the mid-1960s and is still continuing.

As brought out by Philip Kotler, buyers want more adequate information about products.[25] They want protection against questionable products and marketing practices. They want the right to influence products and marketing practices in directions that will improve the quality of life. For example, they are concerned about detergents, gasoline, and soft drink containers. Consumerists make the point that the world's resources are limited and that the public interest does not permit their indiscriminate use.

Another important factor that concerns consumers relates to the cost of marketing and thus the cost of goods. The great increase in population in countless communities has added greatly to the complexity and the cost of marketing channels and distribution. Shipping, storing, wholesaling, and retailing have become more complex. The cost of marketing, including advertising and promotional efforts, comes under continuing attack by consumers and government. One constantly learns of new investigations as to why the cost of goods to consumers is so high compared, for example, with the price paid to farmers. Ways must be found to make distribution more economical and to keep the costs as low as possible.

For many businesses, as E. Jerome McCarthy points out, marketing does cost too much from a public viewpoint.[26] This should be a concern of public relations management (as well as of top management and marketing management). Many factors contribute to unjustifiably high marketing costs. For example, overaggressive promotion is used to sell products that

[24] E. Jerome McCarthy, *Basic Marketing, 4th ed.,* Homewood, Ill.: Richard D. Irwin, 1971.

[25] *Harvard Business Review,* May/June 1972, p. 63.

[26] E. Jerome McCarthy, *Basic Marketing,* 4th ed., Homewood, Ill.: Richard D. Irwin, 1971.

really do not meet the consumers' needs and therefore are hard to sell without expensive, overly aggressive, and sometimes tricky promotion. The failure by businesses to examine excessively expensive distribution channels, including inefficient and ineffective wholesalers and retailers, increases marketing costs.

The failure to coordinate advertising and promotion with sales activity was discussed earlier in this book. Products may be advertised and promoted heavily, but they may be not available in retail outlets because of failure on the part of the producer's or wholesaler's sales people. Misdirected or poor marketing efforts or the absence of marketing strategy accounts for some of the excessive costs. The lack of quality control by a large percentage of businesses, with the resulting need for replacement or repair of goods, adds greatly to cost as well as customer discontent.

Organizations that are production- or operations-oriented, selling what the organization wishes to produce rather than what the customer wishes or really needs, add to the cost of promotion, handling complaints, and so on.

A major effort will be needed to manage changes in marketing so that its costs are no higher than need be. Much will depend on changing organizations from being production- and operations-oriented to being centered on the customer and the public.

To ignore or attack protest signals from consumers (voters) is an invitation to deepening social strains. What is needed is problem solving, not social rhetoric. Properly recognized, consumerism will have a positive effect on business and the professions by developing customer orientation aimed at customer satisfaction as the key to long-term profitability.

Recognition of the need to manage change in the area of consumer relations and to meet consumer needs as consumers see them should be of great importance to the public relations management in business, the professions, government, and the academic world especially.

ATTITUDES TOWARD PROFIT AND BUSINESS

In Chapter 3, which examined the public environment, we discussed the importance of profit to all business institutions. Business cannot exist without profit. We also pointed out that business must produce enough food, shelter, and all other goods and services to supply itself and its people and also a surplus to supply all the rest of society, including the nonbusiness sector. The surplus is the difference between the value produced by business activity and the cost. It is profit. Thus business profits and wages make possible all nonbusiness institutions and activities, including government, which is supported by taxes, the money for which is initially derived from business profits and wages. Also included are the schools and churches.

There must be enough profit to increase capacity and to constantly modernize and keep up business plants and equipment to make possible all of tomorrow's jobs. Work must produce not only a living for the worker but also the resources (profit and capital) to make possible economic activity in the future, including the jobs of the future. Peter Drucker makes the point that the rapid improvement in wages of workers has been owing to a large degree to the steadily increasing capital investment in business enterprises.[27] Profit at any given time averages at most only about 10 percent of the cost of wages.

We have discussed the hostility toward profit, the negative attitudes toward business, and some of the reasons for them. One primary contributor to negative attitudes toward profit is the concept held by many business people that the only purpose of business is to maximize profits. However, the function of business is not only profit. As said before, the key to the situation is the requirement for the proper balance between profit on the one hand and the public interest on the other.

As suggested by Daniel Yankelovich, another cause of hostility toward profit may be that some business people do not distinguish between profit making and profiteering.[28] The difference lies in how the profits are made. Yankelovich says that the public does distinguish between profit making and profiteering. He points out that people in general are not resentful of large profits if they are perceived as being made as a result of rendering a real service. But people are very resentful of even small profit if they think it is made because business "has its hand in the consumers' pockets." Yankelovich cites the recent oil embargo situation as a classical instance of people seeing very large profits made not in rendering a service but for exploiting a situation.

One of the causes of hostility toward business is the frequent failure of marketing to be in the public interest. As defined by J. B. McKitterick, the principal task of marketing is to be skillful in perceiving and then making business do what suits the interests of the customer.[29] We pointed out in an earlier chapter that too often business attempts to make the customer do what suits the interests of the business.

The attitudes toward profit and business are an area in which public rela-

---

[27] *Management: Tasks, Responsibilities, Practices.* New York: Harper and Row, 1974.
[28] The Conference Board, Report No. 701, *Business Credibility: The Critical Factors.* New York, 1976.
[29] "What is the Marketing Management Concept," in *The Frontiers of Marketing Thought and Science.* Chicago: American Marketing Association, 1958.

tions managements should take the initiative in the management of change, because the present attitudes are a great danger to society and to both business and nonbusiness institutions. The area is fraught with controversy. Politically it is popular to attack business and profit. Business is a convenient whipping boy for society's ills.

The problem is a dual one requiring concerted work to change the attitudes of many businesses on the one hand and a large segment of the public on the other. Thus it is change requiring careful management with well-conceived and well-executed plans. It will require good organizing, good coordination, integration of efforts, and excellent leadership. This problem will not be remedied in a day, but the sooner it is tackled the better.

THE CAPITAL REQUIREMENTS CRISIS

The capital requirements crisis is closely allied with the attitudes toward businesses and toward profit. New investment capital is required to make possible new businesses, increases in industrial and business capacity, and much of the modernization necessary to provide the jobs for increasing numbers of people. It is also a requirement if we are to continue to improve standards of living for all parts of society.

Capital fuels the economy, even in communist countries. For example, in the early days of Stalin in the Soviet Union, he directed that all available capital be used in building heavy industry. This was done at the expense of sacrificing better living conditions for the Soviet people.

Although continual additions of capital are essential for providing jobs and for improving standards of living, capital requirements are not being met in the United States. As brought out in a speech by Edward I. O'Brien, president of the Securities Industry Association, in the 10 years from 1965 to 1974, the United States devoted only 13.6 percent of its gross national product to nonresidential fixed investment,[30] compared with 29 percent for Japan, 20 percent for West Germany, and 18.2 percent for France. *Capacity in the United States has failed to grow rapidly enough to make possible absorbing the growth in the labor force.*

The capital crisis is the result of several things. The first is insufficient profit to permit putting sufficient money back into the businesses. Retained earnings in the United States as a percentage of the gross national product declined from 5.6 percent in 1965 to only 3.9 percent in 1974.. By 1975, with

[30] Speech delivered to the Commonwealth Club of California in San Francisco, August 8, 1975.

a gross national product of $1516.3 billion, retained earnings came to only $33.3 billion or 2.2 percent.[31]

The second cause of the capital crisis is heavy taxation of both individuals and businesses to support large government. Thus the money needed to increase productive ability has gone instead to countless government projects.

The third factor causing the capital requirements crisis is inflation, which stems primarily from government deficit spending and is in reality a subtle form of taxation. Before-tax profits of $111 billion were reported by nonfinancial corporations in 1974, as compared with $66 billion in 1965. This appears to be a 68 percent increase, but because of the effects of inflation and taxes, in reality after-tax profits actually fell by 56 percent.

Borrowing from banks and selling bonds can be a source of capital, but unfortunately many businesses have already borrowed all that they safely can either from the viewpoint of the people who buy the bonds or the businesses themselves. The fixed charges (interest, and so on) of too high a percentage of bonds can bring bankruptcy when the economy turns seriously downward. This is the fourth factor causing the capital requirements crisis.

The fifth factor concerns depreciation. Because of inflation and rapid technical obsolescence of plants and production methods, the charges for depreciation reserves is nowhere near adequate for replacement of old equipment and modernization.

The sixth factor—public confidence in stocks, which is another source of capital—has fallen so that between 1972 and 1975, for example, the number of shareholders in United States businesses dropped by 1½ million individuals—from 32½ to 31 million. People have lost too much money on stocks. The rewards for buying them are too low as compared with the risks involved.

A seventh important related factor is the erosion of business management's confidence in the future (as well as that of many parts of the general public), which comes from the cleavage between business and government caused by mutual mistrust and also to some extent by our tax laws.

Walter E. Hoadley, executive vice president and chief economist of the Bank of America, pointed out in a speech delivered to the Commonwealth Club of California that managers feel they must have "three lawyers with them" when they talk with government.[32] Thus many managements' view of the future is not secure enough to warrant the risk of enough money (capital) for sufficient expansion and modernization. This also affects the

[31] U.S. Department of Commerce, Washington, D.C.
[32] January 7, 1977.

general public's confidence in stocks and other securities. Yet, as Hoadley commented, just in the area of small business alone, if every small business were able to put just one more person to work, it would amount to between half a million and a million more people employed.

At first one may not see the connection between the capital requirements crisis and public relations. However, two primary causes are directly in the public relation realm. First, as discussed earlier, a large number of people do not understand the close relationship between government spending, inflation, taxes, profit, and the ability of business to finance expanded productive ability. Second, the unethical acts, the acts contrary to the public interest, and poor performance of some business organizations constantly cause lowered public confidence in business, which reduces public support of business in the legislature. It is one reason why many people do not desire to invest their savings in business stocks and bonds.

One of public relations managements' important tasks will be to develop specific objectives and specific plans needed in the management of change to remedy this serious situation. It will be a long-term task. The objectives and plans should encompass the overall public relations function, public affairs, community relations, and financial public relations.

THE ENERGY CRISIS

In Chapter 3 we discussed the energy crisis, which is also a very important area requiring the management of change. The increasingly rapid diminishment of the petroleum resources of the world can have tremendous impact on organizations of every kind. Beginning during the next decade, its effects and ramifications will probably bring many great changes that will require management from a public relations viewpoint.

For example, the entire marketing function may be greatly affected, including the products offered to consumers, the places where products are produced and offered, the prices charged for them, the kinds of promotions used to get them through the marketing channels, and performance.

Marketing distributing channels now require the shipment of many goods over large distances utilizing trucks, railroad trains, and airplanes, all powered by petroleum products. With an insufficient supply of petroleum and much higher costs, more dependence on coal-burning railroads and much less on trucks and planes may be necessary. Complete restructuring of freight rates may be required. The location and size of producers and their work forces could be involved.

People may, of necessity, have to live closer to the place they work. Automobile commuting may be seriously reduced, requiring much more effective public transportation. Larger volumes of passenger traffic on railroads may be restored. Some businesses may have to go out of existence. The political and social systems could undergo upheavals. Among other things, people may have fewer freedoms in areas involving the use of energy.

As discussed in Chapter 3, many of the problems connected with the energy crisis may be blamed on business and government. Many people will not believe the seriousness of the crisis. They may balk at restricting their "freedoms." They may protest price changes and possible slower availability of goods. The energy crisis requires the best thinking of public relations management and the managements of all other competences to manage the changes that may be necessary and to minimize public relations problems.

CONCERN FOR THE PHYSICAL ENVIRONMENT

Concern for the physical environment is related to consumerism. This relatively new concern represents a change from the general lack of concern over the past centuries. Many are surprised by it and resist it, but conditions are not the same as they were even 30 years ago. Along with the greatly increased population growth, according to a 1974 Commonwealth Club of California study, *the amount of solid waste had increased from 2.5 pounds per day per person in 1920 to from 6.5 to 8 pounds per day per person in 1970.*[33] This increase has not only strained the refuse disposal systems in many places but has also added to the waste dumped into rivers and bays and the litter spread along streets, highways, railroad lines, beaches, and in vacant property. Not only has the volume of waste increased but the number of individuals and organizations that are thoughtless and careless in the disposal of waste has also increased.

There has been a vast increase in the number of automobiles and trucks and the amount of gaseous and other waste they create. Growth in industry has brought with it larger amounts of liquid and gaseous waste.

The concern for the physical environment also stems from the almost sudden realization that the earth and its resources are not infinite. There are no more geographic frontiers where people may go to escape the crowd. The supplies of pure air, clean water, scenery, and other resources are not infinite. They are finite.

People are coming to realize that they must protect their physical environment as they would protect their front yards. As this realization has

[33] Commonwealth Club of California, report, *Incentives or Penalties for Solid Waste Producers.* San Francisco, 1974.

become more general, public pressures have caused the enactment of protective laws. As the population grows, the competition for living, recreation, business, and industrial space becomes more intense and makes pure air and clean water harder to preserve.

The need to manage changes concerning the protection of the physical environment should be of great importance to business and government public relations managements particularly. What can they do about it? Business and industry public relations managements can make certain that their firms are aware of the serious need for protecting the physical environment. Plans can be reviewed to spot potential problems. Managers in other departments can be made aware of what ought to be done or avoided. Attention can be called to existing situations with realistic recommendations being made for corrective action.

Government public relations people can keep the general public and special publics informed about the problem, its results, and its costs to government and to the public in taxes. Special publics include industry, legislative bodies, police organizations, political parties, schools of all levels, and civic organizations. Government public relations people can also take the same steps as business and industry people in regard to government operating departments such as the military, the Corps of Engineers, forestry people, and so on.

Government public relations people particularly may believe that these suggestions are unrealistic in regard to their responsibilities and authority. However, if they are unable to perform such functions, they should consider themselves publicists rather than public relations people.

EQUAL OPPORTUNITY AND EQUAL TREATMENT

The need for equal opportunity and equal treatment has come to the forefront in the last few years. For example, social pressures have led to the enactment of laws that prescribe equal treatment without discrimination based on a person's sex, age, race, or religion in regard to employment, housing, recreational facilities, schooling, and so on. Change in this area will require the best possible management because of the strong feelings that are involved. The long-range public interest must be balanced with the interests of the organization, minority groups, and majority groups. Rhetoric must be backed up by fact. This is an area of change of special importance to public relations management.

Discrimination in favor of is as undesirable as discrimination against a person or people of any particular sex, age, race, religion, education, or social background. Although laws and regulations have been enacted to prevent many kinds of discrimination, it still exists in various forms. Sometimes in employment, for example, the discrimination may be in reverse.

As John H. Bunzel, president of San Jose State University, discussed in a speech delivered to the Commonwealth Club of California in San Francisco, the use of sex and race quotas to guarantee equal results instead of equal opportunity is the worst form of condescension.[34] It would distribute societies' rewards and benefits on the basis of group affiliation rather than merit. Rights should be held by individuals, not groups.

There has been a shift from a call for equality of opportunity toward a view that equality of results is a right to be given rather than a right to be earned. *The scorekeeper should not be asked to ensure that minorities or any other group of people win a certain percentage of the races.* This would imply the principle that to make some people equal, we must use the authority of the state to make others unequal, and it can only result in harm for organizations and governments that espouse such viewpoints. Such an approach will destroy the will to achieve by many of the more able, whereas in reality these people should be encouraged.

Organizations can afford to employ, promote, or reward only the best available persons. Otherwise, particularly in this day of fast communication and knowledgeable people, they may find themselves to be considered undesirable employers. The result will be that neither the organization nor the nation will be able to compete successfully.

Public relations management in the proper way may call the attention of other departments' managements, or higher management if need be, to discrimination with which those in the organization may be involved. It can also help to ensure that all parts of the organization are fully cognizant of the organization's policies and of government regulations against discrimination as well as the steps needed to prevent it.

THE SHIFT IN EMPHASIS FROM TECHNOLOGY TO HUMANISM

An important change that technically oriented organizations especially should heed is the shift from emphasis on technology to emphasis on humanism, on people—even in technical matters. This shift had its origin in the last part of the nineteenth century and the early part of the twentieth century. One of the leaders in pointing the way was George Elton Mayo of Harvard University who was involved in the Hawthorne experiments at Western Electric Company, which we briefly discussed in Chapter 2.

[34] February 10, 1975.

However, the shift to humanism is still going on. Humanism puts emphasis on people and their needs, on human welfare, on social man, as against emphasis on mathematical, machine, and financial efficiency. No doubt a balance is needed between technical efficiency on the one hand and humanism of the other. Public opinion is still pushing for more emphasis on humanism and demanding that organizations give it increasing attention.

You will recall our earlier reference to Peter Drucker's suggestion that today there is a split between two cultures of business and industry—the world of the scientifically trained and the world of the humanistically trained person. He said that we cannot tolerate such a split any longer.[35]

The indications are that the shift in emphasis to humanism will continue to grow. One can see the impact it will have on public relations management. The shift in emphasis comes to some degree because there is no longer quite the struggle to fill the elementary biological needs—to get enough to eat, a place to live, to keep warm—for most people in the developed countries. Thus people's time and energy have been released to give more emphasis to the human aspects of business and government. Those who have not experienced a time when filling elementary biological needs was difficult may have trouble understanding why the world has progressed so slowly on matters of humanism. Their failure to understand can present major public relations problems.

Recognizing the need to shift and progress from technical emphasis to emphasis on humanism can present opportunities. It is an area in which the management of change is important and may sometimes be difficult.

Abraham Maslow's hierarchy of human needs[36] (see page 41) relate directly to the shift to humanism. The needs for safety, love, esteem, and self-actualization also are important in our discussion of motivation that follows.

THE NEED FOR DESIRABLE MOTIVATION

Motivation is usually thought of in terms of the theories expressed by such men as Rensis Likert, Frederick Herzberg, and Abraham H. Maslow. However, to throw a different light on motivation, we can translate Maslow's hierarchy of needs, for example, into other terms and considerations. That is, motivation as concerns work can also be thought of in terms of psychological, physiological, social (relations), economic (pay), and power (position) considerations.

[35] *The Age of Discontinuity.* New York: Harper and Row, 1969.
[36] *Motivation and Personality.* New York: Harper and Row, 1954.

Motivation has deep significance. Civilized cultures and the lack of civilized cultures may be the result of motivation or the lack of motivation. One can observe the results in some undeveloped parts of the world where down through the years some peoples have not had the motivation even to raise crops. Yet they may have rubbed elbows and associated with the world's great cultures and civilizations.

Investigation by David C. McClelland found that a high need for achievement in a society is significantly correlated with rapid economic development.[37] Wealth and status are ways of keeping score relative to the need for this achievement; they are not the achievement objectives. Historically, McClelland's research indicated that the need for achievement appeared in a culture some 50 or more years before a rapid rate of economic growth. He found this to be true in ancient Greece before its golden age, in Spain before the age of exploration, in England in the years from 1500 to 1625, and again in the eighteenth century before the Industrial Revolution. A people's desire to achieve may depend to a considerable extent on what is expected by the society in which they live. The high need for achievement emphasizes self-reliance and independence (rather than reliance on others), aspirations, ambitions, and a positive attitude toward work—deriving satisfaction from work itself.

Many people react positively to the motivating abilities of leadership. Thus a person may be "turned on" and motivated to do good work and to strive for achievement by one leader. The same person may be a sloth producing unsatisfactory work and little achievement with another leader. This is an important reason why leadership should be a planned effort.

The reactions to various incentives vary greatly among people. Thus careful planning for motivation by supervisors and higher management is important. The use of special incentives and rewards to different people in an organization may cause feelings of dissatisfaction, injustice, and resentment among some of its members. The demotivation caused by what people perceive as inequalities in incentives or rewards may be more important than the satisfaction and motivation the incentives bring.

Continuous training to improve the overall job and to provide people with a view of the organization as a whole, its problems, objectives, and work may produce desirable motivation. Work kept productive and important to the group, the organization, and society can provide motivation to achieve. Keeping people informed about their own performance, their group's performance, and the organization's performance can also help.

With industrialization and the lessening of the struggle to fill the elementary biological needs, desirable motivation or its lack has become one

[37] David C. McClelland, *The Achieving Society,* New York: Van Nostrand Reinhold, 1961.

of the vital influences on public relations. *Desirable motivation is the key to employees who take an interest and to the good performance without which good public relations will not be possible.* It is the ultimate key to both desirable and undesirable interaction by the citizenry concerning economic, political, community, educational, religious, and other factors.

The subject is too complex to discuss in a few pages, and it offers no simple solutions. However, it is an area about which public relations managers should be knowledgeable. It is closely related to "communicative openness"—a climate of trust, integrity and ethics that permits and encourages the growth of openness. It is an important area requiring the management of change so that organizations may optimize desirable motivation.

THE INFORMATION EXPLOSION

We have discussed the information explosion in earlier chapters. Organizations operate on information. The information explosion has a great impact on education and learning. Yet, to paraphrase Peter Drucker, information tends to be expensive, late, and unreliable, notwithstanding the vast and ever-increasing amount of information on all manner of subjects available somewhere.[38]

The vast quantity of written and spoken material now available presents a problem. One has to determine which is correct, which has validity, which has value, which is up to date, which is slanted or biased, and which is complete. Of all the information and misinformation that comes from every side by word of mouth, through newspapers, television, radio, books, and so on, how can one be sure which to accept, which to believe?

"Garbage in, garbage out" is a saying concerning computer information. If you feed the computer poor quality information, you will get poor quality information out. *"Garbage in, garbage out"* also applies to the human brain. In this day of the proliferation of "information," one must use a great deal of care in sorting out the good from the bad.

Information and knowledge are the organization's most important and most productive resources when properly used, but they are the most expensive and unproductive resources when improperly used or wasted. The proper use of information and knowledge is so important that the organization must employ the most knowledgeble and effective staff people it can afford and make the best possible use of these people in setting objectives and formulating plans. Staff management must be by people who recognize the importance of the authority of ideas rather than of persons.

[38] Peter F. Drucker, *The Age of Discontinuity.* New York: Harper and Row, 1969.

The great increase in the amount of information obtainable and the need to find ways to manage it and make it available will require much change.

Robert W. Sarnoff, former president of RCA Corporation, predicted in a speech delivered to the Commonwealth Club of California that at the present rate, the supply of data will increase by another 1000 times by the end of this century.[39] He added that unless we master the information problem, we face a breakdown at all levels of management.

We still do not have effective information systems, but the computer can be used to build them by providing low-cost, reliable, and fast information. Information, Peter Drucker suggests, is the energy of mind work.[40] The computer, he proposes, is analogous to an electric generator. Ways to use the information from the computer can be likened to the use of electric energy from generators to operate electric lights, tools, and appliances. We need more and better ways to use information from the computer. The work of finding those ways is in its infancy. However, it is certain we will find them and understand information systems much better.

Drucker suggests that with the computer "there is no technical reason why someone like Sears Roebuck should not come out with an appliance, selling for less than a television set, giving immediate access to all of the information needed for schoolwork from the first grade through college."[41]

One can see the important implications of easy access to information to public relations managers in the management of change. First, as suggested in Chapter 4, public relations management will need to learn to use the computer in the storage and correlation of information of all kinds and in day-to-day work on a much more sophisticated level. The storage and retrieval made possible by the computer can add vastly to the amount of usable information available. Among other things, computer information may vastly improve the ability to perceive trends. By being able quickly to assemble accurate information from many sources and correlate many different factors, one may gain a better understanding of the relationships among the factors. The effect of actions in trial areas may be more easily examined relative to the entire territory. The managers' perception of changing situations will improve and thus may greatly improve his ability to manage change.

The information explosion has another important effect. The public receives information more rapidly and more fully. People can be better informed. In turn they can inform others of their views quickly and easily. For example, political and business actions that may not have caused problems in the past may now occasion considerable public reaction. Changes in

[39] San Francisco, September 26, 1969.
[40] Peter F. Drucker, *The Age of Discontinuity*. New York: Harper and Row, 1969.
[41] Peter F. Drucker, *The Age of Discontinuity*. New York: Harper and Row, 1969.

public thinking and attitudes can happen more often and more quickly, which will require ability to manage change and to manage it more quickly and more effectively.

THE MANAGEMENT OF CHANGE—A CONCERN OF ALL PARTS OF THE ORGANIZATION

Every department of an organization should be concerned with and actively assist in the management of change. The opportunities inherent in the effective management of change and the problems caused by failure to be effective deeply concern the interface between the organization and the public. For this reason public relations management should have a key part in the responsibility for the planning and the management of change.

RECOGNIZING CHANGE AND THE NEED FOR CHANGE

The question arises: How does one recognize change or the need for change? The handwriting is almost always on the wall. Our problem is not recognizing the need for change is so often one of being blinded by the past, by the organization's doctrinaire, or by some vested interest.

Changes arising outside the organization can frequently be seen most quickly by good perception. Clues to them may be discovered by analysis of such things as the reports of talks, magazine articles, and new books by leading thinkers. For example, several years ago some writers recognized the coming energy shortage, but government and business paid no attention. Those responsible for planning and for the management of change failed to take action. As another example, knowledgeable people in the food industry recognize the effect of increased world population on food supplies, but there has been little planning or action as a result.

Change or the need for change may sometimes be discerned by careful analysis of press clippings over a period of time, of legislation introduced, of testimony at congressional hearings and at investigations by regulatory bodies such as the Federal Trade Commission. Change or its need may be discovered by a look at the difficulties encountered by other organizations and other industries. Analysis of changes and trends shown by opinion research can also be helpful.

The problem then becomes one of taking effective action to guide the organization to good decisions that recognize the need for change and for managing it. Some parts of the oil business recognized the potential energy shortage before it became a crisis, but the knowledge was academic because they took no effective action as a result.

To discover, to perceive, and to search out by every possible means the sociological and other changes that will affect the organization while those changes are still on the horizon, to perceive necessary changes that should be made, to help steer management decisions at every level to make the necessary changes, and to manage change effectively are among the public relations managers' foremost responsibilities.

SUMMARY

Management is primarily concerned with results in the future. The future will require many changes. Thus the key to good management is the effective management of change. Yet the future is not predictable. The management of change requires a knowledge of the past. It also requires determining what changes are desirable, what changes are necessary, and also what changes due to outside forces are inevitable.

The management of change should be greatly concerned with the public environment in which the organization will exist in the future. A key responsibility of public relations management is correctly to perceive and advise the rest of management on the environment and also to use this information to help set organizational objectives, policies, and plans. Public relations management should be tremendously concerned and involved with the management of change.

Those person with public relations responsibilities cannot be people with buckets of whitewash figuratively attempting to paint out the scars caused by a failure of the organization properly to manage change. Rather, they should use all the tools and trained perception available to help guide the organization to success in its own and in the public interest.

TWELVE

Conclusions and Summary

There is a prevalent viewpoint that good public relations is primarily the result of activity by public relations specialists with emphasis on publicity, but the responsibilities of public relations management are of tremendously greater importance than simply publicity. Managers frequently fail to recognize the vital importance of public relations considerations in every decision and every action in every part of the organization.

Good relations with the public and with each of the special publics is an organizationwide opportunity or problem and cannot be achieved merely through the activities of a public relations department or public relations counsel. Research conducted by the Pacific Telephone Company into what really determines customer attitudes showed that they are usually the result of experiences—in other words they are generally the result of an organization's performance or lack of performance.

It would be desirable to conduct additional fundamental research on the determinants of attitudes to broaden our knowledge in the field. Such research could include further examination of possible psychographic influences as well as demographic influences which were considered in the original research. This would be a worthwhile undertaking for both the business world and the academic world.

Good public relations results from good performance publicly acknowledged and appreciated. Good performance from a public viewpoint is the job of every department and every person from the chief executive officer on down to the newly hired janitor. Thus the public relations function is an aspect of every part of an organization and it has become one of the key considerations in the management of both business and nonbusiness

234

institutions. Yet relations with the public is an important area generally overlooked in the study of management.

Because good public relations requires careful consideration of the publics by every part of the organization, organizational structure and viewpoints can have a tremendous bearing on ability to achieve good public relations. For example, the decisions of businesses that are primarily production- or operations-oriented are not likely to give proper consideration to public viewpoints. They are more apt to be internally centered and concerned mostly with the problems and conveniences of production and operating groups. Such organizations also usually have little real understanding of what determines the quality of public relations.

Production- and operations-oriented businesses are also apt to lack understanding of marketing, placing primary emphasis on selling what the organization wishes to produce rather than what the customer wishes or really needs, which usually results in a large undesirable impact on public relations. Such organizations are prone many times to take a negative viewpoint toward staff functions, to make them relatively ineffective and greatly subservient to the production groups. Yet, as brought out in Chapter 11, information and knowledge are the organization's most important and productive resources when properly used, but they are the most expensive and unproductive when improperly used or wasted. The proper use of information and knowledge is so important that the organization must employ and use the most knowledgeable and effective staff people it can afford in order to plan effectively.

Throughout this book we have discussed the importance of public relations management's taking the initiative in counseling their colleagues in other departments and in top-level management. This course will be especially necessary and especially difficult when it comes to the necessity for suggesting changes in organizational structure and organization viewpoint, for frequently businesses that are production- and operations-oriented are also guided by strong organizational doctrinaire and bias. They frequently have strong production or operating departments firmly in control. If the organization has a knowledgeable marketing manager, the public relations manager may be able to team up with him in working with top-level management to change the situation.

Our discussion of production- and operations-oriented organizations and their problems may indicate that they are primarily business organizations, but this is not the case. The problems are also found in the nonbusiness world. For instance, the person in charge of development at a college or a university may be thought of as really being engaged in a marketing activity. He may find that the organization is production- and operations-oriented. Doctrinaire and organization bias may have a considerable influence on the viewpoints and functioning of the organization. Thus the "product", may be bound by tradition and what the organization wishes to "produce" rather than what the "customer" and society really need. This bias can greatly influence the "marketing" and the public relations of the institution and can greatly affect the results of the development function.

The quality of a management can be judged by its ability to perceive correctly its environment and to do something effective about it. Correctly perceiving the environment is essential for the organization to make good decisions that will enable it to prosper.

In perceiving the environment we must forever look outward to find out what the public thinks rather than inward at the machinations, problems, and viewpoints within the organization. This is of particular importance to public relations management since the purpose of the public relations function is to develop and maintain a social climate or environment in which the organization can prosper best.

Thus one of the primary duties of public relations management is (1) to correctly perceive the environment in which the organization now exists and as much as possible the environment in which it will exist in the future, (2) to make the proper parts of the organization aware of the environment, and (3) to counsel and help ensure that this information is taken into account in setting objectives, making plans, and in running the operations.

It follows that the management of the public relations function in large organizations should have three separate primary channels for advising and counseling. The first of these is to top-level management, whose primary functions include such things as defining the purpose of the organization (for example, defining the business, defining the purpose of the university, etc.), making the financing decisions of the organization, and public relations. Thus the public relations manager of the organization should, in effect, sit next to the throne. The second channel is to the top managements of the operating and staff departments and groups. The third is to all the other parts of the organization. In medium-sized and small organization, of course, top-level management and the top management of departments are usually the same people, in which case only two primary channels would be used.

Good public relations results from good performance publicly acknowledged and appreciated. Actions speak louder than words. Communicative efforts cannot for long overcome problems of performance, but this does not imply that the communicative function is not important to good public relations. One of the responsibilities of public relations management is to get public acknowledgment and appreciation for good performance through effective communicative efforts (publicity, advertising, etc.). It should effectively and efficiently interpret the organization's philosophy, actions, results, operations, ethics, and programs both to employees and to the other publics.

However, the misuse of the communicative function can destroy credibility. Too often people in business, government, and politics feel that rhetoric alone will suffice. Once lost, credibility is hard to regain. Thereafter, whatever the organization says, right or wrong, becomes suspect. Unfortunately, that is the predicament in which a great many organizations find themselves. This principle applies not only to business but to government, the professions, and most other groups. Loss of credibility will make the work of public relations management infinitely more difficult. Public relations activity devoted primarily to communication is not only apt to be ineffective; it is also apt to be a hazard.

An example of loss of credibility by both business and government is the prevalent view by a large number of people that there is really no petroleum shortage. Many of these people feel that the whole matter has been "cooked up" by the oil companies and utilities so that they can raise prices. There is a serious lack of credibility by many organizations, including government.

Sometimes the problem of the misuse of the communicative function stems from spokesmen with too narrow, incomplete, or outdated educations and knowledge of the subjects about which they speak, or it may come from a failure continually to reeducate themselves over the years.

Political scientists and politicians may have little real knowledge of the economy, management, or communication. The clergy is usually educated mostly in matters related to religion, and they rarely have knowledge of economics or the sciences. Many economists tend to ignore social and political matters which cannot be separated from economic considerations. Management is apt to ignore almost all else but its business. Engineers' knowledge is likely to be limited primarily to engineering subjects, lawyers' to legal matters, and so on. This condition might be expected of those whose educations are limited, but it seems frequently to be more true the higher the academic level of schooling (and degree) attained. Sometimes it may be the result of an attempt to make education "relevant" without determining what is really relevant.

Our point, again, is that communication must be based on performance. It must really be backed up by all the facts, not just part of them. It must be in the public interest.

The lack of ethics or the failure to understand the need for ethics is behind some public relations problems. A good example of the failure to understand ethics and the need for them was shown in 1975 when those taking the bar examination to become lawyers in California were given questions related to ethics for the first time. The lawyers who created the examination thought that the ethics portion of the exam would easily be passed by almost all those taking it. Instead, a large percentage of the predominantly young, affluent, and "well-educated" people failed to pass it.

The lack of understanding of the need for ethics is a reflection on society and presents an important problem to public relations managements in that some of those within their organizations may not be ethical. It will then be necessary for public relations management to make clear the need for ethical conduct. It also makes it imperative that public relations management make certain the public relations staff is not afflicted with problems of ethics.

Little has been said about the other responsibilities of the public relations function or about its management. The primary concern of public relations management is public attitudes, public opinion, and their effects. Basically, attitudes are determined by what one conceives of as his best interests, but we should remember that economic well being and physical comfort must sometimes take a back seat to other interests, such as interpersonal relationships.

We have emphasized that the organization exists only by public consent, and its existence is justified only in terms of its contribution to society as viewed by society. In this respect we should recognize that consumers, the public, and the voters are all the same group of people. And we must realize that even now public confidence in and the credibility of most organizations is low. Referring to businesses, for example, one important complaint is that large businesses use all of the loopholes they can find to circumvent the law.

When the public is unhappy, more government regulation is imposed, which is then likely to reduce public confidence even further. The voters through their representatives in legislative bodies can adopt legislation that is harmful both to organizations and to the public.

The voters can withdraw public consent for organizations, for institutions, and even for ways of life as we know them. And by overreacting, legislative and regulatory bodies can lead to the destruction of our organizations, institutions, and ways of life. This destruction, like a cancer, may not be perceived in the beginning, but once started, a major effort is needed to overcome it.

Thus public relations management has the responsibility to study the proposed decisions, actions, and operations of the organization and to ensure that they are in the public interest. For business, it should ensure that there is the proper balance between profit and the public interest. In determining public attitudes, in correctly perceiving the public environment, in helping to ensure that there is a proper balance between profit and the public interest—in nearly every other aspect of the job—the public relations manager must be an analyst, for his work requires careful and constant analysis.

Consumerism is an outgrowth of the failure to operate in the public interest as viewed by the public. It is caused to a major extent by the disregard of voiced and unvoiced customer complaints. Many businesses operate in the public interest and do not disregard customer complaints. However, from a broad viewpoint, disregarded customer complaints (complaints concerning which corrective action is not taken) are at the heart of a large percentage of public relations problems. Notwithstanding discussions to the contrary, from an overall standpoint, consumer complaints are justified.

In the area of consumerism we are still prone to think primarily of business, but the professions are deeply involved as well. And in a broader sense, government, most schools, the courts, and other parts of the nonbusiness world are greatly involved. They are unregulated monopolies and are not subject to quality and price selection by their "customers." Thus they have no competitive stimulation to cause quality performance. It is of tremendous importance whether their performance is good, whether it is really in the public interest, and whether their costs are proper as related to their values.

At one point in history, when government was relatively small, performance and cost may not have been a great problem to society. However, in a society such as ours, in which half the total income of a country goes through or to nonbusiness institutions, the quality of performance and the cost present serious public relations problems to both business and nonbusiness institutions.

Another factor involving the consumer is what may be termed the crisis of scarcity. The energy crisis, discussed in Chapter 11, is now perhaps its most visible part. It is the part with the greatest near-future impact on organizations and society. For that reason we discussed its impact separately earlier. However, the potential not-too-distant-future scarcity of many other vital resources could cause serious dislocations in business, government, and society in general. Water, food, and metals are examples.

Society in the developed portion of the world has existed for many years in an environment of relative abundance and oversupply. Some people now realize that the world's resources are not unlimited, but most of society is still living only for today, with little or no thought of the future. The developed world is still busy promoting the greater use of goods and materials that are approaching the day of short supply. When that day arrives, or perhaps sooner, there will of necessity to tremendous changes in the economic environment and of economic and marketing theory. Marketing in some fields may become distribution with little or no sales advertising or promotion. Already that is true to a considerable extent of petroleum products and electrical and gas energy. The problem may become one of the equitable distribution of goods based on the public interest. With regard to some goods, this may replace reliance on the law of supply and demand. Some products may have to be promoted part of the time and equitably distributed at other times.

Obviously both business and government will encounter upheaval and difficult public relations problems. Public relations management should assess what is happening and help to cause a more prudent use of all resources now. Prudence is a matter of survival and is in the self-interest of individuals, businesses, and government. The problem of diminishing resources is another reason why maximization of profit cannot be the sole objective of business.

What are some of the other responsibilities of public relations management? It should evaluate and anticipate the effect of every proposed objective, policy, plan, and important action of the organization on each of its important publics. It should also evaluate and anticipate the effects of each of the publics on the organization. It should consider whether proposals ought to be implemented and the best method for doing so from a public relations viewpoint.

What is in the public interest may not always be popular when viewed in the short term. There can be a great difference between the long-term public interest and what the public desires at a given time. Doing what is in the public interest rather than what gives the public short-term pleasure requires good public leadership.

Public relations management should define the public relations opportunities, problems, and potential problems, and obtain agreement among the top management on the public relations objectives, policies, and plans of the organization.

Public relations management is concerned with three kinds of objectives. The first relates to the degree of public satisfaction with the products and services of the organization. The second concerns the policies set by management, such as those relating to the organization as a place to work. The third kind of performance relates to the communicative function.

Public relations management has the responsibility for the favorableness of the organization's relations with all its publics, even though it may not be directly involved with the publics in many matters under consideration. With responsibility goes accountability. Merely because a desired result requires decisions beyond the authority of public relations management to implement does not mean that it should not be held accountable, for authority to analyze a problem or an opportunity and to recommend decisions is an important kind of authority. To do these things effectively, public relations management needs to be well acquainted with the objectives, operations, viewpoints, and results of all the other parts of the organization. In turn the other parts should be informed of public relations management's objectives, operations, viewpoints, and results. Both are necessary for the efforts of the organization to be well integrated, coordinated, and effective.

To carry out its responsibilities the public relations function must be managed well. Its management consists of four steps:

1. Analyzing and defining opportunities and problems.
2. Making decisions as to what should be done.
3. Getting the decisions carried out.
4. Analyzing the other three steps and their results after decisions are partly or fully implemented.

These four steps include staffing, planning, budgeting, organizing, directing, supervising, coordinating, integrating, controlling, and providing good leadership.

The public relations function is an investment in the privilege to operate. It is more an investment in the future than an operating expenditure. Without this investment an organization can lose its freedom to operate at all or have its freedom curtailed by a multitude of laws and government regulations.

The day when the management of the function can be successfully performed on the basis of philosophical goals and generalization is gone. Such goals, against which one is unable to measure results, are too indefinite. One needs specific objectives and specific plans for reaching those objectives.

A specific objective is one against which one can measure results. Objectives should always relate to underlying problem causes or to the underlying obstacles to achieving opportunities. Management by objectives requires tackling the underlying problem causes rather than symptoms. It requires well-thought-out definition of the underlying problems.

Opinion research and allied kinds of research are primary tools for use in problem analysis. The purpose of research is to provide information that may be used along with other information and judgment in making decisions. It helps one to perceive the environment correctly. It should find out why people have the attitudes and viewpoints they have, as well as what their attitudes are. Public relations objectives should be set to reduce or eliminate problem causes. Through the proper use of research, public relations management can also make the communicative function infinitely more effective.

Research provides information necessary for good management. The essence of good management is the efficient, effective use of information.

The primary source of information is communication. For effective communication, a message must be stated in terms of the interests of its audience.

A person's reactions to communications depend to a large extent on how he sees and perceives things. His views depend on his biases, interpretations, and impressions—his attitudes. They depend on his emotions, prejudices, abilities, ambitions, religion, education, mores, and problems. Attitudes are a key element that bias a person's evaluation of any communicative effort. An individual's attitudes will determine how much attention he will pay to communication or whether he will screen it out through his selective perception barrier. The most important determinant of a person's views, behavior, perception, and reception of communication is his needs.

A key element of communication that is often neglected is listening. This is true in communication between individuals and is also true between organizations and groups or publics. Opinion research provides one way of "listening" to groups or publics. Another way is through discussion with and feedback from opinion leaders.

Opinion leaders influence the judgments and actions of others in their groups through their attitudes, actions, and interpretations of events. In searching for opinion leaders, it is not wise to rely on titles and include mostly business executives and elected officials. In reality opinion leaders may be members of any profession, trade, race, religion, or degree of education. Some may be prominent; others may seldom be visible. They are often without an important title. A knowledge of the community, considerable inquiry, good perception and judgement are needed in determining who the opinion leaders are.

We should measure and determine whether we are communicating well with the public or with special publics—for example, employees. Tools for doing so include readership and comprehension survey studies and the use of tests such as those devised by Rudolph Flesch.

Specific objectives and specific plans for reaching them are important to communicating the organization's purposes and what is to be done to achieve them. They help to ensure that efforts are directed toward reaching objectives and that they are properly coordinated and integrated for the most effective results. They provide written references to let people know exactly what is to be done, who is responsible for doing it, and when it is to be done.

Public relation's objectives and plans should always be tied to the objectives and plans of the organization as a whole. The need for higher management acceptance of a plan should be considered while the plan is being prepared. The need for the approval and active support of the other parts of the organization should also be considered in the planning stage.

Top management clearance of important plans is essential, and its active involvement is also the first requirement in successfully and effectively implementing them.

Good supervision is important to success in carrying out plans. Everyone involved should realize that he is accountable for the results in the areas for which he is responsible.

One of the areas in which planning is of special importance is that of the management of change because management is primarily concerned with results in the future. Cultural, social, political, and economic changes greatly affect the environment in which organizations exist and operate. Therefore, such changes should be of great concern to public relations management.

The past is a prologue to and the foundation of the future. It is desirable for management people to know about and recognize the major changes that have taken place and are taking place. A knowledge of where we are and how we got there is essential in correctly perceiving the present and in planning change for the future. However, the management of change is not concerned with decisions in the future. It is concerned with decisions in the present that will affect the future. The opportunity today is to manage change so that as much as possible it will have favorable and beneficial results for the organization and society and fewer unfavorable and harmful ones.

Peter Drucker predicts that the future concern will be to make organizations fully effective as major instruments and tools of man and central organs of human society.[1] He comments, though, that no matter how perceptive a reporter may be, he is no more capable of predicting the future than the next person.

There is a split between two cultures in business and industry. The split is between the world of the scientifically trained person and the world of the humanistically trained person. We cannot tolerate such a split. We will have to demand of the scientifically trained person that he become a humanist. Otherwise he will lack the perception needed to make the science effective. On the other hand, we have to demand of the humanist that he acquire an understanding of science, or the humanistics will be irrelevant and ineffectual.

Many of the changes taking place are in the direction of greater social responsibility. It is the duty of the organization to look ahead and think through which of its impacts are likely to become or cause social problems. Then it is their duty to prevent these side effects. As the world becomes more populous and complex, and people through necessity become more

[1] Peter Drucker, *The Age of Discontinuity*. New York: Harper and Row, 1969.

interdependent, the need for social responsibility will become greater. Many organizations both business and nonbusiness, and many individuals feel that in our social system they should be free to do whatever they please. They do not understand or heed the requirement of responsibility and the need for society's interests to be served.

The question is sometimes raised as to whether the assumption of social responsibility conflicts with the need for profitability. Profit is of primary importance. Without it business is unable to assume any kind of responsibility, but consideration of the public interest and social responsibility are a part of the expense of doing business. In today's world business organizations are accountable not only for the goods and services they produce but also for the quality of life in their areas of competence. Failure will only bring government intervention.

Business and profit are popular targets for attack by many politicians who vie for votes. They are convenient whipping boys for many of society's ills. Yet business profits and savings from past profits not only finance all business, economic growth, ane jobs; they also make possible and finance all nonbusiness institutions and activities, including government, schools, churches, and other social institutions.

One of the primary causes of the deep-rooted hostility toward profit is the concept held by many business people that the only responsibility of business is the maximization of profit. Of course, profit for both the present and the long run must always be the first requirement of business because without it business will cease to exist. However, the function of business is not solely profit. There should be a balance between profit on the one hand and the public interest on the other. Some business leaders are noteworthy in their concern for the public interest. Unfortunately, they are tarred with the same brush as those who have little regard for the public interest.

A contributor to the negative viewpoint toward business is the failure of marketing to live up to the marketing concept as expressed by J. B. McKitterick. He said that the task of the marketing function is not so much to be skillful in making customers do what suits the interests of business, as to be skillful in perceiving and then making business do what suits the interests of the customer.[2] There is much emphasis on attempting to create customer needs that are not really in their best interests. Too often business attempts to be skillful in making customers do what suits the interests of business, but business should do what is in the interests of the customer. Careful management is badly needed to help overcome the hostility toward profit and the negative viewpoints toward business.

[2] "What is the Marketing Management Concept," in *The Frontiers of Marketing Thought and Science.* Chicago: American Marketing Association, 1958.

The great increase in the amount of information obtainable and the need to find ways to manage it and make it available will require much change. It has been predicted that at the present rate, the amount of data will increase by 1,000 times by the end of the century. Unless we master the information problem, we face a breakdown at all levels of management.

IN CONCLUSION

In concluding this book let us reemphasize some of the more important concepts we have tried to convey.

First, the public relations function should be concerned with vastly more than communication. Good public relations results from good performance and then effectively telling people about it.

Second, the purpose of the public relations function is to develop and maintain a social climate or environment in which the organization can prosper best.

Third, the organization exists only by public consent. Its existence is justified only in terms of its contribution to society as viewed by society. Operating in the public interest is in the enlightened self-interest of the organization in the long run.

Fourth, the public relations function demands the keen use of perceptive powers and effective analytical ability.

Last, the public relations function must emphasize effective, efficient management. Its responsibilities include correctly perceiving the environment and effectively informing the rest of management about it. Its responsibility is to influence decisions so that they will result in good relations with the publics.

Effective management of public relations is a matter of survival not only for the organization but also for society as we know it.

Reference Index

2   DANIEL A. WREN, *The Evolution of Management Thought.* New
    York: Ronald Press, 1972.   24

3   JOSEPH R. DAUGHEN AND PETER BENZEN, *The Wreck of The
    Penn Central.* Boston: Little, Brown, 1971.   30

4   *The Wall Street Journal.* New York: Dow-Jones, August 26,
    1968.   30

CHAPTER THREE

1   PAUL R. ERLICH AND ANNE H. ERLICH, *Population, Resources
    and Environment.* San Francisco: Freeman, 1970.   34

2   A. GERLOF HOMAN, speech delivered to the San Francisco
    Chapter, Society for the Advancement of Management. San
    Francisco: November 21, 1974.   38

3   ABRAHAM MASLOW, *Motivation and Personality.* New York:
    Harper and Row, 1954.   41

4   PETER F. DRUCKER, *Management: Tasks, Responsibilities,
    Practices.* New York: Harper and Row, 1974.   42

5   J. B. MCKITTERICK, "What is the Marketing Management
    Concept," in *The Frontiers of Marketing Thought and Science.*
    Chicago: American Marketing Association, 1958.   43

6   E. JEROME MCCARTHY, *Basic Marketing,* 4th ed. Homewood,
    Ill.: Richard D. Irwin, 1971.   43

7   PHILIP KOTLER, *Marketing Management,* 3rd ed. Englewood
    Cliffs, N.J.: Prentice-Hall, 1976.   43

8   JAMES T. DOUDIET, speech delivered to the San Francisco
    Chapter, Society for the Advancement of Management. San
    Francisco: March, 1975.   44

CHAPTER FOUR

1   PETER F. DRUCKER, *Management: Tasks, Responsibilities,
    Practices.* New York: Harper and Row, 1974.   55

2 PETER F. DRUCKER, *Management: Tasks, Responsibilities, Practices.* New York: Harper and Row, 1974.   56

3 J. D. MOONEY, *Principles of Organization.* New York: Harper and Row, 1947.   56

4 HAROLD L. WILENSKY, *Organizational Intelligence.* New York: Basic Books, 1967.   63

5 HAROLD L. WILENSKY, *Organizational Intelligence.* New York: Basic Books, 1967.   63

6 WILLIAM V. HANEY, *Communication and Organizational Behavior.* Homewood, Ill.: Richard D. Irwin, 1967.   64, 65

CHAPTER FIVE

1 GEORGE S. ODIORNE, *Management by Objectives.* New York: Pitman, 1965.   70

2 W. J. REDDIN, *Effective Management by Objectives.* New York: McGraw-Hill, 1971.   70

3 RUSSELL H. COLLEY, *Defining Advertising Goals for Measured Advertising Results.* New York: Association of National Advertisers, 1964.   70

4 PETER F. DRUCKER, *Management: Tasks, Responsibilities, Practices.* New York: Harper and Row, 1974.   71

5 ERNEST C. MILLER, *Objectives and Standards: An Approach to Planning.* New York: American Management Association, 1966.   76

6 CHARLES H. KEPNER AND BENJAMIN B. TREGOE, *The Rational Manager.* New York: McGraw-Hill, 1965.   78

7 M. SCOTT MYERS, *Every Employee A Manager.* New York: McGraw-Hill, 1970.   85

CHAPTER SIX

1 ABRAHAM MASLOW, *Motivation and Personality.* New York: Harper and Row, 1954.   92

2   DAVID C. MCCLELLAND, *The Achieving Society*. New York: Van
    Nostrand Reinhold, 1961.   93

3   MASON HAIRE, "Projective Techniques in Marketing Research,"
    Journal of Marketing, April 1950.   96

4   *Standard Rate and Data*. Skokie, Ill.: Standard Rate and Data
    Services. Annual.   103

5   *Ayer's Directory of Newspapers*. Philadelphia: N. W. Ayer
    Advertising Company. Annual.   103

6   RUDOLPH FLESCH, *How to Test Readability*. New York: Harper,
    1951.   108

CHAPTER SEVEN

1   GLENN A. BASSETT, *The New Face of Communication*. New
    York: American Management Association, 1968.   112

2   GLENN A. BASSETT, *The New Face of Communication*. New
    York: American Management Association, 1968.   115

3   GLENN A. BASSETT, *The New Face of Communication*. New
    York: American Management Association, 1968.   116

4   GLENN A. BASSETT, *The New Face of Communication*. New
    York: American Management Association, 1968.   116

5   THE PACIFIC TELEPHONE AND TELEGRAPH COMPANY,
    unpublished study, *What Really Determines Customer Attitudes*.
    San Francisco. 1967.   120

6   THE PACIFIC TELEPHONE AND TELEGRAPH COMPANY,
    unpublished study, *What Really Determines Consumer Attitudes*.
    San Francisco, 1967.   121

7   *The World Book Encyclopedia*. Chicago: Field Enterprises
    Educational Corp., 1968.   122

8   GLENN A. BASSETT, *The New Face of Communication*. New
    York: American Management Association, 1968.   127

9   GLENN A. BASSETT, *The New Face of Communication.* New
    York: American Management Association, 1968.   128

10 RALPH G. NICHOLS AND LEONARD A. STEVENS, *Are You
    Listening?* New York: McGraw-Hill, 1957.   132

11 WILLIAM V. HANEY, *Communication and Organizational
    Behavior.* Homewood, Ill.: Richard D. Irwin, 1967.   132

12 GLENN A. BASSETT, *The New Face of Communications.* New
    York: American Management Association, 1968.   135

13 GEORGE S. ODIORNE, *Management by Objectives.* New York:
    Pitman, 1968.   137

14 EARL BROOKS, Cornell University Business School, class lecture. 137

15 RENSIS LIKERT, *New Patterns of Management.* New York:
    McGraw-Hill, 1961.   138

16 WILLIAM V. HANEY, *Communication and Organizational
    Behavior.* Homewood, Ill.: Richard D. Irwin, 1967.   138

    CHAPTER EIGHT   None

    CHAPTER NINE

1   E. JEROME MCCARTHY, *Basic Marketing,* 4th ed. Homewood
    Ill.: Richard D. Irwin, 1971.   163

2   PETER F. DRUCKER, *Management: Tasks, Responsibilities,
    Practices.* New York: Harper and Row, 1974.   165

3   *1976 Budget of the U.S. Government,* Office of the President of
    the United States, Washington, D. C.   167

4   PETER F. DRUCKER, *The Age of Discontinuity,* New York:
    Harper and Row, 1969.   167

5   PETER F. DRUCKER, *The Age of Discontinuity.* New York:
    Harper and Row, 1969.   172

13 PETER F. DRUCKER, *The Age of Discontinuity.* New York: Harper and Row, 1969. 208

14 JEROME HARDY, speech delivered to the Commonwealth Club of California. San Francisco: July 19, 1968. 210

15 DANIEL A. WREN, *The Evolution of Management Thought.* New York: Ronald Press, 1972. 212

16 PETER F. DRUCKER, *The Age of Discontinuity.* New York: Harper and Row, 1969. 214

17 PETER F. DRUCKER, *The Age of Discontinuity.* New York: Harper and Row, 1969. 214

18 PETER F. DRUCKER, *The Age of Discontinuity.* New York: Harper and Row, 1969. 214

19 PETER F. DRUCKER, *The Age of Discontinuity.* New York: Harper and Row, 1969. 214

20 PETER F. DRUCKER, *The Age of Discontinuity.* New York: Harper and Row, 1969. 215

21 PETER F. DRUCKER, *Management: Tasks, Responsibilities, Practices.* New York: Harper and Row, 1974. 215

22 PETER F. DRUCKER, *The Age of Discontinuity.* New York: Harper and Row, 1969. 216

23 PETER F. DRUCKER, *Management: Tasks, Responsibilities, Practices.* New York: Harper and Row, 1974. 217

24 E. JEROME McCARTHY, *Basic Marketing,* 4th ed. Homewood, Ill.: Richard D. Irwin, 1971. 219

25 PHILIP KOTLER, "What Consumerism Means for Marketers," *Harvard Business Review,* May/June 1972. 219

26 E. JEROME McCARTHY, *Basic Marketing,* 4th ed. Homewood Ill.: Richard D. Irwin, 1971. 219

27 PETER F. DRUCKER, *Management: Tasks, Responsibilities,*
    Practices. New York: Harper and Row, 1974.   221

28 THE CONFERENCE BOARD, Report No. 701, *Business Credibility:*
    The Critical Factors. New York, 1976.   221

29 J. B. MCKITTERICK, "What is the Marketing Management
    Concept," in *The Frontiers of Marketing Thought and Science.*
    Chicago: American Marketing Association, 1958.   221

30 EDWARD I. O'BRIEN, President, Securities Industry Association,
    speech delivered to the Commonwealth Club of California. San
    Francisco: August 8, 1975.   222

31 U.S. Department of Commerce, Washington, D.C.   223

32 WALTER E. HOADLEY, Executive Vice President and Chief
    Economist, Bank of America, speech delivered to the
    Commonwealth Club of California. San Francisco: January 7,
    1977.   223

33 COMMONWEALTH CLUB OF CALIFORNIA, report, *Incentives or*
    Penalties for Solid Waste Producers. San Francisco, 1974.   225

34 JOHN H. BUNZEL, speech delivered to the Commonwealth Club
    of California. San Francisco: February 10, 1975.   227

35 PETER F. DRUCKER, *The Age of Discontinuity.* New York:
    Harper and Row, 1969.   228

36 ABRAHAM MASLOW, *Motivation and Personality.* New York:
    Harper and Row, 1954.   228

37 DAVID C. MCCLELLAND, *The Achieving Society.* New York: Van
    Nostrand Reinhold, 1961.   229

38 PETER F. DRUCKER, *The Age of Discontinuity.* New York:
    Harper and Row, 1969.   230

39 ROBERT W. SARNOFF, former President, RCA Corporation,
    speech delivered to the Commonwealth Club of California, San
    Francisco: September 26, 1969.   231

40   PETER F. DRUCKER, *The Age of Discontinuity.* New York:
     Harper and Row, 1969.   231

41   PETER F. DRUCKER, *The Age of Discontinuity.* New York:
     Harper and Row, 1969.   231

     CHAPTER TWELVE

1   PETER F. DRUCKER, *The Age of Discontinuity.* New York:
     Harper and Row, 1969.   243

2   J. B. MCKITTERICK, "What is the Marketing Management
     Concept," in *The Frontiers of Marketing Thought and Science.*
     Chicago: American Marketing Association, 1958.   244

Subject Index